N. Gregory Mankiw

PRINCIPLES OF ECONOMICS
(8TH EDITION)

清华经济学系列英文版教材

经济学原理
宏观部分
第8版

[美] N.格雷戈里·**曼昆** 著
（N. Gregory Mankiw）

PRINCIPLES OF ECONOMICS
(8TH EDITION)

清华大学出版社
北京

北京市版权局著作权合同登记号　图字：01-2025-2164

Principles of Economics，8e

N. Gregory Mankiw

Copyright © 2018 South-Western, Cengage Learning

ISBN：978-1-305-58512-6

Cengage Learning Asia Pte. Ltd.

30A Kallang Place #12-06 Singapore 339213

图书在版编目（CIP）数据

经济学原理. 宏观部分：第 8 版 = Principles of Economics, 8th Edition：英文 /（美）N. 格雷戈里·曼昆 (N. Gregory Mankiw) 著 . -- 北京：清华大学出版社，2025. 3.
（清华经济学系列英文版教材）. --ISBN 978-7-302-68921-8

Ⅰ. F0

中国国家版本馆 CIP 数据核字第 2025AE6465 号

责任编辑：高晓蔚
封面设计：常雪影
责任印制：刘　菲

出版发行：清华大学出版社
　　　　　网　　　址：https://www.tup.com.cn，https://www.wqxuetang.com
　　　　　地　　　址：北京清华大学学研大厦 A 座　　　　邮　　　编：100084
　　　　　社 总 机：010-83470000　　　　　　　　　　邮　　　购：010-62786544
　　　　　投稿与读者服务：010-62776969，c-service@tup.tsinghua.edu.cn
　　　　　质 量 反 馈：010-62772015，zhiliang@tup.tsinghua.edu.cn
印 装 者：大厂回族自治县彩虹印刷有限公司
经　　销：全国新华书店
开　　本：210mm×260mm　　　　印　张：13.75　　插　页：2
版　　次：2025 年 5 月第 1 版　　　印　次：2025 年 5 月第 1 次印刷
定　　价：59.00 元

产品编号：109790-01

出版说明

　　为了适应经济全球化的发展趋势，满足国内广大读者了解、学习和借鉴国外先进管理经验和掌握经济理论前沿动态的需要，清华大学出版社与国外著名出版公司合作影印出版一系列英文版经济管理方面的图书。我们所选择的图书，基本上是已再版多次、在国外深受欢迎并被广泛采用的优秀教材，是该领域中具有权威性的经典之作。

　　曼昆教授的这本《经济学原理》，自1997年首次出版以来，被全世界数以百万计的学生使用，深受学生和教师的喜爱，被翻译成20多种语言。很多学生因学习这本书而深深地爱上了经济学。这本书的中文翻译版也已经在我国出版。

　　感谢圣智学习出版公司对清华大学出版社独家授予本书的影印版版权，使我们能够将这本深受读者喜爱的经济学教科书原汁原味地奉献给更多的中国读者，使读者能够既轻松地学习经济学，又感受到曼昆教授的语言魅力。

　　应原版图书出版方的要求，并适应我国的教学实际情况，我们删减了少数章节，使本书的篇幅和内容更适合广大学生。在对原版图书进行删节的同时保留了原书的页码，并按顺序编制了新的页码，望读者予以注意。删减的章节，读者可以从电子书中阅读。

　　在本书的审阅过程中，我们得到了清华大学经济管理学院钟笑寒老师的热心帮助和支持，在此表示感谢！

　　由于原作者所处国家的政治、经济和文化背景等与我国不同，对书中所持观点，敬请广大读者在阅读过程中注意分析和鉴别。

　　欢迎广大读者给我们提出宝贵的意见和建议，也欢迎有关专业人士向我们推荐您所接触到的国外优秀图书。

清华大学出版社

About the Author

N. Gregory Mankiw is the Robert M. Beren Professor of Economics at Harvard University. As a student, he studied economics at Princeton University and MIT. As a teacher, he has taught macroeconomics, microeconomics, statistics, and principles of economics. He even spent one summer long ago as a sailing instructor on Long Beach Island.

Professor Mankiw is a prolific writer and a regular participant in academic and policy debates. His work has been published in scholarly journals, such as the *American Economic Review, Journal of Political Economy,* and *Quarterly Journal of Economics*, and in more popular forums, such as the *New York Times* and *The Wall Street Journal*. He is also author of the best-selling intermediate-level textbook *Macroeconomics* (Worth Publishers). In addition to his teaching, research, and writing, Professor Mankiw has been a research associate of the National Bureau of Economic Research, an adviser to the Congressional Budget Office and the Federal Reserve Banks of Boston and New York, and a member of the ETS test development committee for the Advanced Placement exam in economics. From 2003 to 2005, he served as chairman of the President's Council of Economic Advisers.

Professor Mankiw lives in Wellesley, Massachusetts, with his wife, Deborah, three children, Catherine, Nicholas, and Peter, and their border terrier, Tobin.

Preface: to the Student

"Economics is a study of mankind in the ordinary business of life." So wrote Alfred Marshall, the great 19th-century economist, in his textbook, *Principles of Economics*. We have learned much about the economy since Marshall's time, but this definition of economics is as true today as it was in 1890, when the first edition of his text was published.

Why should you, as a student in the 21st century, embark on the study of economics? There are three reasons.

The first reason to study economics is that it will help you understand the world in which you live. There are many questions about the economy that might spark your curiosity. Why are apartments so hard to find in New York City? Why do airlines charge less for a round-trip ticket if the traveler stays over a Saturday night? Why is Robert Downey, Jr., paid so much to star in movies? Why are living standards so meager in many African countries? Why do some countries have high rates of inflation while others have stable prices? Why are jobs easy to find in some years and hard to find in others? These are just a few of the questions that a course in economics will help you answer.

The second reason to study economics is that it will make you a more astute participant in the economy. As you go about your life, you make many economic decisions. While you are a student, you decide how many years to stay in school. Once you take a job, you decide how much of your income to spend, how much to save, and how to invest your savings. Someday you may find yourself running a small business or a large corporation, and you will decide what prices to charge for your products. The insights developed in the coming chapters will give you a new perspective on how best to make these decisions. Studying economics will not by itself make you rich, but it will give you some tools that may help in that endeavor.

The third reason to study economics is that it will give you a better understanding of both the potential and the limits of economic policy. Economic questions are always on the minds of policymakers in mayors' offices, governors' mansions, and the White House. What are the burdens associated with alternative forms of taxation? What are the effects of free trade with other countries? What is the best way to protect the environment? How does a government budget deficit affect the economy? As a voter, you help choose the policies that guide the allocation of society's resources. An understanding of economics will help you carry out that responsibility. And who knows: Perhaps someday you will end up as one of those policymakers yourself.

Thus, the principles of economics can be applied in many of life's situations. Whether the future finds you following the news, running a business, or sitting in the Oval Office, you will be glad that you studied economics.

N. Gregory Mankiw
December 2016

简明目录

Brief Contents

Contents

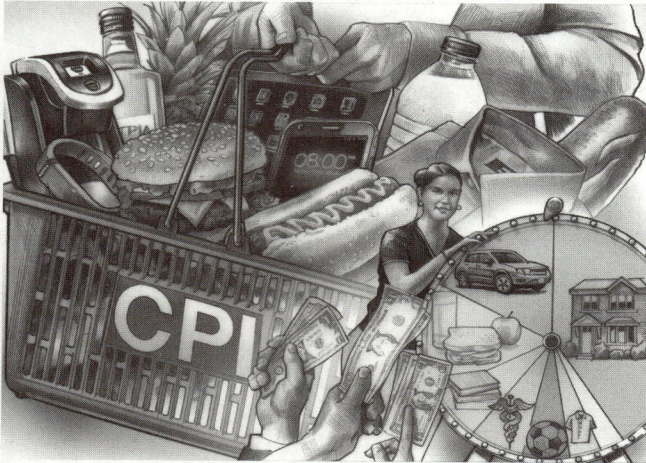

PART IX The Real Economy in the Long Run 43(513)

PART X Money and Prices in the Long Run 91(601)

CHAPTER 30

Money Growth and Inflation 117(627)

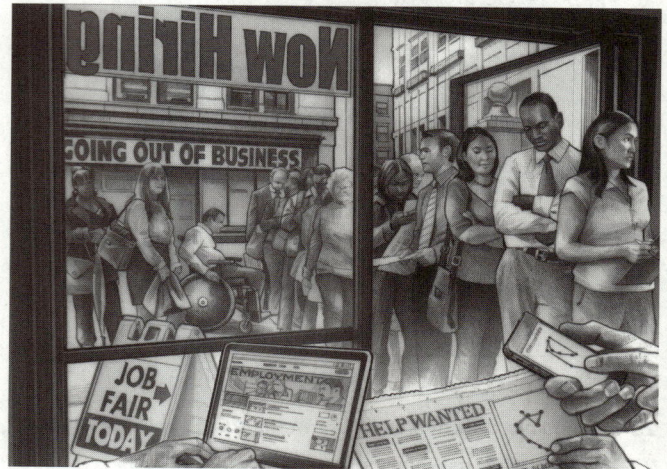

PART XII Short-Run Economic Fluctuations 141(699)

CHAPTER 33

Aggregate Demand and Aggregate Supply 143(701)

CHAPTER 34

The Influence of Monetary and Fiscal Policy on Aggregate Demand 179(737)

PART VIII

The Data of Macroeconomics

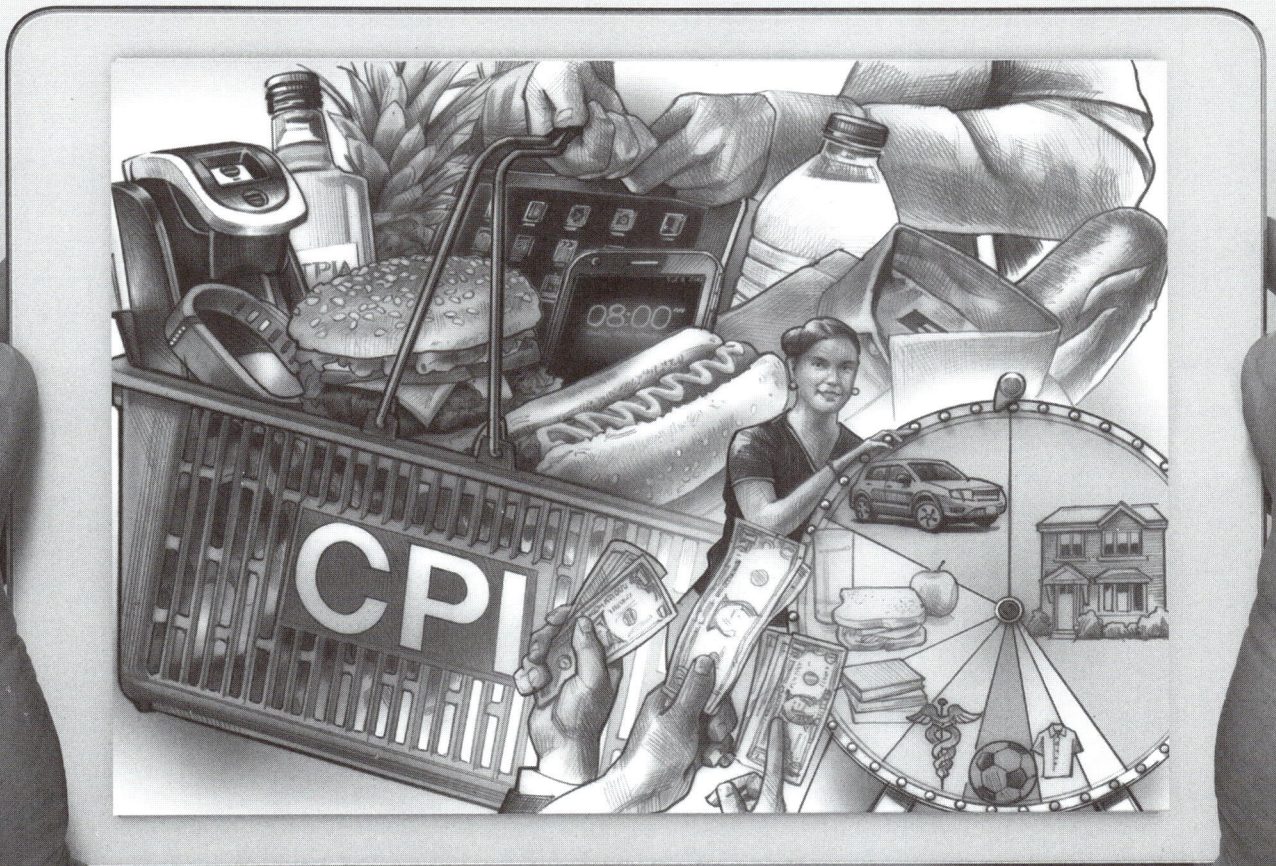

CHAPTER 23

Measuring a Nation's Income

When you finish school and start looking for a full-time job, your experience will, to a large extent, be shaped by prevailing economic conditions. In some years, firms throughout the economy are expanding their production of goods and services, employment is rising, and jobs are easy to find. In other years, firms are cutting back production, employment is declining, and finding a good job takes a long time. Not surprisingly, any college graduate would rather enter the labor force in a year of economic expansion than in a year of economic contraction.

Because the health of the overall economy profoundly affects all of us, changes in economic conditions are widely reported by the

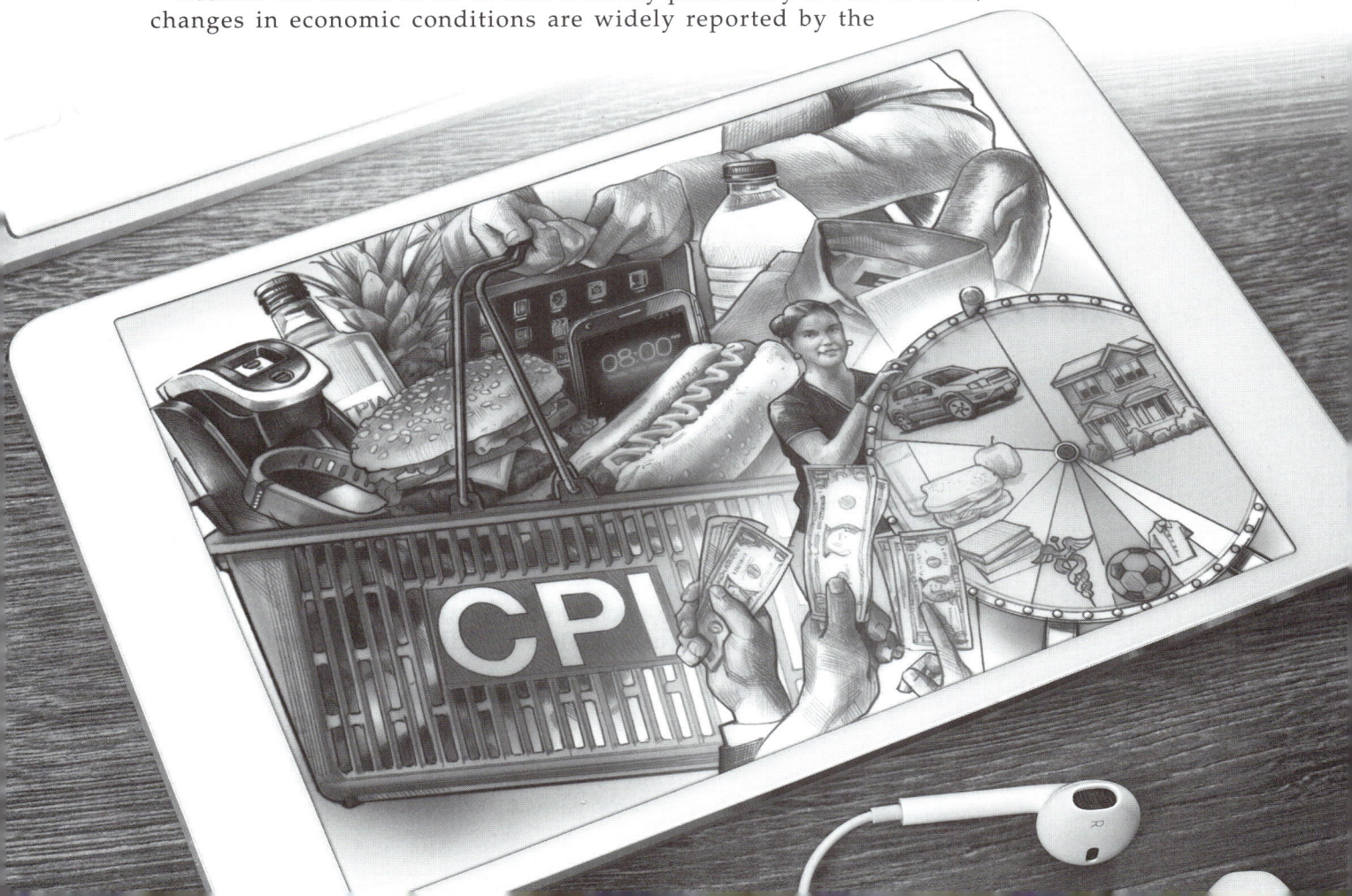

media. Indeed, it is hard to pick up a newspaper, check an online news service, or turn on the TV without seeing some newly reported statistic about the economy. The statistic might measure the total income of everyone in the economy (gross domestic product, or GDP), the rate at which average prices are rising or falling (inflation/deflation), the percentage of the labor force that is out of work (unemployment), total spending at stores (retail sales), or the imbalance of trade between the United States and the rest of the world (the trade deficit). All these statistics are *macroeconomic*. Rather than telling us about a particular household, firm, or market, they tell us something about the entire economy.

As you may recall from Chapter 2, economics is divided into two branches: microeconomics and macroeconomics. **Microeconomics** is the study of how individual households and firms make decisions and how they interact with one another in markets. **Macroeconomics** is the study of the economy as a whole. The goal of macroeconomics is to explain the economic changes that affect many households, firms, and markets simultaneously. Macroeconomists address a broad variety of questions: Why is average income high in some countries and low in others? Why do prices sometimes rise rapidly while at other times they are more stable? Why do production and employment expand in some years and contract in others? What, if anything, can the government do to promote rapid growth in incomes, low inflation, and stable employment? These questions are all macroeconomic in nature because they concern the workings of the entire economy.

Because the economy as a whole is a collection of many households and many firms interacting in many markets, microeconomics and macroeconomics are closely linked. The basic tools of supply and demand, for instance, are as central to macroeconomic analysis as they are to microeconomic analysis. Yet studying the economy in its entirety raises some new and intriguing challenges.

In this and the next chapter, we discuss some of the data that economists and policymakers use to monitor the performance of the overall economy. These data reflect the economic changes that macroeconomists try to explain. This chapter considers *gross domestic product*, which measures the total income of a nation. GDP is the most closely watched economic statistic because it is thought to be the single best measure of a society's economic well-being.

microeconomics
the study of how households and firms make decisions and how they interact in markets

macroeconomics
the study of economy-wide phenomena, including inflation, unemployment, and economic growth

23-1 The Economy's Income and Expenditure

If you were to judge how a person is doing economically, you might first look at her income. A person with a high income can more easily afford life's necessities and luxuries. It is no surprise that people with higher incomes enjoy higher standards of living—better housing, better healthcare, fancier cars, more opulent vacations, and so on.

The same logic applies to a nation's overall economy. When judging whether the economy is doing well or poorly, it is natural to look at the total income that everyone in the economy is earning. That is the task of gross domestic product.

GDP measures two things at once: the total income of everyone in the economy and the total expenditure on the economy's output of goods and services. GDP can perform the trick of measuring both total income and total expenditure because these two things are the same. *For an economy as a whole, income must equal expenditure.*

Why is this true? An economy's income is the same as its expenditure because every transaction has two parties: a buyer and a seller. Every dollar of spending by some buyer is a dollar of income for some seller. Suppose, for instance, that Karen pays Doug $100 to mow her lawn. In this case, Doug is a seller of a service and Karen is a buyer. Doug earns $100 and Karen spends $100. Thus, the transaction contributes equally to the economy's income and to its expenditure. GDP, whether measured as total income or total expenditure, rises by $100.

Another way to see the equality of income and expenditure is with the circular-flow diagram in Figure 1. As you may recall from Chapter 2, this diagram describes all the transactions between households and firms in a simple economy. It simplifies matters by assuming that all goods and services are bought by households and that households spend all of their income. In this economy, when households buy goods and services from firms, these expenditures flow through the markets for goods and services. When the firms use the money they receive from sales to pay workers' wages, landowners' rent, and firm owners' profit, this income flows through the markets for the factors of production. Money continuously flows from households to firms and then back to households.

GDP measures this flow of money. We can compute it for this economy in one of two ways: by adding up the total expenditure by households or by adding up the total income (wages, rent, and profit) paid by firms. Because all expenditure in the economy ends up as someone's income, GDP is the same regardless of how we compute it.

The actual economy is, of course, more complicated than the one illustrated in Figure 1. Households do not spend all of their income; they pay some of it to the government in taxes, and they save some for use in the future. In addition, households do not buy all goods and services produced in the economy; some goods and services are bought by governments, and some are bought by firms that plan to use them in the future to produce their own output. Yet the basic lesson remains the same: Regardless of whether a household, government, or firm buys a good or service, the transaction always has a buyer and a seller. Thus, for the economy as a whole, expenditure and income are the same.

QuickQuiz *What two things does GDP measure? How can it measure two things at once?*

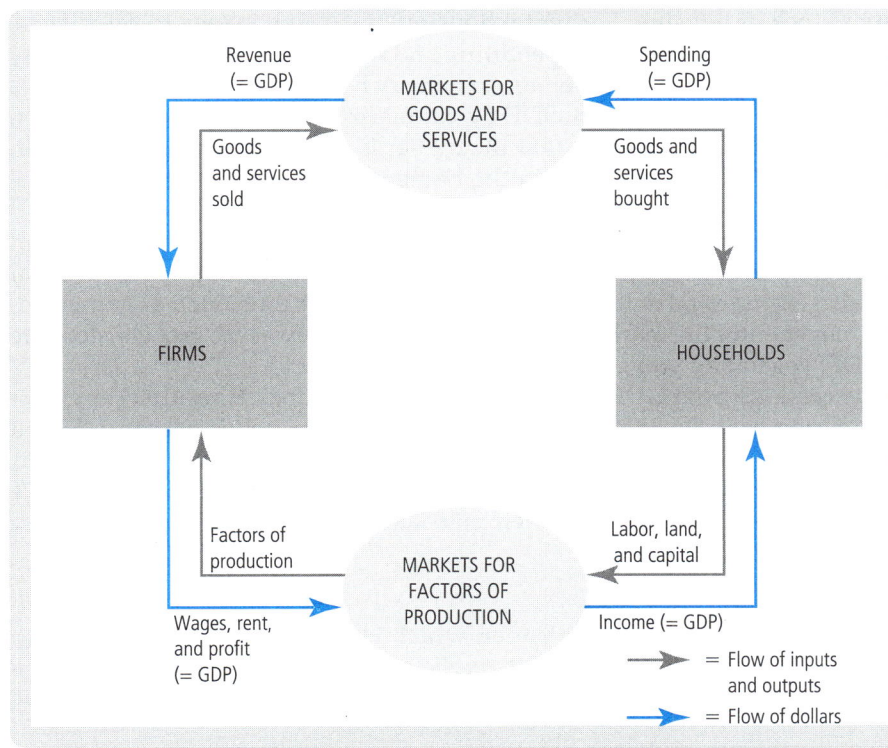

FIGURE 1

The Circular-Flow Diagram
Households buy goods and services from firms, and firms use their revenue from sales to pay wages to workers, rent to landowners, and profit to firm owners. GDP equals the total amount spent by households in the market for goods and services. It also equals the total wages, rent, and profit paid by firms in the markets for the factors of production.

23-2 The Measurement of GDP

**gross domestic product
(GDP)**
the market value of all
final goods and services
produced within a coun-
try in a given period of
time

Having discussed the meaning of gross domestic product in general terms, let's be more precise about how this statistic is measured. Here is a definition of GDP that focuses on GDP as a measure of total expenditure:

- **Gross domestic product (GDP)** is the market value of all final goods and services produced within a country in a given period of time.

This definition might seem simple enough. But in fact, many subtle issues arise when computing an economy's GDP. Let's therefore consider each phrase in this definition with some care.

23-2a "GDP Is the Market Value . . ."

You have probably heard the adage "You can't compare apples and oranges." Yet GDP does exactly that. GDP adds together many different kinds of products into a single measure of the value of economic activity. To do this, it uses market prices. Because market prices measure the amount people are willing to pay for different goods, they reflect the value of those goods. If the price of an apple is twice the price of an orange, then an apple contributes twice as much to GDP as does an orange.

23-2b ". . . of All . . ."

GDP tries to be comprehensive. It includes all items produced in the economy and sold legally in markets. GDP measures the market value of not just apples and oranges but also pears and grapefruit, books and movies, haircuts and healthcare, and so on.

GDP also includes the market value of the housing services provided by the economy's stock of housing. For rental housing, this value is easy to calculate—the rent equals both the tenant's expenditure and the landlord's income. Yet many people own their homes and, therefore, do not pay rent. The government includes this owner-occupied housing in GDP by estimating its rental value. In effect, GDP is based on the assumption that the owner is renting the house to herself. The imputed rent is included both in the homeowner's expenditure and in her income, so it adds to GDP.

There are some products, however, that GDP excludes because measuring them is difficult. GDP excludes most items produced and sold illicitly, such as illegal drugs. It also excludes most items that are produced and consumed at home and, therefore, never enter the marketplace. Vegetables you buy at the grocery store are part of GDP; vegetables you grow in your garden are not.

These exclusions from GDP can at times lead to paradoxical results. For example, when Karen pays Doug to mow her lawn, that transaction is part of GDP. But suppose Doug and Karen marry. Even though Doug may continue to mow Karen's lawn, the value of the mowing is now left out of GDP because Doug's service is no longer sold in a market. Thus, their marriage reduces GDP.

23-2c ". . . Final . . ."

When International Paper makes paper, which Hallmark then uses to make a greeting card, the paper is called an *intermediate good* and the card is called a *final good*. GDP includes only the value of final goods. This is done because the value of intermediate goods is already included in the prices of the final goods. Adding the market value of the paper to the market value of the card would be double counting. That is, it would (incorrectly) count the paper twice.

An important exception to this principle arises when an intermediate good is produced and, rather than being used, is added to a firm's inventory of goods for use or sale at a later date. In this case, the intermediate good is taken to be "final" for the moment, and its value as inventory investment is included as part of GDP. Thus, additions to inventory add to GDP, and when the goods in inventory are later used or sold, the reductions in inventory subtract from GDP.

23-2d "...Goods and Services..."

GDP includes both tangible goods (food, clothing, cars) and intangible services (haircuts, housecleaning, doctor visits). When you buy a CD by your favorite band, you are buying a good, and the purchase price is part of GDP. When you pay to hear a concert by the same band, you are buying a service, and the ticket price is also part of GDP.

23-2e "...Produced..."

GDP includes goods and services currently produced. It does not include transactions involving items produced in the past. When Ford produces and sells a new car, the value of the car is included in GDP. But when one person sells a used car to another person, the value of the used car is not included in GDP.

23-2f "...Within a Country..."

GDP measures the value of production within the geographic confines of a country. When a Canadian citizen works temporarily in the United States, her production is part of U.S. GDP. When an American citizen owns a factory in Haiti, the production at her factory is not part of U.S. GDP. (It is part of Haiti's GDP.) Thus, items are included in a nation's GDP if they are produced domestically, regardless of the nationality of the producer.

23-2g "...In a Given Period of Time."

GDP measures the value of production that takes place within a specific interval of time. Usually, that interval is a year or a quarter (3 months). GDP measures the economy's flow of income, as well as its flow of expenditure, during that interval.

When the government reports the GDP for a quarter, it usually presents GDP "at an annual rate." This means that the figure reported for quarterly GDP is the amount of income and expenditure during the quarter multiplied by 4. The government uses this convention so that quarterly and annual figures on GDP can be compared more easily.

In addition, when the government reports quarterly GDP, it presents the data after they have been modified by a statistical procedure called *seasonal adjustment*. The unadjusted data show clearly that the economy produces more goods and services during some times of the year than during others. (As you might guess, December's holiday shopping season is a high point.) When monitoring the condition of the economy, economists and policymakers often want to look beyond these regular seasonal changes. Therefore, government statisticians adjust the quarterly data to take out the seasonal cycle. The GDP data reported in the news are always seasonally adjusted.

Now let's repeat the definition of GDP:

- Gross domestic product (GDP) is the market value of all final goods and services produced within a country in a given period of time.

This definition focuses on GDP as total expenditure in the economy. But don't forget that every dollar spent by a buyer of a good or service becomes a dollar of income to the seller of that good or service. Therefore, in addition to applying this definition, the government adds up total income in the economy. The two ways of calculating GDP give almost exactly the same answer. (Why "almost"? The two measures should be precisely the same, but data sources are not perfect. The difference between the two calculations of GDP is called the *statistical discrepancy*.)

It should be apparent that GDP is a sophisticated measure of the value of economic activity. In advanced courses in macroeconomics, you will learn more about the subtleties that arise in its calculation. But even now you can see that each phrase in this definition is packed with meaning.

Quick Quiz   *Which contributes more to GDP—the production of a pound of hamburger or the production of a pound of caviar? Why?*

FYI

Other Measures of Income

When the U.S. Department of Commerce computes the nation's GDP, it also computes various other measures of income to get a more complete picture of what's happening in the economy. These other measures differ from GDP by excluding or including certain categories of income. What follows is a brief description of five of these income measures, ordered from largest to smallest.

- *Gross national product* (GNP) is the total income earned by a nation's permanent residents (called *nationals*). It differs from GDP in that it includes income that our citizens earn abroad and excludes income that foreigners earn here. For example, when a Canadian citizen works temporarily in the United States, her production is part of U.S. GDP, but it is not part of U.S. GNP. (It is part of Canada's GNP.) For most countries, including the United States, domestic residents are responsible for most domestic production, so GDP and GNP are quite close.

- *Net national product* (NNP) is the total income of a nation's residents (GNP) minus losses from depreciation. *Depreciation* is the wear and tear on the economy's stock of equipment and structures, such as trucks rusting and old computer models becoming obsolete. In the national income accounts prepared by the Department of Commerce, depreciation is called the "consumption of fixed capital."

- *National income* is the total income earned by a nation's residents in the production of goods and services. It is almost identical to net national product. These two measures differ because of the *statistical discrepancy* that arises from problems in data collection.

- *Personal income* is the income that households and noncorporate businesses receive. Unlike national income, it excludes *retained earnings*, which is income that corporations have earned but have not paid out to their owners. It also subtracts indirect business taxes (such as sales taxes), corporate income taxes, and contributions for social insurance (mostly Social Security taxes). In addition, personal income includes the interest income that households receive from their holdings of government debt and the income that households receive from government transfer programs, such as welfare and Social Security.

- *Disposable personal income* is the income that households and noncorporate businesses have left after satisfying all their obligations to the government. It equals personal income minus personal taxes and certain nontax payments (such as traffic tickets).

Although the various measures of income differ in detail, they almost always tell the same story about economic conditions. When GDP grows rapidly, these other measures of income usually grow rapidly. And when GDP falls, these other measures usually fall as well. For monitoring fluctuations in the overall economy, it does not matter much which measure of income we use. ■

23-3 The Components of GDP

Spending in an economy takes many forms. At any moment, the Smith family may be having lunch at Burger King; Ford may be building a car factory; the U.S. Navy may be procuring a submarine; and British Airways may be buying an airplane from Boeing. GDP includes all of these various forms of spending on domestically produced goods and services.

To understand how the economy is using its scarce resources, economists study the composition of GDP among various types of spending. To do this, GDP (which we denote as Y) is divided into four components: consumption (C), investment (I), government purchases (G), and net exports (NX):

$$Y = C + I + G + NX.$$

This equation is an *identity*—an equation that must be true because of how the variables in the equation are defined. In this case, because each dollar of expenditure included in GDP is placed into one of the four components of GDP, the total of the four components must be equal to GDP. Let's look at each of these four components more closely.

23-3a Consumption

Consumption is spending by households on goods and services, with the exception of purchases of new housing. Goods include durable goods, such as automobiles and appliances, and nondurable goods, such as food and clothing. Services include such intangible items as haircuts and medical care. Household spending on education is also included in consumption of services (although one might argue that it would fit better in the next component).

> **consumption**
> spending by households on goods and services, with the exception of purchases of new housing

23-3b Investment

Investment is the purchase of goods (called *capital goods*) that will be used in the future to produce more goods and services. Investment is the sum of purchases of business capital, residential capital, and inventories. Business capital includes business structures (such as a factory or office building), equipment (such as a worker's computer), and intellectual property products (such as the software that runs the computer). Residential capital includes the landlord's apartment building and a homeowner's personal residence. By convention, the purchase of a new house is the one type of household spending categorized as investment rather than consumption.

> **investment**
> spending on business capital, residential capital, and inventories

As mentioned earlier, the treatment of inventory accumulation is noteworthy. When Apple produces a computer and adds it to its inventory instead of selling it, Apple is assumed to have "purchased" the computer for itself. That is, the national income accountants treat the computer as part of Apple's investment spending. (If Apple later sells the computer out of inventory, Apple's inventory investment will then be negative, offsetting the positive expenditure of the buyer.) Inventories are treated this way because one aim of GDP is to measure the value of the economy's production, and goods added to inventory are part of that period's production.

Notice that GDP accounting uses the word *investment* differently from how you might hear the term in everyday conversation. When you hear the word *investment*, you might think of financial investments, such as stocks, bonds, and mutual funds—topics that we study later in this book. By contrast, because GDP measures expenditure on goods and services, here the word *investment* means

Sex, Drugs, and GDP

Some nations are debating what to include in their national income accounts.

No Sex, Please, We're French

By Zachary Karabell

The government of France has just made what on the face of it appears to be a nonannouncement announcement: It will not include illegal drugs and prostitution in its official calculation of the country's gross domestic product.

What made the announcement odd was that it never has included such activities, nor have most countries. Nor do most governments announce what they do not plan to do. ("The U.S. government has no intention of sending a man to Venus.") Yet the French decision comes in the wake of significant pressure from neighboring countries and from the European Union to integrate these activities into national accounts and economic output. That raises a host of questions: *Should* these activities be included, and if those are, why not others? And what exactly are we measuring—and why?

Few numbers shape our world today more than GDP. It has become the alpha and omega of national success, used by politicians and pundits as the primary gauge of national strength and treated as a numerical proxy for greatness or the lack thereof.

Yet GDP is only a statistic, replete with the limitations of all statistics. Created as an outgrowth of national accounts that were themselves only devised in the 1930s, GDP was never an all-inclusive measure, even as it is treated as such. Multiple areas of economic life were left out, including volunteer work and domestic work.

Now Eurostat, the official statistical agency of the European Union, is leading the drive to include a host of illegal activities in national calculations of GDP, most notably prostitution and illicit drugs. The argument, as a United Nations commission laid out in 2008, is fairly simple: Prostitution and illicit drugs are significant economic activities, and if they're not factored into economic statistics, then we're looking at an incomplete picture—which in turn will make it that much harder to craft smart policy. Additionally, different

---

purchases of goods (such as business capital, residential structures, and inventories) that will be used to produce other goods and services in the future.

23-3c Government Purchases

government purchases
spending on goods and services by local, state, and federal governments

Government purchases include spending on goods and services by local, state, and federal governments. It includes the salaries of government workers as well as expenditures on public works. Recently, the U.S. national income accounts have switched to the longer label *government consumption expenditure and gross investment*, but in this book, we will use the traditional and shorter term *government purchases*.

The meaning of government purchases requires a bit of clarification. When the government pays the salary of an Army general or a schoolteacher, that salary is part of government purchases. But when the government pays a Social Security benefit to a person who is elderly or an unemployment insurance benefit to a worker who was recently laid off, the story is very different: These are called *transfer payments* because they are not made in exchange for a currently produced good or service. Transfer payments alter household income, but they do not reflect the economy's production. (From a macroeconomic standpoint, transfer payments are like negative taxes.) Because GDP is intended to measure income from, and expenditure on, the production of goods and services, transfer payments are not counted as part of government purchases.

23-3d Net Exports

net exports
spending on domestically produced goods by foreigners (exports) minus spending on foreign goods by domestic residents (imports)

Net exports equal the foreign purchases of domestically produced goods (exports) minus the domestic purchases of foreign goods (imports). A domestic firm's sale

countries have different laws: In the Netherlands, for instance, prostitution is legal, as is marijuana. Those commercial transactions (or at least those that are recorded and taxed) are already part of Dutch GDP. Not including them in Italy's or Spain's GDPs can thus make it challenging to compare national numbers.

That is why Spain, Italy, Belgium, and the U.K. have in recent months moved to include illegal drugs and nonlicensed sex trade in their national accounts. The U.K. Office for National Statistics in particular approached its mandate with wonkish seriousness, publishing a 20-page précis of its methodology that explained how it would, say, calculate the dollar amount of prostitution (police records help) or deal with domestically produced drugs versus imported drugs. The result, which will be formally announced in September, will be an additional 10 billion pounds added to Great Britain's GDP.

France, however, has demurred. A nation with a clichéd reputation for a certain savoir faire when it comes to sex and other nocturnal activities has decided (or at least its bureaucrats have) that in spite of an EU directive, it will not calculate the effects of illegal activities that are often nonconsensual or nonvoluntary. That is clearly the case for some prostitution—one French minister stated that "street prostitution" is largely controlled by the Mafia—and the same could be reasonably said of the use of some hard drugs, given their addictive nature.

There is undeniably a strong moralistic component in the French decision. By averring that because they are not voluntary or consensual these exchanges should not be included in GDP, the French government is placing a moral vision of what society *should be* ahead of an economic vision of what society *is*. That in turn makes an already messy statistic far messier, and that serves no one's national interests. . . .

With all of GDP's limitations, adding a new moral dimension would only make the number that much less useful. After all, why stop at not including prostitution because it degrades women? Why not refuse to measure coal production because it degrades the environment? Why not leave out cigarette usage because it causes cancer? The list of possible exclusions on this basis is endless.

If GDP is our current best metric for national output, then at the very least it should attempt to include all measurable output. The usually moralistic United States has actually been including legal prostitution in Nevada and now marijuana sales and consumption in Colorado, California, and Washington without any strong objections based solely on the argument that these are commercial exchanges that constitute this fuzzy entity we call "the economy.". . .

Not measuring drugs and sex won't make them go away, but it will hobble efforts to understand the messy latticework of our economic lives, all in a futile attempt to excise what we do not like. ■

Source: *Slate*, June 20, 2014.

to a buyer in another country, such as Boeing's sale of an airplane to British Airways, increases net exports.

The *net* in *net exports* refers to the fact that imports are subtracted from exports. This subtraction is made because other components of GDP include imports of goods and services. For example, suppose that a household buys a $40,000 car from Volvo, the Swedish carmaker. This transaction increases consumption by $40,000 because car purchases are part of consumer spending. It also reduces net exports by $40,000 because the car is an import. In other words, net exports include goods and services produced abroad (with a minus sign) because these goods and services are included in consumption, investment, and government purchases (with a plus sign). Thus, when a domestic household, firm, or government buys a good or service from abroad, the purchase reduces net exports, but because it also raises consumption, investment, or government purchases, it does not affect GDP.

CASE STUDY

THE COMPONENTS OF U.S. GDP

Table 1 shows the composition of U.S. GDP in 2015. In this year, the GDP of the United States was almost $18 trillion. Dividing this number by the 2015 U.S. population of 321 million yields GDP per person (sometimes called GDP per capita). In 2015 the income and expenditure of the average American was $55,882.

Consumption made up 68 percent of GDP, or $38,218 per person. Investment was $9,402 per person. Government purchases were $9,919 per person. Net exports were −$1,657 per person. This number is negative because Americans spent more on foreign goods than foreigners spent on American goods.

GDP and Its Components
This table shows total GDP for the U.S. economy in 2015 and the breakdown of GDP among its four components. When reading this table, recall the identity $Y = C + I + G + NX$.

	Total (in billions of dollars)	Per Person (in dollars)	Percent of Total
Gross domestic product, Y	$17,938	$55,882	100%
Consumption, C	12,268	38,218	68
Investment, I	3,018	9,402	17
Government purchases, G	3,184	9,919	18
Net exports, NX	−532	−1,657	−3

Source: U.S. Department of Commerce. Parts may not sum to totals due to rounding.

These data come from the Bureau of Economic Analysis, the part of the U.S. Department of Commerce that produces the national income accounts. You can find more recent data on GDP on its website, http://www.bea.gov. ●

QuickQuiz *List the four components of expenditure. Which is the largest?*

23-4 Real versus Nominal GDP

As we have seen, GDP measures the total spending on goods and services in all markets in the economy. If total spending rises from one year to the next, at least one of two things must be true: (1) the economy is producing a larger output of goods and services, or (2) goods and services are being sold at higher prices. When studying changes in the economy over time, economists want to separate these two effects. In particular, they want a measure of the total quantity of goods and services the economy is producing that is not affected by changes in the prices of those goods and services.

To do this, economists use a measure called *real GDP*. Real GDP answers a hypothetical question: What would be the value of the goods and services produced this year if we valued these goods and services at the prices that prevailed in some specific year in the past? By evaluating current production using prices that are fixed at past levels, real GDP shows how the economy's overall production of goods and services changes over time.

To see more precisely how real GDP is constructed, let's consider an example.

23-4a A Numerical Example

Table 2 shows some data for an economy that produces only two goods: hot dogs and hamburgers. The table shows the prices and quantities produced of the two goods in the years 2016, 2017, and 2018.

To compute total spending in this economy, we would multiply the quantities of hot dogs and hamburgers by their prices. In the year 2016, 100 hot dogs are sold at a price of $1 per hot dog, so expenditure on hot dogs equals $100. In the same year, 50 hamburgers are sold for $2 per hamburger, so expenditure on hamburgers also equals $100. Total expenditure in the economy—the sum of expenditure on hot dogs and expenditure on hamburgers—is $200. This amount, the production of goods and services valued at current prices, is called **nominal GDP**.

nominal GDP
the production of goods and services valued at current prices

TABLE 2

Real and Nominal GDP

This table shows how to calculate real GDP, nominal GDP, and the GDP deflator for a hypothetical economy that produces only hot dogs and hamburgers.

Prices and Quantities

Year	Price of Hot Dogs	Quantity of Hot Dogs	Price of Hamburgers	Quantity of Hamburgers
2016	$1	100	$2	50
2017	$2	150	$3	100
2018	$3	200	$4	150

Calculating Nominal GDP

2016	($1 per hot dog × 100 hot dogs) + ($2 per hamburger × 50 hamburgers) = $200
2017	($2 per hot dog × 150 hot dogs) + ($3 per hamburger × 100 hamburgers) = $600
2018	($3 per hot dog × 200 hot dogs) + ($4 per hamburger × 150 hamburgers) = $1,200

Calculating Real GDP (base year 2016)

2016	($1 per hot dog × 100 hot dogs) + ($2 per hamburger × 50 hamburgers) = $200
2017	($1 per hot dog × 150 hot dogs) + ($2 per hamburger × 100 hamburgers) = $350
2018	($1 per hot dog × 200 hot dogs) + ($2 per hamburger × 150 hamburgers) = $500

Calculating the GDP Deflator

2016	($200/$200) × 100 = 100
2017	($600/$350) × 100 = 171
2018	($1,200/$500) × 100 = 240

The table shows the calculation of nominal GDP for these 3 years. Total spending rises from $200 in 2016 to $600 in 2017 and then to $1,200 in 2018. Part of this rise is attributable to the increase in the quantities of hot dogs and hamburgers, and part is attributable to the increase in the prices of hot dogs and hamburgers.

To obtain a measure of the amount produced that is not affected by changes in prices, we use **real GDP**, which is the production of goods and services valued at constant prices. We calculate real GDP by first designating 1 year as a *base year*. We then use the prices of hot dogs and hamburgers in the base year to compute the value of goods and services in all the years. In other words, the prices in the base year provide the basis for comparing quantities in different years.

real GDP
the production of goods and services valued at constant prices

Suppose that we choose 2016 to be the base year in our example. We can then use the prices of hot dogs and hamburgers in 2016 to compute the value of goods and services produced in 2016, 2017, and 2018. Table 2 shows these calculations. To compute real GDP for 2016, we use the prices of hot dogs and hamburgers in 2016 (the base year) and the quantities of hot dogs and hamburgers produced in 2016. (Thus, for the base year, real GDP always equals nominal GDP.) To compute real GDP for 2017, we use the prices of hot dogs and hamburgers in 2016 (the base year) and the quantities of hot dogs and hamburgers produced in 2017. Similarly, to compute real GDP for 2018, we use the prices in 2016 and the quantities in 2018. When we find that real GDP has risen from $200 in 2016 to $350 in 2017 and then to $500 in 2018, we know that the increase is attributable to an increase in the quantities produced because the prices are being held fixed at base-year levels.

To sum up: *Nominal GDP uses current prices to place a value on the economy's production of goods and services. Real GDP uses constant base-year prices to place a value on the economy's production of goods and services.* Because real GDP is not affected by changes in prices, changes in real GDP reflect only changes in the amounts being produced. Thus, real GDP is a measure of the economy's production of goods and services.

Our goal in computing GDP is to gauge how well the overall economy is performing. Because real GDP measures the economy's production of goods and services, it reflects the economy's ability to satisfy people's needs and desires. Thus, real GDP is a better gauge of economic well-being than is nominal GDP. When economists talk about the economy's GDP, they usually mean real GDP rather than nominal GDP. And when they talk about growth in the economy, they measure that growth as the percentage change in real GDP from one period to another.

23-4b The GDP Deflator

As we have just seen, nominal GDP reflects both the quantities of goods and services the economy is producing and the prices of those goods and services. By contrast, by holding prices constant at base-year levels, real GDP reflects only the quantities produced. From these two statistics, we can compute a third, called the GDP deflator, which reflects only the prices of goods and services.

The **GDP deflator** is calculated as follows:

GDP deflator

a measure of the price level calculated as the ratio of nominal GDP to real GDP times 100

Because nominal GDP and real GDP must be the same in the base year, the GDP deflator for the base year always equals 100. The GDP deflator for subsequent years measures the change in nominal GDP from the base year that cannot be attributable to a change in real GDP.

The GDP deflator measures the current level of prices relative to the level of prices in the base year. To see why this is true, consider a couple of simple examples. First, imagine that the quantities produced in the economy rise over time but prices remain the same. In this case, both nominal and real GDP rise at the same rate, so the GDP deflator is constant. Now suppose, instead, that prices rise over time but the quantities produced stay the same. In this second case, nominal GDP rises but real GDP remains the same, so the GDP deflator rises. Notice that, in both cases, the GDP deflator reflects what's happening to prices, not quantities.

Let's now return to our numerical example in Table 2. The GDP deflator is computed at the bottom of the table. For the year 2016, nominal GDP is $200 and real GDP is $200, so the GDP deflator is 100. (The deflator is always 100 in the base year.) For the year 2017, nominal GDP is $600 and real GDP is $350, so the GDP deflator is 171.

Economists use the term *inflation* to describe a situation in which the economy's overall price level is rising. The *inflation rate* is the percentage change in some measure of the price level from one period to the next. Using the GDP deflator, the inflation rate between two consecutive years is computed as follows:

Because the GDP deflator rose in year 2017 from 100 to 171, the inflation rate is $100 \times (171 - 100)/100$, or 71 percent. In 2018, the GDP deflator rose to 240 from 171 the previous year, so the inflation rate is $100 \times (240 - 171)/171$, or 40 percent.

The GDP deflator is one measure that economists use to monitor the average level of prices in the economy and thus the rate of inflation. The GDP deflator gets its name because it can be used to take inflation out of nominal GDP—that is, to "deflate" nominal GDP for the rise that is due to increases in prices. We examine another measure of the economy's price level, called the consumer price index, in the next chapter, where we also describe the differences between the two measures.

CASE STUDY

A HALF CENTURY OF REAL GDP

Now that we know how real GDP is defined and measured, let's look at what this macroeconomic variable tells us about the recent history of the United States. Figure 2 shows quarterly data on real GDP for the U.S. economy since 1965.

The most obvious feature of these data is that real GDP grows over time. The real GDP of the U.S. economy in 2015 was more than four times its 1965 level. Put differently, the output of goods and services produced in the United States has grown on average about 3 percent per year. This continued growth in real GDP enables most Americans to enjoy greater economic prosperity than their parents and grandparents did.

A second feature of the GDP data is that growth is not steady. The upward climb of real GDP is occasionally interrupted by periods during which GDP declines, called *recessions*. Figure 2 marks recessions with shaded vertical bars. (There is no ironclad rule for when the official business cycle dating committee will declare that a recession has occurred, but an old rule of thumb is two consecutive quarters of falling real GDP.) Recessions are associated not only with lower incomes but also with other forms of economic distress: rising unemployment, falling profits, increased bankruptcies, and so on.

Much of macroeconomics is aimed at explaining the long-run growth and short-run fluctuations in real GDP. As we will see in the coming chapters, we need different models for these two purposes. Because the short-run fluctuations represent deviations from the long-run trend, we first examine the behavior of key macroeconomic variables, including real GDP, in the long run. Then in later chapters, we build on this analysis to explain short-run fluctuations. ●

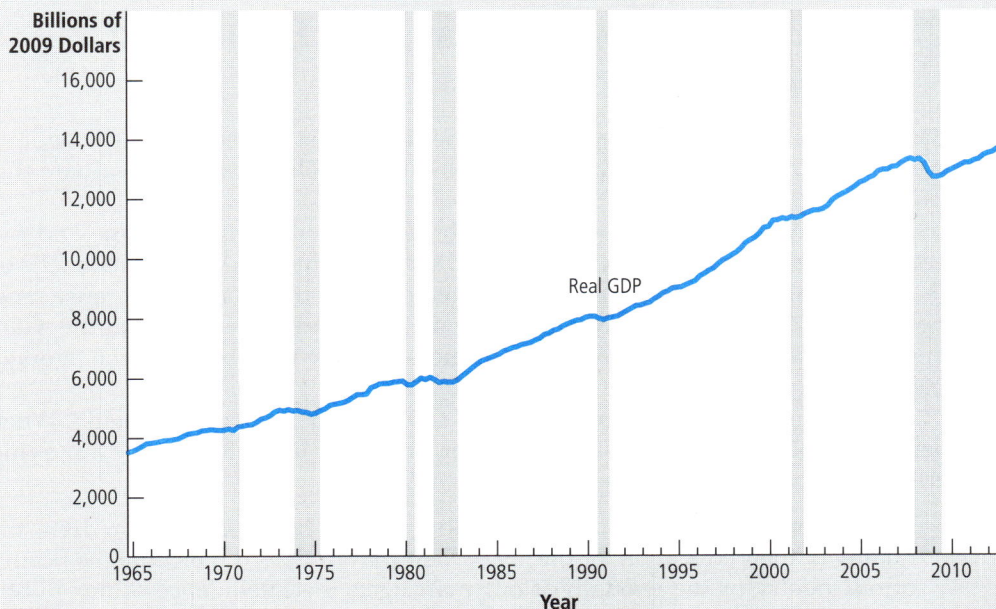

FIGURE 2

Real GDP in the United States
This figure shows quarterly data on real GDP for the U.S. economy since 1965. Recessions— periods of falling real GDP—are marked with the shaded vertical bars.

Source: U.S. Department of Commerce.

IN THE NEWS

Gauging the High-Tech Economy

GDP measures the economy's total output. Labor productivity measures output per unit of labor input. If GDP is incorrectly measured, so is productivity.

Silicon Valley Doesn't Believe U.S. Productivity Is Down

By Timothy Aeppel

MOUNTAIN VIEW, Calif.—Google Inc. chief economist Hal Varian is an evangelist for Silicon Valley's contrarian take on America's productivity slump.

Swiveling to a large screen on the desk behind him, Mr. Varian types in a search for the most commonly asked question on the subject economists elsewhere are wringing their hands over. Up pops, "What is productivity?"

See, he says, vindicated: "Most people don't know what it even means."

To Mr. Varian and other wealthy brains in the world's most innovative neighborhood, productivity means giving people and companies tools to do things better and faster. By that measure, there is an explosion under way, thanks to the shiny gadgets, apps and digital geegaws spewing out of Silicon Valley.

Official U.S. figures tell a different story. For a decade, economic output per hour worked—the federal government's formula for productivity—has barely budged.... Productivity matters, economists point out, because at a 2% annual growth rate, it takes 35 years to double the standard of living; at 1%, it takes 70. Low productivity growth slows the economy and holds down wages.

The 68-year-old Mr. Varian, dressed in a purple hoodie and khaki pants, says the U.S. doesn't have a productivity problem, it has a measurement problem, a sound bite shaping up as the gospel according to Silicon Valley.

"There is a lack of appreciation for what's happening in Silicon Valley," he says, "because we don't have a good way to measure it."

One measurement problem is that a lot of what originates here is free or nearly free. Take, for example, a recent walk Mr. Varian

QuickQuiz *Define* real GDP *and* nominal GDP. *Which is a better measure of economic well-being? Why?*

23-5 Is GDP a Good Measure of Economic Well-Being?

Earlier in this chapter, GDP was called the single best measure of the economic well-being of a society. Now that we know what GDP is, we can evaluate this claim.

As we have seen, GDP measures both the economy's total income and the economy's total expenditure on goods and services. Thus, GDP per person tells us the income and expenditure of the average person in the economy. Because most people would prefer to receive higher income and enjoy higher expenditure, GDP per person seems a natural measure of the economic well-being of the average individual.

Yet some people dispute the validity of GDP as a measure of well-being. When Senator Robert Kennedy was running for president in 1968, he gave a moving critique of such economic measures:

[Gross domestic product] does not allow for the health of our children, the quality of their education, or the joy of their play. It does not include the beauty of our poetry or the strength of our marriages, the intelligence of our public debate or the integrity of our public officials. It measures neither our courage,

arranged with friends. To find each other in the sprawling park nearby, he and his pals used an app that tracked their location, allowing them to meet up quickly. The same tool can track the movement of workers in a warehouse, office or shopping mall.

"Obviously that's a productivity enhancement," Mr. Varian says. "But I doubt that gets measured anywhere."

Consider the efficiency of hailing a taxi with an app on your mobile phone, or finding someone who will meet you at the airport and rent your car while you're away, a new service in San Francisco. Add in online tools that instantly translate conversations or help locate organ donors—the list goes on and on.

Surely, Mr. Varian says, they also make the U.S. more productive....

One problem with the government's productivity measure, Mr. Varian says, is that it is based on gross domestic product, the tally of goods and services produced by the U.S.

economy. GDP was conceived in the 1930s, when economists worried mostly about how much, for example, steel and grain were produced—output easy to measure compared with digital goods and services.

Technological improvements and time-saving apps are trickier. For one thing, it is tough to capture the full impact of quality improvements. For example, if a newer model car breaks down less often than older models but costs the same, the consumers' gain can get lost in the ether....

The U.S. Labor Department has sought to update its GDP measure over the years to include more intangibles, such as adjusting for higher quality. Productivity measures of computer chips, for example, are periodically updated to account for faster speeds. But critics say the process lags behind badly....

Silicon Valley's complaints echo earlier eras. The introduction in the last century of indoor plumbing and household appliances

drastically increased the efficiency of performing domestic chores. But since domestic labor isn't counted in GDP either, the time saved hauling water or washing clothes by hand didn't show up in productivity numbers.

However, these timesaving technologies—among other factors—eventually led to the flood of women into the workforce starting in the 1960s, which, in turn, sent U.S. output soaring.

Mr. Varian is convinced something similar will happen again. At the heart of his argument is the Internet search, cutting short the time to, say, learn how to grow geraniums or find the best Mexican restaurant—a free tool that provides uncounted value at home and at work.... "To be fair," he says, "as we adopt technologies that save time in these nonmarket activities, that frees up time for market-based activities which will show up in GDP." ◼

Source: *The Wall Street Journal*, July 17, 2015.

nor our wisdom, nor our devotion to our country. It measures everything, in short, except that which makes life worthwhile, and it can tell us everything about America except why we are proud that we are Americans.

Much of what Robert Kennedy said is correct. Why, then, do we care about GDP?

The answer is that a large GDP does in fact help us to lead good lives. GDP does not measure the health of our children, but nations with larger GDP can afford better healthcare for their children. GDP does not measure the quality of their education, but nations with larger GDP can afford better educational systems. GDP does not measure the beauty of our poetry, but nations with larger GDP can afford to teach more of their citizens to read and enjoy poetry. GDP does not take account of our intelligence, integrity, courage, wisdom, or devotion to country, but all of these laudable attributes are easier to foster when people are less concerned about being able to afford the material necessities of life. In short, GDP does not directly measure those things that make life worthwhile, but it does measure our ability to obtain many of the inputs for a worthwhile life.

GDP is not, however, a perfect measure of well-being. Some things that contribute to a good life are left out of GDP. One is leisure. Suppose, for instance, that everyone in the economy suddenly started working every day of the week, rather than enjoying leisure on weekends. More goods and services would be produced, and GDP would rise. But despite the increase in GDP, we should not conclude that everyone would be better off. The loss from reduced leisure would offset the gain from producing and consuming a greater quantity of goods and services.

Because GDP uses market prices to value goods and services, it excludes the value of almost all activity that takes place outside markets. In particular, GDP

Measuring Macroeconomic Well-Being

Can we do better than using gross domestic product?

Nations Seek Success Beyond GDP

By Mark Whitehouse

Money isn't everything. But in measuring the success of nations, it isn't easy to find a substitute.

Political leaders are increasingly expressing dissatisfaction with gross domestic product—a monetary measure of all the goods and services a country produces—as a gauge of a nation's success in raising living standards.

In November, British Prime Minister David Cameron announced plans to build measures of national well-being that would take into account factors such as peoples' life satisfaction, following a similar effort by French President Nicolas Sarkozy.

Their efforts cut to the core of what economics is supposed to be about: What makes us better off? How can we all have more of it? Anyone hoping for a clear-cut answer, though, is likely to be disappointed.

"There is more to life than GDP, but it will be hard to come up with a single measure to replace it and we are not sure that a single measure is the answer," said Paul Allin, director of the Measuring National Well-Being

Project at the U.K.'s Office of National Statistics. "Maybe we live in a multidimensional world and we have to get used to handling a reasonable number of bits of information."

After a session on creating a national success indicator at the annual meeting of the American Economic Association on Friday, Carol Graham, fellow at the Brookings Institution, summed up the situation thus: "It's like a new science. There's still a lot of work to be done."

For much of the past four decades, economists have puzzled over a paradox that cast doubt on GDP as the world's main indicator of success.

People in richer countries didn't appear to be any happier than people in poor countries. In research beginning in the 1970s, University of Pennsylvania economist Richard Easterlin found no evidence of a link between countries' income—as measured by GDP per person—and peoples' reported levels of happiness.

More recent research suggests GDP isn't quite so bad. Using more data and different statistical techniques, three economists at the University of Pennsylvania's Wharton School—Daniel Sacks, Betsey Stevenson and Justin Wolfers—found that a given percentage increase in GDP per person tends to coincide with a similar increase in reported well-being. The correlation held across different countries and over time.

Still, for measuring the success of policy, GDP is far from ideal. Making everybody work 120 hours a week could radically boost a country's GDP per capita, but it wouldn't make people happier. Removing pollution limits could boost GDP per hour worked, but wouldn't necessarily lead to a world we'd want to live in.

One approach is to enhance GDP with other objective factors such as inequality, leisure and life expectancy. In a paper presented Saturday at the American Economic Association meeting, Stanford economists Peter Klenow and Charles Jones found that doing so can make a big difference.

By their calculation, accounting for longer life expectancy, additional leisure time and lower levels of inequality makes living standards in France and Germany look almost the same as those in the U.S., which otherwise leads the pack by a large margin.

Mr. Klenow points out that the calculation is fraught with difficulties. For one, many countries have poor data on crucial factors such as life expectancy.

omits the value of goods and services produced at home. When a chef prepares a delicious meal and sells it at her restaurant, the value of that meal is part of GDP. But if the chef prepares the same meal for her family, the value she has added to the raw ingredients is left out of GDP. Similarly, child care provided in day-care centers is part of GDP, whereas child care by parents at home is not. Volunteer work also contributes to the well-being of those in society, but GDP does not reflect these contributions.

Another thing that GDP excludes is the quality of the environment. Imagine that the government eliminated all environmental regulations. Firms could then produce goods and services without considering the pollution they create,

For the purpose of comparing well-being across countries, asking people how they feel might be better than monetary measures. Angus Deaton, an economist at Princeton University, notes that placing values on the extremely different goods and services consumed in the U.S. and, say, Tajikistan, can be impossible to do in a comparable way. Just asking people about their situation could be much easier and no less accurate.

Surveys already play a meaningful role in the way many countries assess their performance, from consumer confidence in the U.S. to the Netherlands's Life Situation Index, which accounts for factors such as relationships and community involvement.

As part of its effort to gauge well-being, the U.K. plans to add more subjective questions to its household surveys.

But surveys can also send misleading policy signals. Mr. Wolfers, for example, has found that surveys of women's subjective well-being in the U.S. suggest that they are less happy than they were four decades ago, despite improvements in wages, education and other objective measures. That, he says, doesn't mean the feminist movement should be reversed. Rather, it could be related to rising expectations or greater frankness among the women interviewed.

Peoples' true preferences are often revealed more by what they do than by what they say. Surveys suggest people with children tend to be less happy than those without, yet people keep having children—and nobody would advocate mass sterilization to improve overall well-being.

"What we care about in the world is not just happiness," says Mr. Wolfers. "If you measure just one part of what makes for a full life you're going to end up harming the other parts."

For the time being, that leaves policy makers to choose the measures of success that seem most appropriate for the task at hand. That's not ideal, but it's the best economics has to offer. ∎

Source: *The Wall Street Journal*, January 10, 2011.

Happily ever after

More wealth doesn't always translate into greater quality of life, when factors such as leisure and length of life are included.

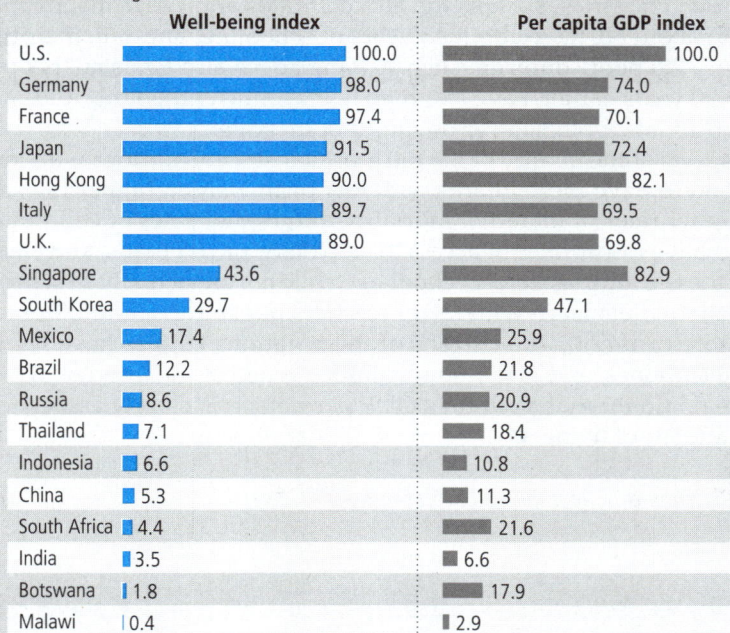

	Well-being index	Per capita GDP index
U.S.	100.0	100.0
Germany	98.0	74.0
France	97.4	70.1
Japan	91.5	72.4
Hong Kong	90.0	82.1
Italy	89.7	69.5
U.K.	89.0	69.8
Singapore	43.6	82.9
South Korea	29.7	47.1
Mexico	17.4	25.9
Brazil	12.2	21.8
Russia	8.6	20.9
Thailand	7.1	18.4
Indonesia	6.6	10.8
China	5.3	11.3
South Africa	4.4	21.6
India	3.5	6.6
Botswana	1.8	17.9
Malawi	0.4	2.9

Source: Peter Klenow and Charles Jones, Stanford University. Data are for 2000.

and GDP might rise. Yet well-being would most likely fall. The deterioration in the quality of air and water would more than offset the gains from greater production.

GDP also says nothing about the distribution of income. A society in which 100 people have annual incomes of $50,000 has GDP of $5 million and, not surprisingly, GDP per person of $50,000. So does a society in which 10 people earn $500,000 and 90 suffer with nothing at all. Few people would look at those two situations and call them equivalent. GDP per person tells us what happens to the average person, but behind the average lies a large variety of personal experiences.

In the end, we can conclude that GDP is a good measure of economic well-being for most—but not all—purposes. It is important to keep in mind what GDP includes and what it leaves out.

CASE STUDY

INTERNATIONAL DIFFERENCES IN GDP AND THE QUALITY OF LIFE
One way to gauge the usefulness of GDP as a measure of economic well-being is to examine international data. Rich and poor countries have vastly different levels of GDP per person. If a large GDP leads to a higher standard of living, then we should observe GDP to be strongly correlated with various measures of the quality of life. And, in fact, we do.

Table 3 shows twelve large nations ranked in order of GDP per person. The table also shows life expectancy at birth, the average years of schooling among adults, and an index of life satisfaction based on asking people to gauge how they feel about their lives on a scale of 0 to 10 (with 10 being the best). These data show a clear pattern. In rich countries, such as the United States and Germany, people can expect to live to about 80, have about 13 years of schooling, and rate their life satisfaction at about 7. In poor countries, such as Bangladesh and Pakistan, people typically die about 10 years earlier, have less than half as much schooling, and rate their life satisfaction about 2 points lower on the 10-point scale.

Data on other aspects of the quality of life tell a similar story. Countries with low GDP per person tend to have more infants with low birth weight, higher rates of infant mortality, higher rates of maternal mortality, and higher rates of child malnutrition. They also have lower rates of access to electricity, paved roads, and clean drinking water. In these countries, fewer school-age children are actually in school, those who are in school must learn with fewer teachers per student, and illiteracy among adults is more common. The citizens of these nations tend to have fewer televisions, fewer telephones, and fewer opportunities to access the Internet. International data leave no doubt that a nation's GDP per person is closely associated with its citizens' standard of living. ●

QuickQuiz   *Why should policymakers care about GDP?*

TABLE 3

GDP and the Quality of Life

The table shows GDP per person and three other measures of the quality of life for twelve major countries.

Source: *Human Development Report 2015,* United Nations. Real GDP is for 2014, expressed in 2011 dollars. Average years of schooling is among adults 25 years and older.

Country	Real GDP per Person	Life Expectancy	Average Years of Schooling	Overall Life Satisfaction (0 to 10 scale)
United States	$52,947	79 years	13 years	7.2
Germany	43,919	81	13	7.0
Japan	36,927	83	12	5.9
Russia	22,352	70	12	6.0
Mexico	16,056	77	9	6.7
Brazil	15,175	74	8	7.0
China	12,547	76	8	5.2
Indonesia	9,788	69	8	5.6
India	5,497	68	5	4.4
Nigeria	5,341	53	6	4.8
Pakistan	4,866	66	5	5.4
Bangladesh	3,191	72	5	4.6

23-6 Conclusion

In this chapter we learned how economists measure the total income of a nation. Measurement is, of course, only a starting point. Much of macroeconomics is aimed at revealing the long-run and short-run determinants of a nation's gross domestic product. Why, for example, is GDP higher in the United States and Japan than in India and Nigeria? What can the governments of the poorest countries do to promote more rapid GDP growth? Why does GDP in the United States rise rapidly in some years and fall in others? What can U.S. policymakers do to reduce the severity of these fluctuations in GDP? These are the questions we will take up shortly.

At this point, it is important to acknowledge the significance of just measuring GDP. We all get some sense of how the economy is doing as we go about our lives. But the economists who study changes in the economy and the policymakers who formulate economic policies need more than this vague sense—they need concrete data on which to base their judgments. Quantifying the behavior of the economy with statistics such as GDP is, therefore, the first step to developing a science of macroeconomics.

CHAPTER QuickQuiz

1. If the price of a hot dog is $2 and the price of a hamburger is $4, then 30 hot dogs contribute as much to GDP as _____ hamburgers.
   a. 5
   b. 15
   c. 30
   d. 60

2. Angus the sheep farmer sells wool to Barnaby the knitter for $20. Barnaby makes two sweaters, each of which has a market price of $40. Collette buys one of them, while the other remains on the shelf of Barnaby's store to be sold later. What is GDP here?
   a. $40
   b. $60
   c. $80
   d. $100

3. Which of the following does NOT add to U.S. GDP?
   a. Air France buys a plane from Boeing, the U.S. aircraft manufacturer.
   b. General Motors builds a new auto factory in North Carolina.
   c. The city of New York pays a salary to a policeman.
   d. The federal government sends a Social Security check to your grandmother.

4. An American buys a pair of shoes made in Italy. How do the U.S. national income accounts treat the transaction?
   a. Net exports and GDP both rise.
   b. Net exports and GDP both fall.
   c. Net exports fall, while GDP is unchanged.
   d. Net exports are unchanged, while GDP rises.

5. Which is the largest component of GDP?
   a. consumption
   b. investment
   c. government purchases
   d. net exports

6. If all quantities produced rise by 10 percent and all prices fall by 10 percent, which of the following occurs?
   a. Real GDP rises by 10 percent, while nominal GDP falls by 10 percent.
   b. Real GDP rises by 10 percent, while nominal GDP is unchanged.
   c. Real GDP is unchanged, while nominal GDP rises by 10 percent.
   d. Real GDP is unchanged, while nominal GDP falls by 10 percent.

SUMMARY

- Because every transaction has a buyer and a seller, the total expenditure in the economy must equal the total income in the economy.
- Gross domestic product (GDP) measures an economy's total expenditure on newly produced goods and services and the total income earned from the production of these goods and services. More precisely, GDP is the market value of all final goods and services produced within a country in a given period of time.
- GDP is divided among four components of expenditure: consumption, investment, government purchases, and net exports. Consumption includes spending on goods and services by households, with the exception of purchases of new housing. Investment includes spending on business capital, residential capital, and inventories. Government purchases include spending

on goods and services by local, state, and federal governments. Net exports equal the value of goods and services produced domestically and sold abroad (exports) minus the value of goods and services produced abroad and sold domestically (imports).
- Nominal GDP uses current prices to value the economy's production of goods and services. Real GDP uses constant base-year prices to value the economy's production of goods and services. The GDP deflator—calculated from the ratio of nominal to real GDP—measures the level of prices in the economy.
- GDP is a good measure of economic well-being because people prefer higher to lower incomes. But it is not a perfect measure of well-being. For example, GDP excludes the value of leisure and the value of a clean environment.

KEY CONCEPTS

microeconomics, p. 474
macroeconomics, p. 474
gross domestic product (GDP), p. 476
consumption, p. 479

investment, p. 479
government purchases, p. 480
net exports, p. 480
nominal GDP, p. 482

real GDP, p. 483
GDP deflator, p. 484

QUESTIONS FOR REVIEW

1. Explain why an economy's income must equal its expenditure.

2. Which contributes more to GDP—the production of an economy car or the production of a luxury car? Why?

3. A farmer sells wheat to a baker for $2. The baker uses the wheat to make bread, which is sold for $3. What is the total contribution of these transactions to GDP?

4. Many years ago, Peggy paid $500 to put together a record collection. Today, she sold her albums at a garage sale for $100. How does this sale affect current GDP?

5. List the four components of GDP. Give an example of each.

6. Why do economists use real GDP rather than nominal GDP to gauge economic well-being?

7. In the year 2017, the economy produces 100 loaves of bread that sell for $2 each. In the year 2018, the economy produces 200 loaves of bread that sell for $3 each. Calculate nominal GDP, real GDP, and the GDP deflator for each year. (Use 2017 as the base year.) By what percentage does each of these three statistics rise from one year to the next?

8. Why is it desirable for a country to have a large GDP? Give an example of something that would raise GDP and yet be undesirable.

PROBLEMS AND APPLICATIONS

1. What components of GDP (if any) would each of the following transactions affect? Explain.
    a. Uncle Henry buys a new refrigerator from a domestic manufacturer.
    b. Aunt Jane buys a new house from a local builder.
    c. The Jackson family buys an old Victorian house from the Walker family.
    d. You pay a hairdresser for a haircut.
    e. Ford sells a Mustang from its inventory to the Martinez family.
    f. Ford manufactures a Focus and sells it to Avis, the car rental company.
    g. California hires workers to repave Highway 101.
    h. The federal government sends your grandmother a Social Security check.
    i. Your parents buy a bottle of French wine.
    j. Honda expands its factory in Ohio.

2. Fill in the blanks:

Year	Real GDP (in 2000 dollars)	Nominal GDP (in current dollars)	GDP Deflator (base year 2000)
1970	3,000	1,200	_____
1980	5,000	_____	60
1990	_____	6,000	100
2000	_____	8,000	_____
2010	_____	15,000	200
2020	10,000	_____	300
2030	20,000	50,000	_____

3. The government purchases component of GDP does not include spending on transfer payments such as Social Security. Thinking about the definition of GDP, explain why transfer payments are excluded.

4. As the chapter states, GDP does not include the value of used goods that are resold. Why would including such transactions make GDP a less informative measure of economic well-being?

5. Below are some data from the land of milk and honey.

Year	Price of Milk	Quantity of Milk	Price of Honey	Quantity of Honey
2016	$1	100 quarts	$2	50 quarts
2017	1	200	2	100
2018	2	200	4	100

    a. Compute nominal GDP, real GDP, and the GDP deflator for each year, using 2016 as the base year.
    b. Compute the percentage change in nominal GDP, real GDP, and the GDP deflator in 2017 and 2018 from the preceding year. For each year, identify the variable that does not change. Explain why your answer makes sense.
    c. Did economic well-being increase more in 2017 or 2018? Explain.

6. Consider an economy that produces only chocolate bars. In year 1, the quantity produced is 3 bars and the price is $4. In year 2, the quantity produced is 4 bars and the price is $5. In year 3, the quantity produced is 5 bars and the price is $6. Year 1 is the base year.
    a. What is nominal GDP for each of these three years?
    b. What is real GDP for each of these years?
    c. What is the GDP deflator for each of these years?
    d. What is the percentage growth rate of real GDP from year 2 to year 3?
    e. What is the inflation rate as measured by the GDP deflator from year 2 to year 3?
    f. In this one-good economy, how might you have answered parts (d) and (e) without first answering parts (b) and (c)?

7. Consider the following data on U.S. GDP:

Year	Nominal GDP (in billions of dollars)	GDP Deflator (base year 2009)
2014	17,419	108.3
1994	7,309	73.8

    a. What was the growth rate of nominal GDP between 1994 and 2014? (*Hint*: The growth rate of a variable X over an N-year period is calculated as $100 \times [(X_{final}/X_{initial})^{1/N} - 1]$.)
    b. What was the growth rate of the GDP deflator between 1994 and 2014?
    c. What was real GDP in 1994 measured in 2009 prices?
    d. What was real GDP in 2014 measured in 2009 prices?
    e. What was the growth rate of real GDP between 1994 and 2014?
    f. Was the growth rate of nominal GDP higher or lower than the growth rate of real GDP? Explain.

8. Revised estimates of U.S. GDP are usually released by the government near the end of each month. Find a newspaper article that reports on the most recent release, or read the news release yourself at http://www.bea.gov, the website of the U.S. Bureau of Economic Analysis. Discuss the recent changes in real and nominal GDP and in the components of GDP.

9. A farmer grows wheat, which she sells to a miller for $100. The miller turns the wheat into flour, which she sells to a baker for $150. The baker turns the wheat

23

into bread, which she sells to consumers for $180. Consumers eat the bread.

   a. What is GDP in this economy? Explain.

   b. *Value added* is defined as the value of a producer's output minus the value of the intermediate goods that the producer buys to make the output. Assuming there are no intermediate goods beyond those described above, calculate the value added of each of the three producers.

   c. What is total value added of the three producers in this economy? How does it compare to the economy's GDP? Does this example suggest another way of calculating GDP?

10. Goods and services that are not sold in markets, such as food produced and consumed at home, are generally not included in GDP. Can you think of how this might cause the numbers in the second column of Table 3 to be misleading in a comparison of the economic well-being of the United States and India? Explain.

11. The participation of women in the U.S. labor force has risen dramatically since 1970.

   a. How do you think this rise affected GDP?

   b. Now imagine a measure of well-being that includes time spent working in the home and taking leisure. How would the change in this measure of well-being compare to the change in GDP?

   c. Can you think of other aspects of well-being that are associated with the rise in women's labor-force participation? Would it be practical to construct a measure of well-being that includes these aspects?

12. One day, Barry the Barber, Inc., collects $400 for haircuts. Over this day, his equipment depreciates in value by $50. Of the remaining $350, Barry sends $30 to the government in sales taxes, takes home $220 in wages, and retains $100 in his business to add new equipment in the future. From the $220 that Barry takes home, he pays $70 in income taxes. Based on this information, compute Barry's contribution to the following measures of income.

   a. gross domestic product

   b. net national product

   c. national income

   d. personal income

   e. disposable personal income

To find additional study resources, visit cengagebrain.com, and search for "Mankiw."

Measuring the Cost of Living

In 1931, as the U.S. economy was suffering through the Great Depression, the New York Yankees paid famed baseball player Babe Ruth a salary of $80,000. At the time, this pay was extraordinary, even among the stars of baseball. According to one story, a reporter asked Ruth whether he thought it was right that he made more than President Herbert Hoover, who had a salary of $75,000. Ruth replied, "I had a better year."

In 2015, the average salary earned by major league baseball players was about $4 million, and Los Angeles Dodgers pitcher Clayton Kershaw was paid $31 million. At first, this fact might lead you to think that baseball has become vastly more lucrative over the past eight decades. But as everyone knows, the prices of goods and services have also risen. In 1931, a

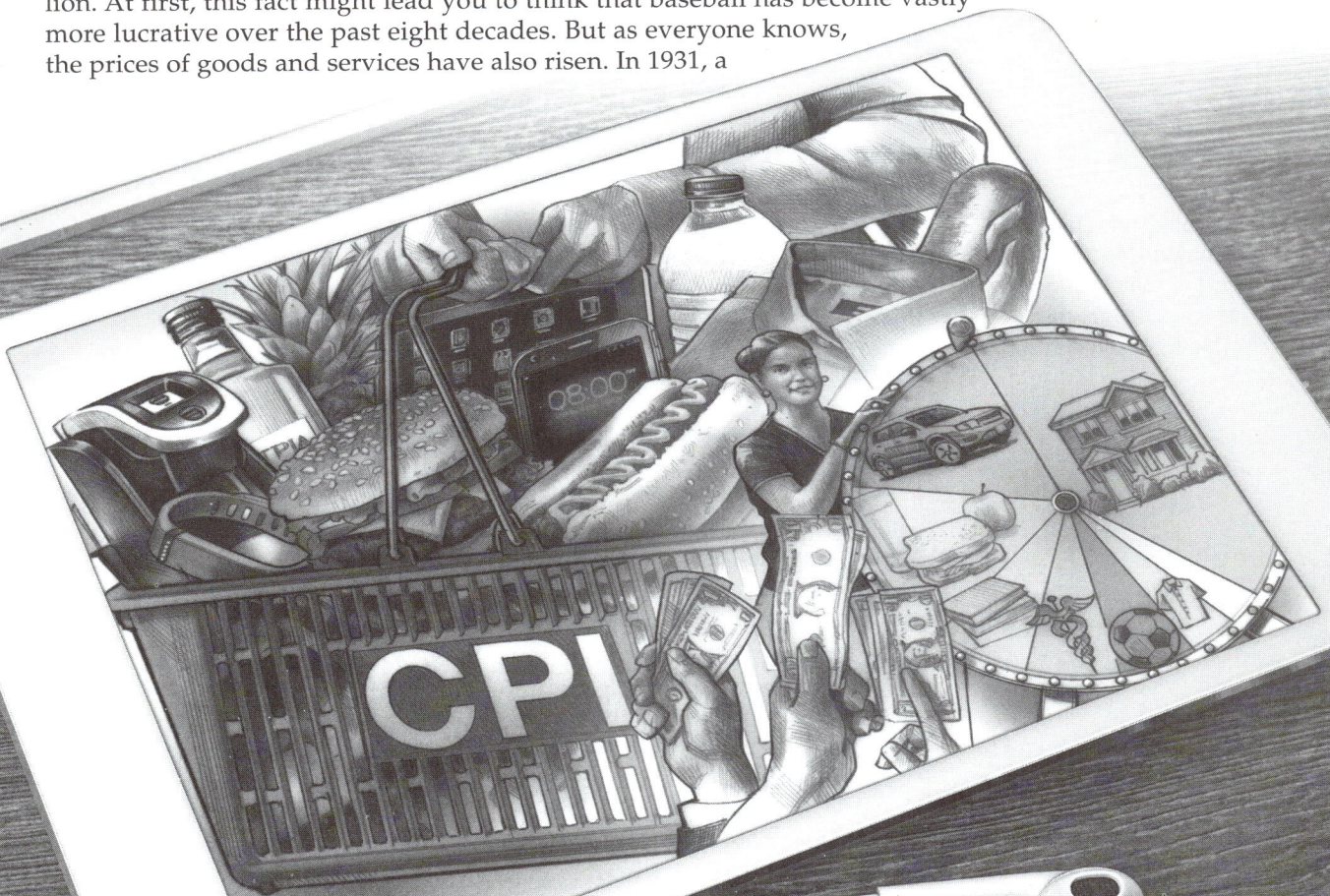

nickel would buy an ice-cream cone and a quarter would buy a ticket at the local movie theater. Because prices were so much lower in Babe Ruth's day than they are today, it is not clear whether Ruth enjoyed a higher or lower standard of living than today's players.

In the preceding chapter, we looked at how economists use gross domestic product (GDP) to measure the quantity of goods and services that the economy is producing. This chapter examines how economists measure the overall cost of living. To compare Babe Ruth's salary of $80,000 to salaries from today, we need to find some way of turning dollar figures into meaningful measures of purchasing power. That is exactly the job of a statistic called the *consumer price index*, or simply the CPI. After seeing how the CPI is constructed, we discuss how we can use such a price index to compare dollar figures from different points in time.

The CPI is used to monitor changes in the cost of living over time. When the CPI rises, the typical family has to spend more money to maintain the same standard of living. Economists use the term *inflation* to describe a situation in which the economy's overall price level is rising. The *inflation rate* is the percentage change in the price level from the previous period. The preceding chapter showed how economists can measure inflation using the GDP deflator. The inflation rate you are likely to hear on the nightly news, however, is calculated from the CPI, which better reflects the goods and services bought by consumers.

As we will see in the coming chapters, inflation is a closely watched aspect of macroeconomic performance and is a key variable guiding macroeconomic policy. This chapter provides the background for that analysis by showing how economists measure the inflation rate using the CPI and how this statistic can be used to compare dollar figures from different times.

24-1 The Consumer Price Index

consumer price index (CPI)
a measure of the overall cost of the goods and services bought by a typical consumer

The **consumer price index (CPI)** is a measure of the overall cost of the goods and services bought by a typical consumer. Every month, the Bureau of Labor Statistics (BLS), which is part of the Department of Labor, computes and reports the CPI. In this section, we discuss how the CPI is calculated and what problems arise in its measurement. We also consider how this index compares to the GDP deflator, another measure of the overall level of prices, which we examined in the preceding chapter.

24-1a How the CPI Is Calculated

When the BLS calculates the CPI and the inflation rate, it uses data on the prices of thousands of goods and services. To see exactly how these statistics are constructed, let's consider a simple economy in which consumers buy only two goods: hot dogs and hamburgers. Table 1 shows the five steps that the BLS follows.

1. *Fix the basket.* Determine which prices are most important to the typical consumer. If the typical consumer buys more hot dogs than hamburgers, then the price of hot dogs is more important than the price of hamburgers and, therefore, should be given greater weight in measuring the cost of living. The BLS sets these weights by surveying consumers to find the basket of goods and services bought by the typical consumer. In the example in the table, the typical consumer buys a basket of 4 hot dogs and 2 hamburgers.
2. *Find the prices.* Find the prices of each of the goods and services in the basket at each point in time. The table shows the prices of hot dogs and hamburgers for three different years.

Step 1: Survey Consumers to Determine a Fixed Basket of Goods

Basket = 4 hot dogs, 2 hamburgers

Step 2: Find the Price of Each Good in Each Year

Year	Price of Hot Dogs	Price of Hamburgers
2016	$1	$2
2017	2	3
2018	3	4

Step 3: Compute the Cost of the Basket of Goods in Each Year

2016	($1 per hot dog × 4 hot dogs) + ($2 per hamburger × 2 hamburgers) = $8 per basket
2017	($2 per hot dog × 4 hot dogs) + ($3 per hamburger × 2 hamburgers) = $14 per basket
2018	($3 per hot dog × 4 hot dogs) + ($4 per hamburger × 2 hamburgers) = $20 per basket

Step 4: Choose One Year as a Base Year (2016) and Compute the CPI in Each Year

2016	($8/$8) × 100 = 100
2017	($14/$8) × 100 = 175
2018	($20/$8) × 100 = 250

Step 5: Use the CPI to Compute the Inflation Rate from Previous Year

2017	(175 − 100)/100 × 100 = 75%
2018	(250 − 175)/175 × 100 = 43%

TABLE 1

Calculating the Consumer Price Index and the Inflation Rate: An Example This table shows how to calculate the CPI and the inflation rate for a hypothetical economy in which consumers buy only hot dogs and hamburgers.

3. *Compute the basket's cost.* Use the data on prices to calculate the cost of the basket of goods and services at different times. The table shows this calculation for each of the three years. Notice that only the prices in this calculation change. By keeping the basket of goods the same (4 hot dogs and 2 hamburgers), we are isolating the effects of price changes from the effects of any quantity changes that might be occurring at the same time.
4. *Choose a base year and compute the index.* Designate one year as the base year, the benchmark against which other years are to be compared. (The choice of base year is arbitrary. The index is used to measure percentage changes in the cost of living, and these changes are the same regardless of the choice of base year.) Once the base year is chosen, the index is calculated as follows:

That is, the price of the basket of goods and services in each year is divided by the price of the basket in the base year, and this ratio is then multiplied by 100. The resulting number is the CPI.

In the example in Table 1, 2016 is the base year. In this year, the basket of hot dogs and hamburgers costs $8. Therefore, to calculate the CPI, the price of the basket in each year is divided by $8 and multiplied by 100. The CPI is 100 in 2016. (The index is always 100 in the base year.) The CPI is 175 in 2017. This means that the price of the basket in 2017 is 175 percent of its price in the base year. Put differently, a basket of goods that costs $100 in the base year costs

inflation rate

the percentage change in
the price index from the
preceding period

$175 in 2017. Similarly, the CPI is 250 in 2018, indicating that the price level in 2018 is 250 percent of the price level in the base year.

5. *Compute the inflation rate.* Use the CPI to calculate the **inflation rate**, which is the percentage change in the price index from the preceding period. That is, the inflation rate between two consecutive years is computed as follows:

As shown at the bottom of Table 1, the inflation rate in our example is 75 percent in 2017 and 43 percent in 2018.

Although this example simplifies the real world by including only two goods, it shows how the BLS computes the CPI and the inflation rate. The BLS collects and processes data on the prices of thousands of goods and services every month and, by following the five foregoing steps, determines how quickly the cost of living for the typical consumer is rising. When the BLS makes its monthly announcement of the CPI, you can usually hear the number on the evening television news or see it in the next day's newspaper.

In addition to the CPI for the overall economy, the BLS calculates several other price indexes. It reports the index for some narrow categories of goods and services, such as food, clothing, and energy. It also calculates the CPI for all goods

FYI

What's in the CPI's Basket?

When constructing the consumer price index, the Bureau of Labor Statistics tries to include all the goods and services that the typical consumer buys. Moreover, it tries to weight these goods and services according to how much consumers buy of each item.

Figure 1 shows the breakdown of consumer spending into the major categories of goods and services. By far the largest category is housing, which makes up 42 percent of the typical consumer's budget. This category includes the cost of shelter (33 percent), fuel and utilities (5 percent), and household furnishings and operation (4 percent). The next largest category, at 16 percent, is transportation, which includes spending on cars, gasoline, buses, subways, and so on. The next category, at 15 percent, is food and beverages; this includes food at home (8 percent), food away from home (6 percent), and alcoholic beverages (1 percent). Next are medical care at 8 percent, education and communication at 7 percent, and recreation at 6 percent. Apparel, which includes clothing, footwear, and jewelry, makes up 3 percent of the typical consumer's budget.

Also included in the figure, at 3 percent of spending, is a category for other goods and services. This is a catchall for consumer purchases (such as cigarettes, haircuts, and funeral expenses) that do not naturally fit into the other categories. ■

FIGURE 1

The Typical Basket of Goods and Services

This figure shows how the typical consumer divides spending among various categories of goods and services. The Bureau of Labor Statistics calls each percentage the "relative importance" of the category.

Source: Bureau of Labor Statistics.

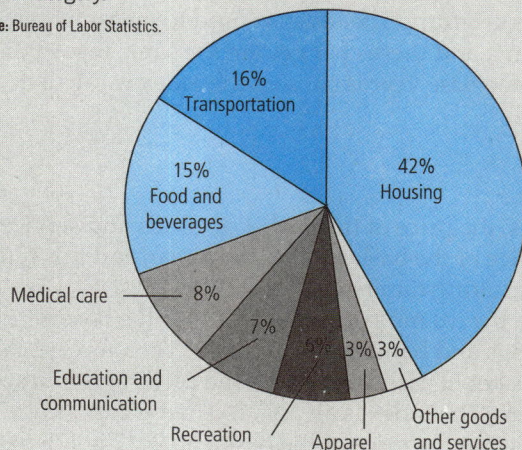

and services excluding food and energy, a statistic called the **core CPI**. Because food and energy prices show substantial short-run volatility, the core CPI better reflects ongoing inflation trends. Finally, the BLS also calculates the **producer price index** (PPI), which measures the cost of a basket of goods and services bought by firms rather than consumers. Because firms eventually pass on their costs to consumers in the form of higher consumer prices, changes in the PPI are often thought to be useful in predicting changes in the CPI.

core CPI
a measure of the overall cost of consumer goods and services excluding food and energy

producer price index
a measure of the cost of a basket of goods and services bought by firms

24-1b Problems in Measuring the Cost of Living

The goal of the consumer price index is to measure changes in the cost of living. In other words, the CPI tries to gauge how much incomes must rise to maintain a constant standard of living. The CPI, however, is not a perfect measure of the cost of living. Three problems with the index are widely acknowledged but difficult to solve.

The first problem is called *substitution bias*. When prices change from one year to the next, they do not all change proportionately: Some prices rise more than others. Consumers respond to these differing price changes by buying less of the goods whose prices have risen by relatively large amounts and by buying more of the goods whose prices have risen less or perhaps even have fallen. That is, consumers substitute toward goods that have become relatively less expensive. If a price index is computed assuming a fixed basket of goods, it ignores the possibility of consumer substitution and, therefore, overstates the increase in the cost of living from one year to the next.

Let's consider a simple example. Imagine that in the base year, apples are cheaper than pears, so consumers buy more apples than pears. When the BLS constructs the basket of goods, it will include more apples than pears. Suppose that next year pears are cheaper than apples. Consumers will naturally respond to the price changes by buying more pears and fewer apples. Yet when computing the CPI, the BLS uses a fixed basket, which in essence assumes that consumers continue buying the now expensive apples in the same quantities as before. For this reason, the index will measure a much larger increase in the cost of living than consumers actually experience.

The second problem with the CPI is the *introduction of new goods*. When a new good is introduced, consumers have more variety from which to choose, and this in turn reduces the cost of maintaining the same level of economic well-being. To see why, consider a hypothetical situation: Suppose you could choose between a $100 gift certificate at a large store that offered a wide array of goods and a $100 gift certificate at a small store with the same prices but a more limited selection. Which would you prefer? Most people would pick the store with greater variety. In essence, the increased set of possible choices makes each dollar more valuable. The same is true with the evolution of the economy over time: As new goods are introduced, consumers have more choices, and each dollar is worth more. But because the CPI is based on a fixed basket of goods and services, it does not reflect the increase in the value of the dollar that arises from the introduction of new goods.

Again, let's consider an example. When the iPod was introduced in 2001, consumers found it more convenient to listen to their favorite music. Devices to play music were available previously, but they were not nearly as portable and versatile. The iPod was a new option that increased consumers' set of opportunities. For any given number of dollars, the introduction of the iPod made people better off; conversely, achieving the same level of economic well-being required a smaller number of dollars. A perfect cost-of-living index would have reflected the introduction of the iPod with a decrease in the cost of living. The CPI, however, did not decrease in response to the introduction of the iPod. Eventually, the BLS revised the basket of goods to include the iPod, and subsequently, the index reflected changes in iPod prices. But the reduction in the cost of living associated with the initial introduction of the iPod never showed up in the index.

The third problem with the CPI is *unmeasured quality change*. If the quality of a good deteriorates from one year to the next while its price remains the same, the value of a dollar falls, because you are getting a lesser good for the same amount of money. Similarly, if the quality rises from one year to the next, the value of a dollar rises. The BLS does its best to account for quality change. When the quality of a good in the basket changes—for example, when a car model has more horsepower or gets better gas mileage from one year to the next—the Bureau adjusts the price of the good to account for the quality change. It is, in essence,

IN THE NEWS

Monitoring Inflation in the Internet Age

The web is providing alternative ways to collect data on the overall level of prices.

Do We Need Google to Measure Inflation?

By Annie Lowrey

At some 23,000 retailers and businesses in 90 U.S. cities, hundreds of government workers find and mark down prices on very precise products. And I'm not kidding when I say "very precise."

Say the relevant worker is finding the price for a motel room. She might write a report like this: *Occupancy*—two adults; *Type of accommodation*—deluxe room; *Room classification/location*—ocean view, room 306; *Time of stay*—weekend; *Length of stay*—one night; *Bathroom facilities*—one full bathroom; *Kitchen facilities*—none; *Television*—one, includes free movie channel; *Telephone*—one telephone, free local calls; *Air-conditioned*—yes; *Meals included*—breakfast; *Parking*—free self parking; *Transportation*—Transportation to airport, no charge; *Recreation facilities*—an indoor and an outdoor pool, a private beach, three tennis courts, and an exercise room.

This mind-numbingly tedious process goes on for a dizzying panoply of items:

wine, takeaway meals, bedroom furniture, surgical procedures, pet dogs, college tuition, cigarettes, haircuts, funerals. When all of the prices are marked down, the workers submit forms that are collated, checked, and input into massive spreadsheets. Then the government boils all those numbers down to one. It weights certain prices, taking into account that consumers spend more on rent than cereal, for instance. It considers product improvements and changes in spending habits. Then it comes up with a master number showing how much a customer's spending needed to increase to buy the same goods, month-on-month. That number is the Consumer Price Index, the government's main gauge of inflation.

Each month, the Bureau of Labor Statistics goes through all that hassle because knowing the rate of inflation is such an important measure of economic health—and it's important to the government's own budget. High inflation? Savers panic, watching the spending power of their accounts erode. Deflation? Everyone saves, awaiting cheaper prices in a few months. And wildly changing inflation makes it difficult for businesses and consumers to make economic decisions. Moreover, the government needs to know the rate of inflation to index certain payments, like Social Security benefits or interest payments on TIPS bonds.

But just because the government expends so much energy determining the rate of inflation does not mean it is tallying it in the smartest or most accurate way. The reigning methodology is, well, clunky. It costs Washington around $234 million a year to get all those people to go and bear witness to a $1.57 price increase in a packet of tube socks and then to massage those individual data points down to one number. Moreover, there is a weekslong lag between the checkers tallying up the numbers and the government announcing the changes: The inflation measure comes out only 12 times a year, though prices change, sometimes dramatically, all the time. Plus, the methodology is archaic, given that we live in the Internet age. Prices are easily available online and a lot of shopping happens on the Web rather than in stores.

But there might be a better way. In the last few months, economists have come up with new methods for calculating inflation at Internet speed—nimbler, cheaper, faster, and perhaps even more accurate than Washington's. The first comes from the Massachusetts Institute of Technology. In

trying to compute the price of a basket of goods of constant quality. Despite these efforts, changes in quality remain a problem because quality is hard to measure.

There is still much debate among economists about how severe these measurement problems are and what should be done about them. Several studies written during the 1990s concluded that the CPI overstated inflation by about 1 percentage point per year. In response to this criticism, the BLS adopted several technical changes to improve the CPI, and many economists believe that the bias is now only about half as large as it once was. The issue is important because many government programs use the CPI to adjust for changes in the overall level of prices. Recipients of Social Security, for instance, get annual increases in benefits that are tied to the CPI. Some economists have suggested modifying these programs to correct for the measurement problems by, for instance, reducing the magnitude of the automatic benefit increases.

2007, economists Roberto Rigobon and Alberto Cavallo started tracking prices online and inputting them into a massive database. Then, last month, they unveiled the Billion Prices Project, an inflation measure based on 5 million items sold by 300 online retailers in 70 countries. (For the United States, the BPP collects about 500,000 prices.)

The BPP's inflation measure is markedly different from the government's. The economists just average all the prices culled online, meaning the basket of goods is whatever you can buy on the Web. (Some things, like books, are most often bought online. Some items, like cats, are not.) Plus, the researchers do not weight certain items' prices, even if they tend to make up a bigger proportion of household spending.

Still, thus far, the BPP has tracked the CPI closely. And the online-based measure has additional advantages. It comes out daily, giving a better sense of inflation's direction. It also lets researchers examine minute, day-to-day price changes. For instance, this month Rigobon and Cavallo noted that Black Friday discounts "had a smaller effect on average prices in 2010 than in 2009," contrary to reports of deeper discounting this year. And it has already produced some academic insights. For instance, Cavallo found that retailers change prices less often, but more, percentage-wise, than economists previously thought.

A second inflation measure comes from Web behemoth Google and is a pet project of

the company's chief economist, Hal Varian. As reported by the *Financial Times*, earlier this year, Varian decided to use Google's vast database of Web prices to construct the "Google Price Index," a constantly updated measure of price changes and inflation. (The idea came to him when he was searching for a pepper grinder online.) Google has not yet decided whether it will publish the price index, and has not released its methodology. But Varian said that his preliminary index tracked CPI closely, though it did show periods of

"I wonder how much this costs online."

deflation—the worrisome incidence of prices actually falling—where the CPI did not.

The new indices lead to the big question of whether the government *needs* to update its methods to account for changes in the economy—taking new pricing trends into consideration, rejiggering its formula, updating more frequently. The answer might be yes. (Economists have reformed the CPI before.) But the CPI and its Stone Age method of calculation boasts one huge benefit: It's a stable, tested measure, consistent over time, since its methodology doesn't change much. Moreover, and somewhat remarkably, the Google and Billion Prices Project indices actually seem to confirm the accuracy of the old-fashioned CPI, tracking it closely rather than showing it to be off-base.

Ultimately, there is a good argument for *more* inflation measures, not just better or newer ones. The government already calculates a number of rates of inflation to give a fuller picture of price changes, the value of money, and the economy. Most notably, the BLS publishes a "core inflation" number, a measure of inflation outside volatile food and energy prices. There are dozens of other measures, as well. The new Web-based yardsticks provide even more alternatives and opportunities to examine the accuracy of the CPI—and to make new findings. That means, for now, those detective-like government rubes painstakingly checking prices on clipboards get to stay in work. ■

Source: *Slate*, December 20, 2010.

24-1c The GDP Deflator versus the Consumer Price Index

In the preceding chapter, we examined another measure of the overall level of prices in the economy—the GDP deflator. The GDP deflator is the ratio of nominal GDP to real GDP. Because nominal GDP is current output valued at current prices and real GDP is current output valued at base-year prices, the GDP deflator reflects the current level of prices relative to the level of prices in the base year.

Economists and policymakers monitor both the GDP deflator and the CPI to gauge how quickly prices are rising. Usually, these two statistics tell a similar story. Yet two important differences can cause them to diverge.

The first difference is that the GDP deflator reflects the prices of all goods and services *produced domestically*, whereas the CPI reflects the prices of all goods and services *bought by consumers*. For example, suppose that the price of an airplane produced by Boeing and sold to the Air Force rises. Even though the plane is part of GDP, it is not part of the basket of goods and services bought by a typical consumer. Thus, the price increase shows up in the GDP deflator but not in the CPI.

As another example, suppose that Volvo raises the price of its cars. Because Volvos are made in Sweden, the car is not part of U.S. GDP. But U.S. consumers buy Volvos, so the car is part of the typical consumer's basket of goods. Hence, a price increase in an imported consumption good, such as a Volvo, shows up in the CPI but not in the GDP deflator.

This first difference between the CPI and the GDP deflator is particularly important when the price of oil changes. The United States produces some oil, but much of the oil we use is imported. As a result, oil and oil products such as gasoline and heating oil make up a much larger share of consumer spending than of GDP. When the price of oil rises, the CPI rises by much more than does the GDP deflator.

The second and subtler difference between the GDP deflator and the CPI concerns how various prices are weighted to yield a single number for the overall level of prices. The CPI compares the price of a *fixed* basket of goods and services to the price of the basket in the base year. Only occasionally does the BLS change the basket of goods. By contrast, the GDP deflator compares the price of *currently produced* goods and services to the price of the same goods and services in the base year. Thus, the group of goods and services used to compute the GDP deflator changes automatically over time. This difference is not important when all prices are changing proportionately. But if the prices of different goods and services are changing by varying amounts, the way we weight the various prices matters for the overall inflation rate.

Figure 2 shows the inflation rate as measured by both the GDP deflator and the CPI for each year since 1965. You can see that sometimes the two measures diverge. When they do diverge, it is possible to go behind these numbers and explain the divergence with the two differences we have discussed. For example, in 1979 and 1980, CPI inflation spiked up more than the GDP deflator largely because oil prices more than doubled during these two years. Yet divergence between these two measures is the exception rather than the rule. In the 1970s, both the GDP deflator and the CPI show high rates of inflation. In the late 1980s, 1990s, and the first decade of the 2000s, both measures show low rates of inflation.

THE WALL STREET JOURNAL

| AUDIO - VIDEO |

"The price may seem a little high, but you have to remember that's in today's dollars."

QuickQuiz *Explain briefly what the CPI measures and how it is constructed.* • *Identify one reason why the CPI is an imperfect measure of the cost of living.*

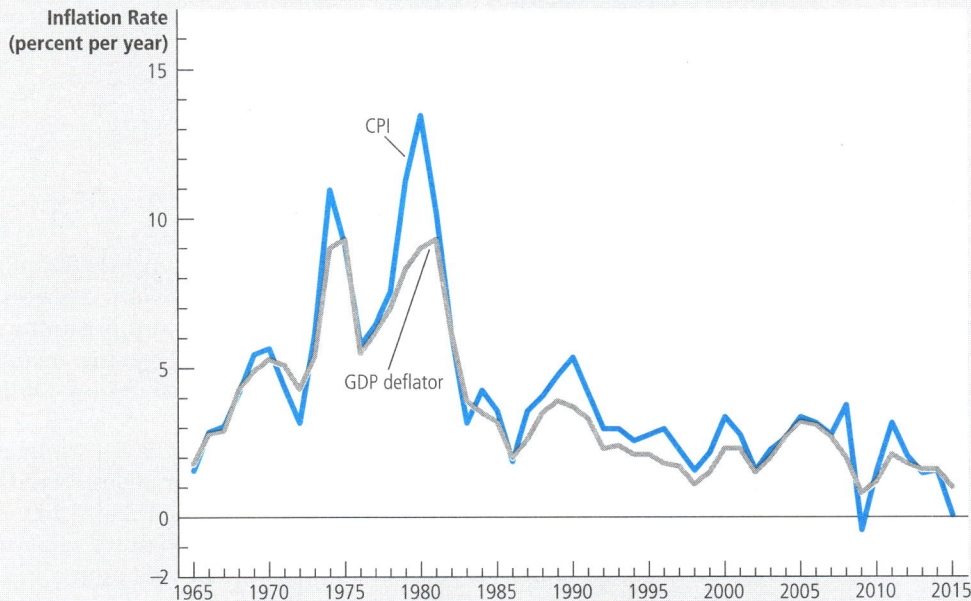

FIGURE 2

Two Measures of Inflation
This figure shows the inflation rate—the percentage change in the level of prices—as measured by the GDP deflator and the CPI using annual data since 1965. Notice that the two measures of inflation generally move together.

Source: U.S. Department of Labor; U.S. Department of Commerce.

24-2 Correcting Economic Variables for the Effects of Inflation

The purpose of measuring the overall level of prices in the economy is to allow us to compare dollar figures from different times. Now that we know how price indexes are calculated, let's see how we might use such an index to compare a dollar figure from the past to a dollar figure in the present.

24-2a Dollar Figures from Different Times

We first return to the issue of Babe Ruth's salary. Was his salary of $80,000 in 1931 high or low compared to the salaries of today's players?

To answer this question, we need to know the level of prices in 1931 and the level of prices today. Part of the increase in baseball salaries compensates players for higher prices today. To compare Ruth's salary to those of today's players, we need to inflate Ruth's salary to turn 1931 dollars into today's dollars.

The formula for turning dollar figures from year T into today's dollars is the following:

.

A price index such as the CPI measures the price level and thus determines the size of the inflation correction.

Let's apply this formula to Ruth's salary. Government statistics show a CPI of 15.2 for 1931 and 237 for 2015. Thus, the overall level of prices has risen by a factor of 15.6 (calculated from 237/15.2). We can use these numbers to measure Ruth's salary in 2015 dollars, as follows:

We find that Babe Ruth's 1931 salary is equivalent to a salary today of over $1.2 million. That is a good income, but it is only a third of the average player's salary today and only 4 percent of what the Dodgers pay Clayton Kershaw. Various forces, including overall economic growth and the increasing income shares earned by superstars, have substantially raised the living standards of the best athletes.

Let's also examine President Hoover's 1931 salary of $75,000. To translate that figure into 2015 dollars, we again multiply the ratio of the price levels in the two years. We find that Hoover's salary is equivalent to $75,000(237/15.2), or $1,169,408 in 2015 dollars. This is well above President Barack Obama's salary of $400,000. It seems that President Hoover did have a pretty good year after all.

FYI

Mr. Index Goes to Hollywood

What is the most popular movie of all time? The answer might surprise you.

Movie popularity is usually gauged by box office receipts. By that measure, *Star Wars: The Force Awakens* is the number-one movie of all time with domestic receipts of $923 million, followed by *Avatar* ($761 million) and *Titanic* ($659 million). But this ranking ignores an obvious but important fact: Prices, including those of movie tickets, have been rising over time. Inflation gives an advantage to newer films.

When we correct box office receipts for the effects of inflation, the story is very different. The number-one movie is now *Gone with the Wind* ($1,758 million), followed by the original *Star Wars* ($1,550 million) and *The Sound of Music* ($1,239 million). *Star Wars: The Force Awakens* falls to number 11.

Gone with the Wind was released in 1939, before everyone had televisions in their homes. In the 1930s, about 90 million Americans went to the cinema each week, compared to about 25 million today. But the movies from that era don't show up in conventional popularity rankings because ticket prices were only a quarter. And indeed, in the ranking based on nominal box office receipts, *Gone with the Wind* does not make the top 100 films. Scarlett and Rhett fare a lot better once we correct for the effects of inflation. ■

"May the force of inflation be with you."

LUCAS FILMS/BAD ROBOT/WALT DISNEY PRODUCTIONS / ALBUM/NEWSCOM

REGIONAL DIFFERENCES IN THE COST OF LIVING

CASE STUDY

When you graduate from college, you may well have several job offers from which to choose. Not surprisingly, some jobs pay more than others. If the jobs are located in different places, however, be careful when comparing them. The cost of living varies not only over time but also over geography. What seems like a larger paycheck might not turn out to be so once you take into account regional differences in the prices of goods and services.

The Bureau of Economic Analysis has used the data collected for the CPI to compare prices around the United States. The resulting statistic is called *regional price parities*. Just as the CPI measures variation in the cost of living from year to year, regional price parities measure variation in the cost of living from state to state.

Figure 3 shows the regional price parities for 2013. For example, living in the state of New York costs 115.3 percent of what it costs to live in the typical place in the United States (that is, New York is 15.3 percent more expensive than average).

2013 Regional Price Parities by State (US = 100)

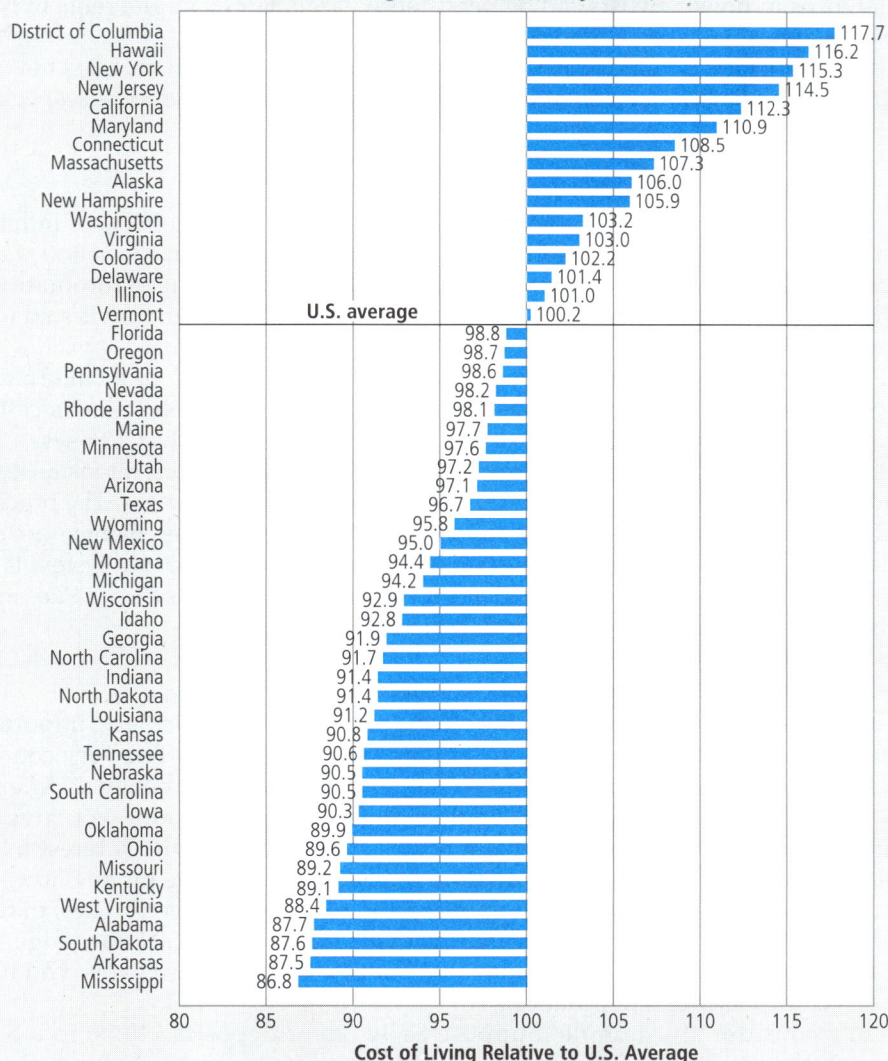

District of Columbia	117.7
Hawaii	116.2
New York	115.3
New Jersey	114.5
California	112.3
Maryland	110.9
Connecticut	108.5
Massachusetts	107.3
Alaska	106.0
New Hampshire	105.9
Washington	103.2
Virginia	103.0
Colorado	102.2
Delaware	101.4
Illinois	101.0
Vermont	100.2
U.S. average	
Florida	98.8
Oregon	98.7
Pennsylvania	98.6
Nevada	98.2
Rhode Island	98.1
Maine	97.7
Minnesota	97.6
Utah	97.2
Arizona	97.1
Texas	96.7
Wyoming	95.8
New Mexico	95.0
Montana	94.4
Michigan	94.2
Wisconsin	92.9
Idaho	92.8
Georgia	91.9
North Carolina	91.7
Indiana	91.4
North Dakota	91.4
Louisiana	91.2
Kansas	90.8
Tennessee	90.6
Nebraska	90.5
South Carolina	90.5
Iowa	90.3
Oklahoma	89.9
Ohio	89.6
Missouri	89.2
Kentucky	89.1
West Virginia	88.4
Alabama	87.7
South Dakota	87.6
Arkansas	87.5
Mississippi	86.8

Cost of Living Relative to U.S. Average

FIGURE 3

Regional Variation in the Cost of Living

This figure shows how the cost of living in the fifty U.S. states and the District of Columbia compares to the U.S. average.

Source: U.S. Department of Commerce. Data are for 2013.

Living in Mississippi costs 86.8 percent of what it costs to live in the typical place (that is, Mississippi is 13.2 percent less expensive than average).

What accounts for these differences? It turns out that the prices of goods, such as food and clothing, explain only a small part of these regional differences. Most goods are tradable: They can be easily transported from one state to another. As a consequence of regional trade, large price disparities are unlikely to persist for long.

Services explain a larger part of these regional differences. A haircut, for example, can cost more in one state than another. If barbers were willing to move to where the price of a haircut is high, or if customers were willing to fly across the country in search of cheap haircuts, then the prices of haircuts across regions might well converge. But because transporting haircuts is so costly, large price disparities can persist.

Housing services are particularly important for understanding regional differences in the cost of living. Such services represent a large share of a typical consumer's budget. Moreover, once built, a house or apartment building can't easily be moved, and the land on which it sits is completely immobile. As a result, differences in housing costs can be persistently large. For example, rents in New York are almost twice what they are in Mississippi.

Keep these facts in mind when it comes time to compare job offers. Look not only at the dollar salaries but also at the local prices of goods and services, especially housing. ●

24-2b Indexation

As we have just seen, price indexes are used to correct for the effects of inflation when comparing dollar figures from different times. This type of correction shows up in many places in the economy. When some dollar amount is automatically corrected for changes in the price level by law or contract, the amount is said to be **indexed** for inflation.

indexation
the automatic correction by law or contract of a dollar amount for the effects of inflation

For example, many long-term contracts between firms and unions include partial or complete indexation of the wage to the CPI. Such a provision, called a *cost-of-living allowance* (or COLA), automatically raises the wage when the CPI rises.

Indexation is also a feature of many laws. Social Security benefits, for instance, are adjusted every year to compensate the elderly for increases in prices. The brackets of the federal income tax—the income levels at which the tax rates change—are also indexed for inflation. There are, however, many ways in which the tax system is not indexed for inflation, even when perhaps it should be. We discuss these issues more fully when we discuss the costs of inflation later in this book.

24-2c Real and Nominal Interest Rates

Correcting economic variables for the effects of inflation is particularly important, and somewhat tricky, when we look at data on interest rates. The very concept of an interest rate necessarily involves comparing amounts of money at different points in time. When you deposit your savings in a bank account, you give the bank some money now, and the bank returns your deposit with interest in the future. Similarly, when you borrow from a bank, you get some money now, but you will have to repay the loan with interest in the future. In both cases, to fully understand the deal between you and the bank, it is crucial to acknowledge that future dollars could have a different value than today's dollars. That is, you have to correct for the effects of inflation.

Let's consider an example. Suppose Sally Saver deposits $1,000 in a bank account that pays an annual interest rate of 10 percent. A year later, after Sally has accumulated $100 in interest, she withdraws her $1,100. Is Sally $100 richer than she was when she made the deposit a year earlier?

The answer depends on what we mean by "richer." Sally does have $100 more than she had before. In other words, the number of dollars in her possession has risen by 10 percent. But Sally does not care about the amount of money itself: She cares about what she can buy with it. If prices have risen while her money was in the bank, each dollar now buys less than it did a year ago. In this case, her purchasing power—the amount of goods and services she can buy—has not risen by 10 percent.

To keep things simple, let's suppose that Sally is a movie fan and buys only DVDs. When Sally made her deposit, a DVD cost $10. Her deposit of $1,000 was equivalent to 100 DVDs. A year later, after getting her 10 percent interest, she has $1,100. How many DVDs can she buy now? It depends on what has happened to the price of a DVD. Here are some examples:

- Zero inflation: If the price of a DVD remains at $10, the amount she can buy has risen from 100 to 110 DVDs. The 10 percent increase in the number of dollars means a 10 percent increase in her purchasing power.
- Six percent inflation: If the price of a DVD rises from $10 to $10.60, then the number of DVDs she can buy has risen from 100 to approximately 104. Her purchasing power has increased by about 4 percent.
- Ten percent inflation: If the price of a DVD rises from $10 to $11, she can still buy only 100 DVDs. Even though Sally's dollar wealth has risen, her purchasing power is the same as it was a year earlier.
- Twelve percent inflation: If the price of a DVD increases from $10 to $11.20, the number of DVDs she can buy has fallen from 100 to approximately 98. Even with her greater number of dollars, her purchasing power has decreased by about 2 percent.

And if Sally were living in an economy with deflation—falling prices—another possibility could arise:

- Two percent deflation: If the price of a DVD falls from $10 to $9.80, then the number of DVDs she can buy rises from 100 to approximately 112. Her purchasing power increases by about 12 percent.

These examples show that the higher the rate of inflation, the smaller the increase in Sally's purchasing power. If the rate of inflation exceeds the rate of interest, her purchasing power actually falls. And if there is deflation (that is, a negative rate of inflation), her purchasing power rises by more than the rate of interest.

To understand how much a person earns in a savings account, we need to consider both the interest rate and the change in prices. The interest rate that measures the change in dollar amounts is called the **nominal interest rate**, and the interest rate corrected for inflation is called the **real interest rate**. The nominal interest rate, the real interest rate, and inflation are related approximately as follows:

$$\text{Real interest rate} = \text{Nominal interest rate} - \text{Inflation rate}.$$

The real interest rate is the difference between the nominal interest rate and the rate of inflation. The nominal interest rate tells you how fast the number of dollars in your bank account rises over time, while the real interest rate tells you how fast the purchasing power of your bank account rises over time.

nominal interest rate
the interest rate as usually reported without a correction for the effects of inflation

real interest rate
the interest rate corrected for the effects of inflation

FIGURE 4

Real and Nominal Interest Rates

This figure shows nominal and real interest rates using annual data since 1965. The nominal interest rate is the rate on a three-month Treasury bill. The real interest rate is the nominal interest rate minus the inflation rate as measured by the CPI. Notice that nominal and real interest rates often do not move together.

Source: U.S. Department of Labor; U.S. Department of Treasury.

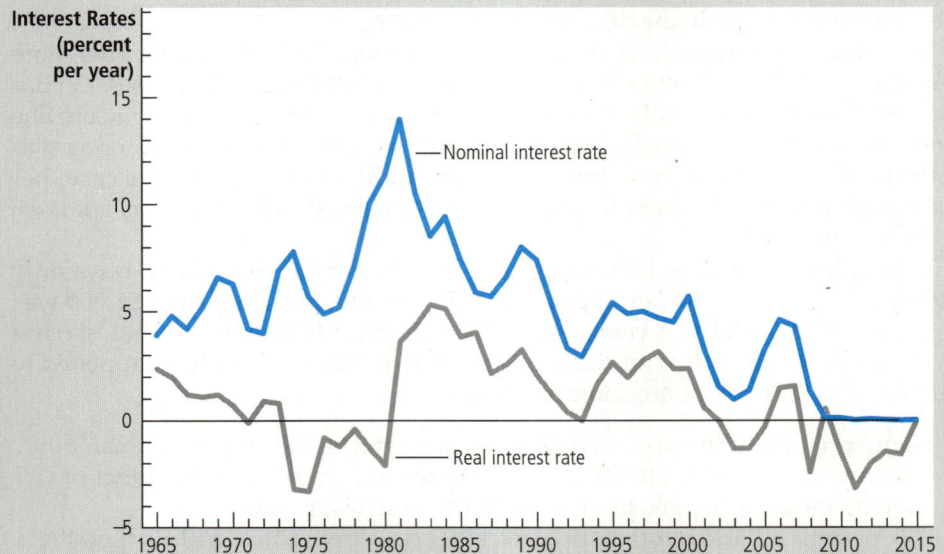

INTEREST RATES IN THE U.S. ECONOMY

CASE STUDY

Figure 4 shows real and nominal interest rates in the U.S. economy since 1965. The nominal interest rate in this figure is the rate on three-month Treasury bills (although data on other interest rates would be similar). The real interest rate is computed by subtracting the rate of inflation from this nominal interest rate. Here the inflation rate is measured as the percentage change in the CPI.

One feature of this figure is that the nominal interest rate almost always exceeds the real interest rate. This reflects the fact that the U.S. economy has experienced rising consumer prices in almost every year during this period. By contrast, if you look at data for the U.S. economy during the late 19th century or for the Japanese economy in some recent years, you will find periods of deflation. During deflation, the real interest rate exceeds the nominal interest rate.

The figure also shows that because inflation is variable, real and nominal interest rates do not always move together. For example, in the late 1970s, nominal interest rates were high. But because inflation was very high, real interest rates were low. Indeed, during much of the 1970s, real interest rates were negative, for inflation eroded people's savings more quickly than nominal interest payments increased them. By contrast, in the late 1990s, nominal interest rates were lower than they had been two decades earlier. But because inflation was much lower, real interest rates were higher. In the coming chapters, we will examine the economic forces that determine both real and nominal interest rates. ●

QuickQuiz *Henry Ford paid his workers $5 a day in 1914. If the CPI was 10 in 1914 and 237 in 2015, how much is the Ford paycheck worth in 2015 dollars?*

24-3 Conclusion

"A nickel ain't worth a dime anymore," the late, great baseball player Yogi Berra once observed. Indeed, throughout recent history, the real values behind the nickel, the dime, and the dollar have not been stable. Persistent increases in the overall level of prices have been the norm. Such inflation reduces the purchasing power of each unit of money over time. When comparing dollar figures from different times, it is important to keep in mind that a dollar today is not the same as a dollar 20 years ago or, most likely, 20 years from now.

This chapter has discussed how economists measure the overall level of prices in the economy and how they use price indexes to correct economic variables for the effects of inflation. Price indexes allow us to compare dollar figures from different points in time and, therefore, get a better sense of how the economy is changing.

The discussion of price indexes in this chapter, together with the preceding chapter's discussion of GDP, is only the first step in the study of macroeconomics. We have not yet examined what determines a nation's GDP or the causes and effects of inflation. To do that, we need to go beyond issues of measurement. Indeed, that is our next task. Having explained how economists measure macroeconomic quantities and prices in the past two chapters, we are now ready to develop the models that explain movements in these variables.

Here is our strategy in the upcoming chapters. First, we look at the long-run determinants of real GDP and related variables, such as saving, investment, real interest rates, and unemployment. Second, we look at the long-run determinants of the price level and related variables, such as the money supply, inflation, and nominal interest rates. Last of all, having seen how these variables are determined in the long run, we examine the more complex question of what causes short-run fluctuations in real GDP and the price level. In all of these chapters, the measurement issues we have just discussed will provide the foundation for the analysis.

CHAPTER QuickQuiz

1. The CPI measures approximately the same economic phenomenon as
   a. nominal GDP.
   b. real GDP.
   c. the GDP deflator.
   d. the unemployment rate.

2. The largest component in the basket of goods and services used to compute the CPI is
   a. food and beverages.
   b. housing.
   c. medical care.
   d. apparel.

3. If a Pennsylvania gun manufacturer raises the price of rifles it sells to the U.S. Army, its price hikes will increase
   a. both the CPI and the GDP deflator.
   b. neither the CPI nor the GDP deflator.
   c. the CPI but not the GDP deflator.
   d. the GDP deflator but not the CPI.

4. Because consumers can sometimes substitute cheaper goods for those that have risen in price,
   a. the CPI overstates inflation.
   b. the CPI understates inflation.
   c. the GDP deflator overstates inflation.
   d. the GDP deflator understates inflation.

5. If the CPI is 200 in year 1980 and 300 today, then $600 in 1980 has the same purchasing power as _____ today.
   a. $400
   b. $500
   c. $700
   d. $900

6. You deposit $2,000 in a savings account, and a year later you have $2,100. Meanwhile, the CPI rises from 200 to 204. In this case, the nominal interest rate is _____ percent, and the real interest rate is _____ percent.
   a. 1, 5
   b. 3, 5
   c. 5, 1
   d. 5, 3

SUMMARY

- The consumer price index (CPI) shows the cost of a basket of goods and services relative to the cost of the same basket in the base year. The index is used to measure the overall level of prices in the economy. The percentage change in the CPI measures the inflation rate.
- The CPI is an imperfect measure of the cost of living for three reasons. First, it does not take into account consumers' ability to substitute toward goods that become relatively cheaper over time. Second, it does not take into account increases in the purchasing power of the dollar due to the introduction of new goods. Third, it is distorted by unmeasured changes in the quality of goods and services. Because of these measurement problems, the CPI overstates true inflation.
- Like the CPI, the GDP deflator measures the overall level of prices in the economy. The two price indexes usually move together, but there are important differences. The GDP deflator differs from the CPI because it includes goods and services produced rather than goods and services consumed. As a result, imported goods affect the CPI but not the GDP deflator. In addition, while the CPI uses a fixed basket of goods, the GDP deflator automatically changes the group of goods and services over time as the composition of GDP changes.
- Dollar figures from different times do not represent a valid comparison of purchasing power. To compare a dollar figure from the past to a dollar figure today, the older figure should be inflated using a price index.
- Various laws and private contracts use price indexes to correct for the effects of inflation. The tax laws, however, are only partially indexed for inflation.
- A correction for inflation is especially important when looking at data on interest rates. The nominal interest rate is the interest rate usually reported; it is the rate at which the number of dollars in a savings account increases over time. By contrast, the real interest rate takes into account changes in the value of the dollar over time. The real interest rate equals the nominal interest rate minus the rate of inflation.

KEY CONCEPTS

consumer price index (CPI), p. 496
inflation rate, p. 498
core CPI, p. 499

producer price index, p. 499
indexation, p. 506

nominal interest rate, p. 507
real interest rate, p. 507

QUESTIONS FOR REVIEW

1. Which do you think has a greater effect on the CPI: a 10 percent increase in the price of chicken or a 10 percent increase in the price of caviar? Why?

2. Describe the three problems that make the CPI an imperfect measure of the cost of living.

3. If the price of imported French wine rises, is the CPI or the GDP deflator affected more? Why?

4. Over a long period of time, the price of a candy bar rose from $0.20 to $1.20. Over the same period, the CPI rose from 150 to 300. Adjusted for overall inflation, how much did the price of the candy bar change?

5. Explain the meaning of *nominal interest rate* and *real interest rate*. How are they related?

PROBLEMS AND APPLICATIONS

1. Suppose that the year you were born someone bought $100 of goods and services for your baby shower. How much would you guess it would cost today to buy a similar amount of goods and services? Now find data on the CPI and compute the answer based on it. (You can find the BLS's inflation calculator here: http://www.bls.gov/data/inflation_calculator.htm).

2. The residents of Vegopia spend all of their income on cauliflower, broccoli, and carrots. In 2016, they spend a total of $200 for 100 heads of cauliflower, $75 for 50 bunches of broccoli, and $50 for 500 carrots. In 2017, they spend a total of $225 for 75 heads of cauliflower, $120 for 80 bunches of broccoli, and $100 for 500 carrots.
   a. Calculate the price of one unit of each vegetable in each year.
   b. Using 2016 as the base year, calculate the CPI for each year.
   c. What is the inflation rate in 2017?

3. Suppose that people consume only three goods, as shown in this table:

	Tennis Balls	Golf Balls	Bottles of Gatorade
2017 price	$2	$4	$1
2017 quantity	100	100	200
2018 price	$2	$6	$2
2018 quantity	100	100	200

   a. What is the percentage change in the price of each of the three goods?
   b. Using a method similar to the CPI, compute the percentage change in the overall price level.
   c. If you were to learn that a bottle of Gatorade increased in size from 2017 to 2018, should that information affect your calculation of the inflation rate? If so, how?
   d. If you were to learn that Gatorade introduced new flavors in 2018, should that information affect your calculation of the inflation rate? If so, how?

4. Go to the website of the Bureau of Labor Statistics (http://www.bls.gov) and find data on the CPI. By how much has the index including all items risen over the past year? For which categories of spending have prices risen the most? The least? Have any categories experienced price declines? Can you explain any of these facts?

5. A small nation of ten people idolizes the TV show *The Voice*. All they produce and consume are karaoke machines and CDs, in the following amounts:

	Karaoke Machines		CDs	
	Quantity	Price	Quantity	Price
2017	10	$40	30	$10
2018	12	60	50	12

   a. Using a method similar to the CPI, compute the percentage change in the overall price level. Use 2017 as the base year and fix the basket at 1 karaoke machine and 3 CDs.
   b. Using a method similar to the GDP deflator, compute the percentage change in the overall price level. Also use 2017 as the base year.
   c. Is the inflation rate in 2018 the same using the two methods? Explain why or why not.

6. Which of the problems in the construction of the CPI might be illustrated by each of the following situations? Explain.
   a. the invention of cell phones
   b. the introduction of air bags in cars
   c. increased personal computer purchases in response to a decline in their price
   d. more scoops of raisins in each package of Raisin Bran
   e. greater use of fuel-efficient cars after gasoline prices increase

7. A dozen eggs cost $0.88 in January 1980 and $2.11 in January 2015. The average wage for production workers was $7.58 per hour in January 1980 and $19.64 in January 2015.
   a. By what percentage did the price of eggs rise?
   b. By what percentage did the wage rise?
   c. In each year, how many minutes did a worker have to work to earn enough to buy a dozen eggs?
   d. Did workers' purchasing power in terms of eggs rise or fall?

8. The chapter explains that Social Security benefits are increased each year in proportion to the increase in the CPI, even though most economists believe that the CPI overstates actual inflation.
   a. If the elderly consume the same market basket as other people, does Social Security provide the elderly with an improvement in their standard of living each year? Explain.
   b. In fact, the elderly consume more healthcare compared to younger people, and healthcare costs have risen faster than overall inflation. What would you do to determine whether the elderly are actually better off from year to year?

9. Suppose that a borrower and a lender agree on the nominal interest rate to be paid on a loan. Then inflation turns out to be higher than they both expected.
   a. Is the real interest rate on this loan higher or lower than expected?
   b. Does the lender gain or lose from this unexpectedly high inflation? Does the borrower gain or lose?
   c. Inflation during the 1970s was much higher than most people had expected when the decade began. How did this affect homeowners who obtained fixed-rate mortgages during the 1960s? How did it affect the banks that lent the money?

To find additional study resources, visit cengagebrain.com, and search for "Mankiw."

PART IX

The Real Economy
in the Long Run

Production and Growth

When you travel around the world, you see tremendous variation in the standard of living. The average income in a rich country, such as the United States, Japan, or Germany, is about ten times the average income in a poor country, such as India, Nigeria, or Nicaragua. These large differences in income are reflected in large differences in the quality of life. People in richer countries have better nutrition, safer housing, better healthcare, and longer life expectancy as well as more automobiles, more telephones, and more computers.

Even within a country, there are large changes in the standard of living over time. In the United States over the past century, average income as measured by real gross domestic product (GDP) per person has grown by about 2 percent per year. Although 2 percent might seem small,

this rate of growth implies that average income doubles every 35 years. Because of this growth, most Americans enjoy much greater economic prosperity than did their parents, grandparents, and great-grandparents.

Growth rates vary substantially from country to country. From 2000 to 2014, GDP per person in China grew at a rate of 11 percent per year, accumulating to a 357 percent increase in average income. A country experiencing such rapid growth can, in one generation, go from being among the poorest in the world to being among the richest. By contrast, in the same time span, income per person in Zimbabwe fell by a total of 13 percent, leaving the typical citizen mired in poverty.

What explains these diverse experiences? How can rich countries maintain their high standard of living? What policies can poor countries pursue to promote more rapid growth and join the developed world? These are among the most important questions in macroeconomics. As the Nobel-Prize-winning economist Robert Lucas put it, "The consequences for human welfare in questions like these are simply staggering: Once one starts to think about them, it is hard to think about anything else."

In the previous two chapters, we discussed how economists measure macroeconomic quantities and prices. We can now begin to study the forces that determine these variables. As we have seen, an economy's GDP measures both the total income earned in the economy and the total expenditure on the economy's output of goods and services. The level of real GDP is a good gauge of economic prosperity, and the growth of real GDP is a good gauge of economic progress. In this chapter we focus on the long-run determinants of the level and growth of real GDP. Later, we study the short-run fluctuations of real GDP around its long-run trend.

We proceed here in three steps. First, we examine international data on real GDP per person. These data will give you some sense of how much the level and growth of living standards vary around the world. Second, we examine the role of *productivity*—the amount of goods and services produced for each hour of a worker's time. In particular, we see that a nation's standard of living is determined by the productivity of its workers, and we consider the factors that determine a nation's productivity. Third, we consider the link between productivity and the economic policies that a nation pursues.

25-1 Economic Growth around the World

As a starting point for our study of long-run growth, let's look at the experiences of some of the world's economies. Table 1 shows data on real GDP per person for thirteen countries. For each country, the data span over a century of history. The first and second columns of the table present the countries and time periods. (The time periods differ somewhat from country to country because of differences in data availability.) The third and fourth columns show estimates of real GDP per person more than a century ago and for a recent year.

The data on real GDP per person show that living standards vary widely from country to country. Income per person in the United States, for instance, is now about four times that in China and about ten times that in India. The poorest countries have average levels of income not seen in the developed world for many decades. The typical resident of Pakistan in 2014 had about the same real income as the typical resident of the United Kingdom in 1870. The typical Bangladeshi in 2014 had considerably less real income than a typical American in 1870.

| Country | Period | Real GDP per Person | | Growth Rate (per year) |
		At Beginning of Period[a]	At End of Period[a]	
Brazil	1900–2014	$ 828	$15,590	2.61%
Japan	1890–2014	1,600	37,920	2.59
China	1900–2014	762	13,170	2.53
Mexico	1900–2014	1,233	16,640	2.31
Germany	1870–2014	2,324	46,850	2.11
Indonesia	1900–2014	948	10,190	2.10
Canada	1870–2014	2,527	43,360	1.99
India	1900–2014	718	5,630	1.82
United States	1870–2014	4,264	55,860	1.80
Pakistan	1900–2014	785	5,090	1.65
Argentina	1900–2014	2,440	12,510	1.44
Bangladesh	1900–2014	663	3,330	1.43
United Kingdom	1870–2014	5,117	39,040	1.42

[a]Real GDP is measured in 2014 dollars.
Source: Robert J. Barro and Xavier Sala-i-Martin, *Economic Growth* (New York: McGraw-Hill, 1995), Tables 10.2 and 10.3; *World Bank* online data; and author's calculations. To account for international price differences, data are PPP-adjusted when available.

TABLE 1

The Variety of Growth Experiences

The last column of the table shows each country's growth rate. The growth rate measures how rapidly real income per person grew in the typical year. In the United States, for example, where real income per person was $4,264 in 1870 and $55,860 in 2014, the growth rate was 1.80 percent per year. This means that if real income per person, beginning at $4,264, were to increase by 1.80 percent for each of 144 years, it would end up at $55,860. Of course, income did not rise exactly 1.80 percent every year: Some years it rose by more, other years it rose by less, and in still other years it fell. The growth rate of 1.80 percent per year ignores short-run fluctuations around the long-run trend and represents an average rate of growth for real income per person over many years.

The countries in Table 1 are ordered by their growth rate from the most to the least rapid. Here you can see the large variety in growth experiences. High on the list are Brazil and China, which went from being among the poorest nations in the world to being among middle-income nations. Also high on the list is Japan, which went from being a middle-income nation to being among the richest nations.

Near the bottom of the list you can find Pakistan and Bangladesh, which were among the poorest nations at the end of the nineteenth century and remain so today. At the bottom of the list is the United Kingdom. In 1870, the United Kingdom was the richest country in the world, with average income about 20 percent higher than that of the United States and more than twice Canada's. Today, average income in the United Kingdom is 30 percent below that of the United States and 10 percent below Canada's.

These data show that the world's richest countries have no guarantee they will stay the richest and that the world's poorest countries are not doomed to remain forever in poverty. But what explains these changes over time? Why do some countries zoom ahead while others lag behind? These are precisely the questions that we take up next.

Quick Quiz *What has been the approximate long-run growth rate of real GDP per person in the United States? Name a country that has had faster growth and a country that has had slower growth.*

25-2 Productivity: Its Role and Determinants

Explaining why living standards vary so much around the world is, in one sense, very easy. The answer can be summarized in a single word—*productivity*. But in another sense, the international variation in living standards is deeply puzzling. To explain why incomes are so much higher in some countries than in others, we must look at the many factors that determine a nation's productivity.

25-2a Why Productivity Is So Important

Let's begin our study of productivity and economic growth by developing a simple model based loosely on Daniel Defoe's famous novel *Robinson Crusoe* about a sailor stranded on a desert island. Because Crusoe lives alone, he

---

FYI

Are You Richer Than the Richest American?

American Heritage magazine once published a list of the richest Americans of all time. The number 1 spot went to John D. Rockefeller, the oil entrepreneur who lived from 1839 to 1937. According to the magazine's calculations, his wealth would today be the equivalent of about $200 billion, almost three times that of Bill Gates, the software entrepreneur who is today's richest American.

Despite his great wealth, Rockefeller did not enjoy many of the conveniences that we now take for granted. He couldn't watch television, play video games, surf the Internet, or send e-mail. During the heat of summer, he couldn't cool his home with air-conditioning. For much of his life, he couldn't travel by car or plane, and he couldn't use a telephone to call friends or family. If he became ill, he couldn't take advantage of many medicines, such as antibiotics, that doctors today routinely use to prolong and enhance life.

John D. Rockefeller

BETTMANN/GETTY IMAGES

Now consider: How much money would someone have to pay you to give up for the rest of your life all the modern conveniences that Rockefeller lived without? Would you do it for $200 billion? Perhaps not. And if you wouldn't, is it fair to say that you are better off than John D. Rockefeller, allegedly the richest American ever?

The preceding chapter discussed how standard price indexes, which are used to compare sums of money from different points in time, fail to fully reflect the introduction of new goods in the economy. As a result, the rate of inflation is overestimated. The flip side of this observation is that the rate of real economic growth is underestimated. Pondering Rockefeller's life shows how significant this problem might be. Because of tremendous technological advances, the average American today is arguably "richer" than the richest American a century ago, even if that fact is lost in standard economic statistics. ■

catches his own fish, grows his own vegetables, and makes his own clothes. We can think of Crusoe's activities—his production and consumption of fish, vegetables, and clothing—as a simple economy. By examining Crusoe's economy, we can learn some lessons that also apply to more complex and realistic economies.

What determines Crusoe's standard of living? In a word, **productivity**, the quantity of goods and services produced from each unit of labor input. If Crusoe is good at catching fish, growing vegetables, and making clothes, he lives well. If he is bad at doing these things, he lives poorly. Because Crusoe gets to consume only what he produces, his living standard is tied to his productivity.

In the case of Crusoe's economy, it is easy to see that productivity is the key determinant of living standards and that growth in productivity is the key determinant of growth in living standards. The more fish Crusoe can catch per hour, the more he eats at dinner. If Crusoe finds a better place to catch fish, his productivity rises. This increase in productivity makes Crusoe better off: He can eat the extra fish, or he can spend less time fishing and devote more time to making other goods he enjoys.

Productivity's key role in determining living standards is as true for nations as it is for stranded sailors. Recall that an economy's GDP measures two things at once: the total income earned by everyone in the economy and the total expenditure on the economy's output of goods and services. GDP can measure these two things simultaneously because, for the economy as a whole, they must be equal. Put simply, an economy's income is the economy's output.

Like Crusoe, a nation can enjoy a high standard of living only if it can produce a large quantity of goods and services. Americans live better than Nigerians because American workers are more productive than Nigerian workers. The Japanese have enjoyed more rapid growth in living standards than Argentineans because Japanese workers have experienced more rapid growth in productivity. Indeed, one of the *Ten Principles of Economics* in Chapter 1 is that a country's standard of living depends its ability to produce goods and services.

Hence, to understand the large differences in living standards we observe across countries or over time, we must focus on the production of goods and services. But seeing the link between living standards and productivity is only the first step. It leads naturally to the next question: Why are some economies so much better at producing goods and services than others?

25-2b How Productivity Is Determined

Although productivity is uniquely important in determining Robinson Crusoe's standard of living, many factors determine Crusoe's productivity. Crusoe will be better at catching fish, for instance, if he has more fishing poles, if he has been trained in the best fishing techniques, if his island has a plentiful fish supply, or if he invents a better fishing lure. Each of these determinants of Crusoe's productivity—which we can call *physical capital, human capital, natural resources,* and *technological knowledge*—has a counterpart in more complex and realistic economies. Let's consider each factor in turn.

Physical Capital per Worker Workers are more productive if they have tools with which to work. The stock of equipment and structures used to produce goods and services is called **physical capital**, or just *capital*. For example,

productivity
the quantity of goods and services produced from each unit of labor input

physical capital
the stock of equipment and structures that are used to produce goods and services

A Picture Is Worth a Thousand Statistics

George Bernard Shaw once said, "It is the mark of a truly intelligent person to be moved by statistics." Most of us, however, have trouble being moved by data on GDP—until we see with our own eyes what these statistics represent.

The three photos on these pages show a typical family from each of three countries—the United Kingdom, Mexico, and Mali. Each family was photographed outside their home, together with all their material possessions.

These nations have very different standards of living, as judged by these photos, GDP, or other statistics.

- The United Kingdom is an advanced economy. In 2014, its income per person was $39,040. A baby born in the United Kingdom can expect a relatively healthy childhood: Only 4 out of 1,000 children die before reaching age 5. Almost the entire population has access to modern sanitation facilities, such as a bathroom and sewer system, to safely remove human waste. Educational attainment is high: Among individuals of college age, 60 percent are enrolled in higher education.

- Mexico is a middle-income country. In 2014, its income per person was $16,640. About 13 out of 1,000 children die before age 5. About 85 percent have access to modern sanitation. Among those of college age, 30 percent are enrolled.

- Mali is a poor country. In 2014, its income per person was only $1,510. Life is often cut short: 115 out of 1,000 children die before age 5. Only 25 percent of the population has access to modern sanitation. And educational attainment in Mali is low: Among those of college age, only 7 percent are enrolled.

Economists who study economic growth try to understand what causes such large differences in the standard of living. ■

A Typical Family in the United Kingdom

DAVID REED - FROM MATERIAL WORLD

A Typical Family in Mexico

A Typical Family in Mali

when woodworkers make furniture, they use saws, lathes, and drill presses. More tools allow the woodworkers to produce their output more quickly and more accurately: A worker with only basic hand tools can make less furniture each week than a worker with sophisticated and specialized woodworking equipment.

As you may recall, the inputs used to produce goods and services—labor, capital, and so on—are called the *factors of production*. An important feature of capital is that it is a *produced* factor of production. That is, capital is an input into the production process that in the past was an output from the production process. The woodworker uses a lathe to make the leg of a table. Earlier, the lathe itself was the output of a firm that manufactures lathes. The lathe manufacturer in turn used other equipment to make its product. Thus, capital is a factor of production used to produce all kinds of goods and services, including more capital.

Human Capital per Worker   A second determinant of productivity is human capital. **Human capital** is the economist's term for the knowledge and skills that workers acquire through education, training, and experience. Human capital includes the skills accumulated in early childhood programs, grade school, high school, college, and on-the-job training for adults in the labor force.

Education, training, and experience are less tangible than lathes, bulldozers, and buildings, but human capital is similar to physical capital in many ways. Like physical capital, human capital raises a nation's ability to produce goods and services. Also like physical capital, human capital is a produced factor of production. Producing human capital requires inputs in the form of teachers, libraries, and student time. Indeed, students can be viewed as "workers" who have the important job of producing the human capital that will be used in future production.

human capital
the knowledge and skills that workers acquire through education, training, and experience

Natural Resources per Worker   A third determinant of productivity is **natural resources**. Natural resources are inputs into production that are provided by nature, such as land, rivers, and mineral deposits. Natural resources take two forms: renewable and nonrenewable. A forest is an example of a renewable resource. When one tree is cut down, a seedling can be planted in its place to be harvested in the future. Oil is an example of a nonrenewable resource. Because oil is produced by nature over many millions of years, there is only a limited supply. Once the supply of oil is depleted, it is impossible to create more.

Differences in natural resources are responsible for some of the differences in standards of living around the world. The historical success of the United States was driven in part by the large supply of land well suited for agriculture. Today, some countries in the Middle East, such as Kuwait and Saudi Arabia, are rich simply because they happen to be on top of some of the largest pools of oil in the world.

Although natural resources can be important, they are not necessary for an economy to be highly productive in producing goods and services. Japan, for instance, is one of the richest countries in the world, despite having few natural resources. International trade makes Japan's success possible. Japan imports many of the natural resources it needs, such as oil, and exports its manufactured goods to economies rich in natural resources.

natural resources
the inputs into the production of goods and services that are provided by nature, such as land, rivers, and mineral deposits

Technological Knowledge   A fourth determinant of productivity is **technological knowledge**—the understanding of the best ways to produce goods and services. A hundred years ago, most Americans worked on farms because farm technology required a high input of labor to feed the entire population. Today, thanks to advances in farming technology, a small fraction of the population can produce enough food to feed the entire country. This technological change made labor available to produce other goods and services.

Technological knowledge takes many forms. Some technology is common knowledge—after one person uses it, everyone becomes aware of it. For example, once Henry Ford successfully introduced assembly-line production, other carmakers quickly followed suit. Other technology is proprietary—it is known only by the company that discovers it. Only the Coca-Cola Company, for instance, knows the secret recipe for making its famous soft drink. Still other technology is proprietary for a short time. When a pharmaceutical company discovers a new drug, the patent system gives that company a temporary right to be its exclusive manufacturer. When the patent expires, however, other companies are allowed to make the drug. All these forms of technological knowledge are important for the economy's production of goods and services.

It is worthwhile to distinguish between technological knowledge and human capital. Although they are closely related, there is an important difference.

technological knowledge society's understanding of the best ways to produce goods and services

FYI

The Production Function

Economists often use a *production function* to describe the relationship between the quantity of inputs used in production and the quantity of output from production. For example, suppose Y denotes the quantity of output, L the quantity of labor, K the quantity of physical capital, H the quantity of human capital, and N the quantity of natural resources. Then we might write

$$Y = AF(L, K, H, N),$$

where $F( )$ is a function that shows how the inputs are combined to produce output. A is a variable that reflects the available production technology. As technology improves, A rises, so the economy produces more output from any given combination of inputs.

Many production functions have a property called *constant returns to scale*. If a production function has constant returns to scale, then doubling all inputs causes the amount of output to double as well. Mathematically, we write that a production function has constant returns to scale if, for any positive number x,

$$xY = AF(xL, xK, xH, xN).$$

A doubling of all inputs would be represented in this equation by $x = 2$. The right side shows the inputs doubling, and the left side shows output doubling.

Production functions with constant returns to scale have an interesting and useful implication. To see this implication, set $x = 1/L$ so that the preceding equation becomes

$$Y/L = AF(1, K/L, H/L, N/L).$$

Notice that Y/L is output per worker, which is a measure of productivity. This equation says that labor productivity depends on physical capital per worker (K/L), human capital per worker (H/L), and natural resources per worker (N/L). Productivity also depends on the state of technology, as reflected by the variable A. Thus, this equation provides a mathematical summary of the four determinants of productivity we have just discussed. ■

Technological knowledge refers to society's understanding about how the world works. Human capital refers to the resources expended transmitting this understanding to the labor force. To use a relevant metaphor, technological knowledge is the quality of society's textbooks, whereas human capital is the amount of time that the population has devoted to reading them. Workers' productivity depends on both.

CASE STUDY

ARE NATURAL RESOURCES A LIMIT TO GROWTH?

Today, the world's population is over 7 billion, more than four times what it was a century ago. At the same time, many people are enjoying a much higher standard of living than did their great-grandparents. A perennial debate concerns whether this growth in population and living standards can continue in the future.

Many commentators have argued that natural resources will eventually limit how much the world's economies can grow. At first, this argument might seem hard to ignore. If the world has only a fixed supply of nonrenewable natural resources, how can population, production, and living standards continue to grow over time? Eventually, won't supplies of oil and minerals start to run out? When these shortages start to occur, won't they stop economic growth and, perhaps, even force living standards to fall?

Despite the apparent appeal of such arguments, most economists are less concerned about such limits to growth than one might guess. They argue that technological progress often yields ways to avoid these limits. If we compare the economy today to the economy of the past, we see various ways in which the use of natural resources has improved. Modern cars have better gas mileage. New houses have better insulation and require less energy to heat and cool. More efficient oil rigs waste less oil in the process of extraction. Recycling allows some nonrenewable resources to be reused. The development of alternative fuels, such as ethanol instead of gasoline, allows us to substitute renewable for nonrenewable resources.

Seventy years ago, some conservationists were concerned about the excessive use of tin and copper. At the time, these were crucial commodities: Tin was used to make many food containers, and copper was used to make telephone wire. Some people advocated mandatory recycling and rationing of tin and copper so that supplies would be available for future generations. Today, however, plastic has replaced tin as a material for making many food containers, and phone calls often travel over fiber-optic cables, which are made from sand. Technological progress has made once crucial natural resources less necessary.

But are all these efforts enough to permit continued economic growth? One way to answer this question is to look at the prices of natural resources. In a market economy, scarcity is reflected in market prices. If the world were running out of natural resources, then the prices of those resources would be rising over time. But in fact, the opposite is more often true. Natural resource prices exhibit substantial short-run fluctuations, but over long spans of time, the prices of most natural resources (adjusted for overall inflation) are stable or falling. It appears that our ability to conserve these resources is growing more rapidly than their supplies are dwindling. Market prices give no reason to believe that natural resources are a limit to economic growth. ●

Quick Quiz   *List and describe four determinants of a country's productivity.*

25-3 Economic Growth and Public Policy

So far, we have determined that a society's standard of living depends on its ability to produce goods and services and that its productivity in turn depends on physical capital per worker, human capital per worker, natural resources per worker, and technological knowledge. Let's now turn to the question faced by policymakers around the world: What can government policy do to raise productivity and living standards?

25-3a Saving and Investment

Because capital is a produced factor of production, a society can change the amount of capital it has. If today the economy produces a large quantity of new capital goods, then tomorrow it will have a larger stock of capital and be able to produce more goods and services. Thus, one way to raise future productivity is to invest more current resources in the production of capital.

One of the *Ten Principles of Economics* presented in Chapter 1 is that people face trade-offs. This principle is especially important when considering the accumulation of capital. Because resources are scarce, devoting more resources to producing capital requires devoting fewer resources to producing goods and services for current consumption. That is, for society to invest more in capital, it must consume less and save more of its current income. The growth that arises from capital accumulation is not a free lunch: It requires that society sacrifice consumption of goods and services in the present to enjoy higher consumption in the future.

The next chapter examines in more detail how an economy's financial markets coordinate saving and investment. It also examines how government policies influence the amount of saving and investment that take place. At this point, it is important to note that encouraging saving and investment is one way that a government can encourage growth and, in the long run, raise an economy's standard of living.

25-3b Diminishing Returns and the Catch-Up Effect

Suppose that a government pursues policies that raise the nation's saving rate—the percentage of GDP devoted to saving rather than consumption. What happens? With the nation saving more, fewer resources are needed to make consumption goods and more resources are available to make capital goods. As a result, the capital stock increases, leading to rising productivity and more rapid growth in GDP. But how long does this higher rate of growth last? Assuming that the saving rate remains at its new, higher level, does the growth rate of GDP stay high indefinitely or only for a period of time?

The traditional view of the production process is that capital is subject to **diminishing returns**: As the stock of capital rises, the extra output produced from an additional unit of capital falls. In other words, when workers already have a large quantity of capital to use in producing goods and services, giving them an additional unit of capital increases their productivity only slightly. This is illustrated in Figure 1, which shows how the amount of capital per worker determines the amount of output per worker, holding constant all the other determinants of output (such as natural resources and technological knowledge).

Because of diminishing returns, an increase in the saving rate leads to higher growth only for a while. As the higher saving rate allows more capital to be accumulated, the benefits from additional capital become smaller over time, and

diminishing returns
the property whereby the benefit from an extra unit of an input declines as the quantity of the input increases

FIGURE 1

Illustrating the Production Function
This figure shows how the amount of capital per worker influences the amount of output per worker. Other determinants of output, including human capital, natural resources, and technology, are held constant. The curve becomes flatter as the amount of capital increases because of diminishing returns to capital.

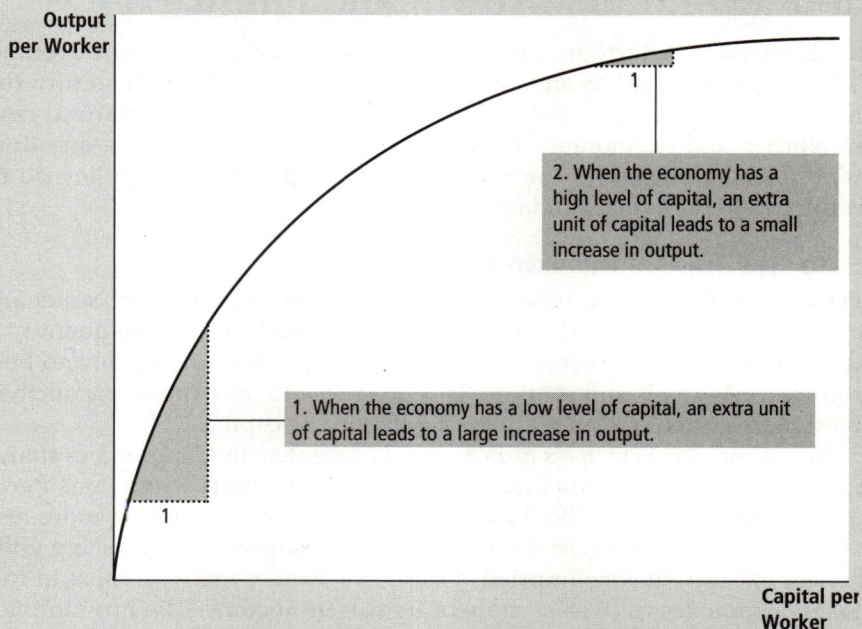

Output per Worker

2. When the economy has a high level of capital, an extra unit of capital leads to a small increase in output.

1. When the economy has a low level of capital, an extra unit of capital leads to a large increase in output.

Capital per Worker

so growth slows down. *In the long run, the higher saving rate leads to a higher level of productivity and income but not to higher growth in these variables.* Reaching this long run, however, can take quite a while. According to studies of international data on economic growth, increasing the saving rate can lead to substantially higher growth for a period of several decades.

The property of diminishing returns to capital has another important implication: Other things being equal, it is easier for a country to grow fast if it starts out relatively poor. This effect of initial conditions on subsequent growth is sometimes called the **catch-up effect**. In poor countries, workers lack even the most rudimentary tools and, as a result, have low productivity. Thus, small amounts of capital investment can substantially raise these workers' productivity. By contrast, workers in rich countries have large amounts of capital with which to work, and this partly explains their high productivity. Yet with the amount of capital per worker already so high, additional capital investment has a relatively small effect on productivity. Studies of international data on economic growth confirm this catch-up effect: Controlling for other variables, such as the percentage of GDP devoted to investment, poor countries tend to grow at faster rates than rich countries.

This catch-up effect can help explain some otherwise puzzling facts. Here's an example: From 1960 to 1990, the United States and South Korea devoted a similar share of GDP to investment. Yet over this time, the United States experienced only mediocre growth of about 2 percent, while South Korea experienced spectacular growth of more than 6 percent. The explanation is the catch-up effect. In 1960, South Korea had GDP per person less than one-tenth the U.S. level, in part because previous investment had been so low. With a small initial capital stock, the benefits to capital accumulation were much greater in South Korea, and this gave South Korea a higher subsequent growth rate.

catch-up effect
the property whereby countries that start off poor tend to grow more rapidly than countries that start off rich

This catch-up effect shows up in other aspects of life. When a school gives an end-of-year award to the "Most Improved" student, that student is usually one who began the year with relatively poor performance. Students who began the year not studying find improvement easier than students who always worked hard. Note that it is good to be "Most Improved," given the starting point, but it is even better to be "Best Student." Similarly, economic growth over the last several decades has been much more rapid in South Korea than in the United States, but GDP per person is still higher in the United States.

25-3c Investment from Abroad

So far, we have discussed how policies aimed at increasing a country's saving rate can increase investment and, thereby, long-term economic growth. Yet saving by domestic residents is not the only way for a country to invest in new capital. The other way is investment by foreigners.

Investment from abroad takes several forms. Ford Motor Company might build a car factory in Mexico. A capital investment that is owned and operated by a foreign entity is called *foreign direct investment*. Alternatively, an American might buy stock in a Mexican corporation (that is, buy a share in the ownership of the corporation), and the corporation can use the proceeds from the stock sale to build a new factory. An investment that is financed with foreign money but operated by domestic residents is called *foreign portfolio investment*. In both cases, Americans provide the resources necessary to increase the stock of capital in Mexico. That is, American saving is being used to finance Mexican investment.

When foreigners invest in a country, they do so because they expect to earn a return on their investment. Ford's car factory increases the Mexican capital stock and, therefore, increases Mexican productivity and Mexican GDP. Yet Ford takes some of this additional income back to the United States in the form of profit. Similarly, when an American investor buys Mexican stock, the investor has a right to a portion of the profit that the Mexican corporation earns.

Investment from abroad, therefore, does not have the same effect on all measures of economic prosperity. Recall that gross domestic product (GDP) is the income earned within a country by both residents and nonresidents, whereas gross national product (GNP) is the income earned by residents of a country both at home and abroad. When Ford opens its car factory in Mexico, some of the income the factory generates accrues to people who do not live in Mexico. As a result, foreign investment in Mexico raises the income of Mexicans (measured by GNP) by less than it raises the production in Mexico (measured by GDP).

Nonetheless, investment from abroad is one way for a country to grow. Even though some of the benefits from this investment flow back to the foreign owners, this investment does increase the economy's stock of capital, leading to higher productivity and higher wages. Moreover, investment from abroad is one way for poor countries to learn the state-of-the-art technologies developed and used in richer countries. For these reasons, many economists who advise governments in less developed economies advocate policies that encourage investment from abroad. Often, this means removing restrictions that governments have imposed on foreign ownership of domestic capital.

An organization that tries to encourage the flow of capital to poor countries is the World Bank. This international organization obtains funds from the world's advanced countries, such as the United States, and uses these resources to make loans to less developed countries so that they can invest in roads, sewer systems, schools, and other types of capital. It also offers the countries advice about how the funds might best be used. The World Bank and its sister organization, the International Monetary Fund, were set up after World War II. One lesson from the war was that economic distress often leads to political turmoil, international tensions, and military conflict. Thus, every country has an interest in promoting economic prosperity around the world. The World Bank and the International Monetary Fund were established to achieve that common goal.

25-3d Education

Education—investment in human capital—is at least as important as investment in physical capital for a country's long-run economic success. In the United States, each year of schooling has historically raised a person's wage by an average of about 10 percent. In less developed countries, where human capital is especially scarce, the gap between the wages of educated and uneducated workers is even larger. Thus, one way government policy can enhance the standard of living is to provide good schools and to encourage the population to take advantage of them.

Investment in human capital, like investment in physical capital, has an opportunity cost. When students are in school, they forgo the wages they could have earned as members of the labor force. In less developed countries, children often drop out of school at an early age, even though the benefit of additional schooling is very high, simply because their labor is needed to help support the family.

Some economists have argued that human capital is particularly important for economic growth because human capital conveys positive externalities. An *externality* is the effect of one person's actions on the well-being of a bystander. An educated person, for instance, might generate new ideas about how best to produce goods and services. If these ideas enter society's pool of knowledge so that everyone can use them, then the ideas are an external benefit of education. In this case, the return from schooling for society is even greater than the return for the individual. This argument would justify the large subsidies to human-capital investment that we observe in the form of public education.

One problem facing some poor countries is the *brain drain*—the emigration of many of the most highly educated workers to rich countries, where these workers can enjoy a higher standard of living. If human capital does have positive externalities, then this brain drain makes those people left behind even poorer. This problem offers policymakers a dilemma. On the one hand, the United States and other rich countries have the best systems of higher education, and it would seem natural for poor countries to send their best students abroad to earn higher degrees. On the other hand, those students who have spent time abroad may choose not to return home, and this brain drain will reduce the poor nation's stock of human capital even further.

25-3e Health and Nutrition

The term *human capital* usually refers to education, but it can also be used to describe another type of investment in people: expenditures that lead to a healthier population. Other things being equal, healthier workers are more productive. The right investments in the health of the population provide one way for a nation to increase productivity and raise living standards.

According to the late economic historian Robert Fogel, improved health from better nutrition has been a significant factor in long-run economic growth. Fogel estimated that in Great Britain in 1780, about one in five people were so malnourished that they were incapable of manual labor. Among those who could work, insufficient caloric intake substantially reduced the work effort they could put forth. As nutrition improved, so did workers' productivity.

Fogel studied these historical trends in part by looking at the height of the population. Short stature can be an indicator of malnutrition, especially during gestation and the early years of life. Fogel found that as nations develop economically, people eat more and the population gets taller. From 1775 to 1975, the average caloric intake in Great Britain rose by 26 percent and the height of the average man rose by 3.6 inches. Similarly, during the spectacular economic growth in South Korea from 1962 to 1995, caloric consumption rose by 44 percent and average male height rose by 2 inches. Of course, a person's height is determined by a combination of genetics and environment. But because the genetic makeup of a population is slow to change, such increases in average height are most likely due to changes in the environment—nutrition being the obvious explanation.

Moreover, studies have found that height is an indicator of productivity. Looking at data on a large number of workers at a point in time, researchers have found that taller workers tend to earn more. Because wages reflect a worker's productivity, this finding suggests that taller workers tend to be more productive. The effect of height on wages is especially pronounced in poorer countries, where malnutrition is a bigger risk.

Fogel won the Nobel Prize in Economics in 1993 for his work in economic history, which includes not only his studies of nutrition but also his studies of American slavery and the role of railroads in the development of the American economy. In the lecture he gave when he was awarded the prize, he surveyed the evidence on health and economic growth. He concluded that "improved gross nutrition accounts for roughly 30 percent of the growth of per capita income in Britain between 1790 and 1980."

Today, malnutrition is fortunately rare in developed nations such as Great Britain and the United States. (Obesity is a more widespread problem.) But for people in developing nations, poor health and inadequate nutrition remain obstacles to higher productivity and improved living standards. The United Nations estimates that almost a third of the population in sub-Saharan Africa is undernourished.

The causal link between health and wealth runs in both directions. Poor countries are poor in part because their populations are not healthy, and their populations are not healthy in part because they are poor and cannot afford adequate healthcare and nutrition. It is a vicious circle. But this fact opens the possibility of a virtuous circle: Policies that lead to more rapid economic growth would naturally improve health outcomes, which in turn would further promote economic growth.

25-3f **Property Rights and Political Stability**

Another way policymakers can foster economic growth is by protecting property rights and promoting political stability. This issue goes to the very heart of how market economies work.

Production in market economies arises from the interactions of millions of individuals and firms. When you buy a car, for instance, you are buying the output of a car dealer, a car manufacturer, a steel company, an iron ore mining company, and so on. This division of production among many firms allows the economy's factors of production to be used as effectively as possible. To achieve this outcome, the economy has to coordinate transactions among these firms, as well as between firms and consumers. Market economies achieve this coordination through market prices. That is, market prices are the instrument with which the invisible hand of the marketplace brings supply and demand into balance in each of the many thousands of markets that make up the economy.

An important prerequisite for the price system to work is an economy-wide respect for *property rights*. Property rights refer to the ability of people to exercise authority over the resources they own. A mining company will not make the effort to mine iron ore if it expects the ore to be stolen. The company mines the ore only if it is confident that it will benefit from the ore's subsequent sale. For this reason, courts serve an important role in a market economy: They enforce property rights. Through the criminal justice system, the courts discourage theft. In addition, through the civil justice system, the courts ensure that buyers and sellers live up to their contracts.

Those of us in developed countries tend to take property rights for granted, but those living in less developed countries understand that a lack of property rights can be a major problem. In many countries, the system of justice does not work well. Contracts are hard to enforce, and fraud often goes unpunished. In more extreme cases, the government not only fails to enforce property rights but actually infringes upon them. To do business in some countries, firms are expected to bribe government officials. Such corruption impedes the coordinating power of markets. It also discourages domestic saving and investment from abroad.

One threat to property rights is political instability. When revolutions and coups are common, there is doubt about whether property rights will be respected in the future. If a revolutionary government might confiscate the capital of some businesses, as was often true after communist revolutions, domestic residents have less incentive to save, invest, and start new businesses. At the same time, foreigners have less incentive to invest in the country. Even the threat of revolution can act to depress a nation's standard of living.

Thus, economic prosperity depends in part on political prosperity. A country with an efficient court system, honest government officials, and a stable constitution will enjoy a higher economic standard of living than a country with a poor court system, corrupt officials, and frequent revolutions and coups.

25-3g Free Trade

Some of the world's poorest countries have tried to achieve more rapid economic growth by pursuing *inward-oriented policies*. These policies attempt to increase productivity and living standards within the country by avoiding interaction with the rest of the world. Domestic firms often advance the infant-industry argument, claiming they need protection from foreign competition to thrive and grow. Together with a general distrust of foreigners, this argument has at times led policymakers in less developed countries to impose tariffs and other trade restrictions.

Most economists today believe that poor countries are better off pursuing *outward-oriented policies* that integrate these countries into the world economy. International trade in goods and services can improve the economic well-being of a country's citizens. Trade is, in some ways, a type of technology. When a country exports wheat and imports textiles, the country benefits as if it had invented a technology for turning wheat into textiles. A country that eliminates trade restrictions will, therefore, experience the same kind of economic growth that would occur after a major technological advance.

The adverse impact of inward orientation becomes clear when one considers the small size of many less developed economies. The total GDP of Argentina, for instance, is about that of Houston, Texas. Imagine what would happen if the Houston city council were to prohibit city residents from trading with people living outside the city limits. Without being able to take advantage of the gains from trade, Houston would need to produce all the goods it consumes. It would also have to produce all its own capital goods, rather than importing state-of-the-art equipment from other cities. Living standards in Houston would fall immediately, and the problem would likely only get worse over time. This is precisely what happened when Argentina pursued inward-oriented policies throughout much of the 20th century. In contrast, countries that pursued outward-oriented policies, such as Republic of Korea and Singapore, enjoyed high rates of economic growth.

The amount that a nation trades with others is determined not only by government policy but also by geography. Countries with natural seaports find trade easier than countries without this resource. It is not a coincidence that many of the world's major cities, such as New York, San Francisco, and Hong Kong, are located next to oceans. Similarly, because landlocked countries find international trade more difficult, they tend to have lower levels of income than countries with easy access to the world's waterways. For example, countries with more than 80 percent of their population living within 100 kilometers of a coast have an average GDP per person about four times as large as countries with less than 20 percent of their population living near a coast. The critical importance of access to the sea helps explain why the African continent, which contains many landlocked countries, is so poor.

25-3h Research and Development

The primary reason that living standards are higher today than they were a century ago is that technological knowledge has advanced. The telephone, the transistor, the computer, and the internal combustion engine are among the thousands of innovations that have improved the ability to produce goods and services.

Most technological advances come from private research by firms and individual inventors, but there is also a public interest in promoting these efforts. To a large extent, knowledge is a *public good*: That is, once one person discovers an idea, the idea enters society's pool of knowledge and other people can freely use it. Just as government has a role in providing a public good such as national defense, it also has a role in encouraging the research and development of new technologies.

The U.S. government has long played a role in the creation and dissemination of technological knowledge. A century ago, the government sponsored research about farming methods and advised farmers how best to use their land. More recently, the U.S. government, through the Air Force and NASA, has supported aerospace research; as a result, the United States is a leading maker of rockets and planes. The government continues to encourage advances in knowledge with research grants from the National Science Foundation and the National Institutes of Health and with tax breaks for firms engaging in research and development.

Yet another way in which government policy encourages research is through the patent system. When a person or firm creates an innovative product, such as a new drug, the inventor can apply for a patent. If the product is deemed truly original,

ASK THE EXPERTS

Innovation and Growth

"Future innovations worldwide will not be transformational enough to promote sustained per-capita economic growth rates in the United States and western Europe over the next century as high as those over the past 150 years."

What do economists say?

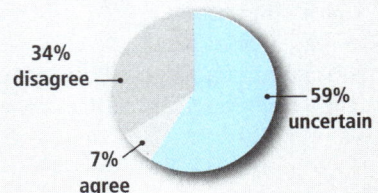

34% disagree

59% uncertain

7% agree

Source: IGM Economic Experts Panel, February 11, 2014.

Curmudgeon versus Optimist

When economists look ahead to future technological progress, their crystal ball is often foggy.

Has All the Important Stuff Already Been Invented?

By Timothy Aeppel

Robert Gordon, a curmudgeonly 73-year-old economist, believes our best days are over. After a century of life-changing innovations that spurred growth, he says, human progress is slowing to a crawl.

Joel Mokyr, a cheerful 67-year-old economist, imagines a coming age of new inventions, including gene therapies to prolong our life span and miracle seeds that can feed the world without fertilizers.

These big-name colleagues at Northwestern University represent opposite poles in the debate over the future of the 21st century economy: rapid innovation driven by robotic manufacturing, 3-D printing and cloud computing, versus years of job losses, stagnant wages and rising income inequality.

The divergent views are more than academic. For many Americans, the recession left behind the scars of lost jobs, lower wages and depressed home prices. The question is whether tough times are here for good. The answer depends on who you ask.

"I think the rate of innovation is just getting faster and faster," Mr. Mokyr said over noodles and spicy chicken at a Thai restaurant near the campus where he and Mr. Gordon have taught for four decades.

"What's the evidence of that?" snapped Mr. Gordon. "There isn't any."

The men get along fine when talk is limited to, say, faculty gossip. About the future, though, they bicker constantly. When Mr. Mokyr described life-prolonging medical advances, Mr. Gordon cut in: "Extending life without curing Alzheimer's means people who can walk but can't think."

Mr. Gordon landed at Northwestern from the University of Chicago in the fall of 1973, a year before Mr. Mokyr arrived there from Yale after finishing his Ph.D. Their tit-for-tat repartee makes them popular speakers—for economists, at least....

The professors headlined a Bank of Korea event in Seoul earlier this month. "We always go mano-a-mano," Mr. Mokyr said. "But we often end up talking about different things. Bob's a macroeconomist, I'm an economic historian."

Mr. Mokyr has long studied how new tools have led to economic breakthroughs. For example, how the development of telescopes allowed for rapid advances in astronomy. History makes him certain his colleague is wrong.

Mr. Gordon's ideas, in fact, fly in the face of modern economic orthodoxy. Since Nobel economist Robert Solow first argued in the 1950s that growth was driven by new technology, most economists have embraced the idea. Progress may be uneven, according to this view, but there is no reason to expect the world to run out of ideas.

"Bob says the low-hanging fruit has been picked, because we won't invent indoor plumbing again," Mr. Mokyr said. In speeches, Mr. Gordon often displays images of a flush toilet and iPhone and asks: Which would you give up?

Mr. Mokyr said many economists before Mr. Gordon have proclaimed the end of progress, but these pessimists have always been proven wrong. It was a popular theme during the Depression, he said, but modern economists now recognize the 1930s as a period of rapid technological progress with such advances as the development of jet engines and radar.

Today, Mr. Mokyr said, fast computing is a new tool that will open the way to new inventions in the future.

The darkness of Mr. Mokyr's family history contrasts with his optimism for the future. His parents were Dutch Jews who survived the Holocaust. His father, a civil servant, died of cancer when Mr. Mokyr was a year old. He was raised by his mother in a small apartment in the port city of Haifa in Israel. "My mother was not an optimist," he said. "She had lived a very tough life."

Mr. Gordon, the more famous of the two men, has the credentials to buck conventional wisdom. His parents and a brother were Ph.D.

Curmudgeon

economists. His father, an expert on business cycles, taught at the University of California, Berkeley, for decades....

If anything, his family should have made him an optimist. Mr. Gordon's father grew up grindingly poor, at one point supporting three younger brothers after his own father died; his eventual success mirrored the larger transformation of the U.S. into the world's richest country.

"His generation saw the move from crowded tenements in the 1920s to suburbia in the 1950s—with everyone having a yard and a car," Mr. Gordon said, a leap showing how much progress has since slowed.

Mr. Gordon sees a hobbled U.S. economy ahead. Americans are getting older, leaving too few workers to support the aging population. The problem is even worse in other Western economies.

An aging citizenry is among a list of troubles, including the declining share of working-age men with jobs; stagnant rates of Americans earning college degrees; jobs lost abroad and high government debt. The biggest obstacle, he said, is growing income inequality.

To compensate, Mr. Gordon said, economies need technological advances. The problem is that the biggest breakthroughs—like electrification or the discovery of antibiotics—are behind us. Electricity changed how people lived and worked, and it spawned hundreds of new industries. The technology that allowed people to communicate instantly or travel quickly over long distances were 19th- and 20th-century innovations.

More recent inventions—including the Internet—won't pack the same punch, he said: "The rapid progress made over the past 250 years could well turn out to be a unique episode in human history."

Cellphones, he said, are just a refinement of the telephone. "Look at what an ideal kitchen looked like in 1955—it's not that different than today," Mr. Gordon said. "It's nothing like moving from clothes lines to clothes dryers."...

Mr. Gordon said his ideas began taking shape between semesters at graduate school. He worked during the summer of 1965 for a team of economists analyzing the dazzling productivity growth that began around 1920 and ran through World War II and the postwar boom.

Except for an upturn in the 1990s, growth has been tepid ever since.

"Everyone has looked for a big overarching factor to explain this," he said. "But it occurred to me, it could be as simple as that we'd run out of the great inventions."

Mr. Gordon said his ideas evolved from there. In 2000, he published a paper saying that computer technology, hailed as the driver of the "new economy," was far less impressive than earlier big inventions. He generated more controversy with a 2012 academic paper titled "Is U.S. Economic Growth Over?"

The paper included a dire prediction: The economy will grow less than half as fast as the remarkable 2% average it notched between 1870 and 2007. "Americans got used to their standard of living doubling from that of their parents. No more," he told investment managers in Germany this year.

If he is right, the standard of living for the average American—measured in per capita income—will in the future take 78 years to double, compared with the 35 years it took between 1972 and 2007....

Much of Mr. Gordon's work focuses on an economy's output. Mr. Mokyr, meanwhile, is more interested in how new inventions improve the quality of life in ways that don't show up in traditional measures: new medicines that treat chronic pain or allow older people to stay active years longer. A hip replacement, he said, let him keep riding his bike to and from work.

"For Bob, it's all about the measure of input and output—especially output," said Mr. Mokyr. That is why the aging population is such a big problem for Mr. Gordon, since retired people stop producing.

Mr. Gordon countered that many of the innovations Mr. Mokyr anticipates—such as new technology to clean air and water pollution—will solve problems created by past economic growth. Those shouldn't be counted the same way as breakthroughs that add to output, he said.

"Maybe the problem is that we didn't measure growth in the past correctly," Mr. Mokyr retorted, "because we didn't account for the costs."

The two men agree on one point. "One of the main missions I have in life is to point out to my students how lucky they are to be born in the 20th century," Mr. Mokyr said. "Compared to what life was like 100 or 200 years ago, we're incredibly fortunate." ■

Source: *The Wall Street Journal*, June 16, 2014.

JOEL MOKYR

Optimist

the government awards the patent, which gives the inventor the exclusive right to make the product for a specified number of years. In essence, the patent gives the inventor a property right over her invention, turning her new idea from a public good into a private good. By allowing inventors to profit from their inventions—even if only temporarily—the patent system enhances the incentive for individuals and firms to engage in research.

25-3i Population Growth

Economists and other social scientists have long debated how population affects a society. The most direct effect is on the size of the labor force: A large population means more workers to produce goods and services. The tremendous size of the Chinese population is one reason China is such an important player in the world economy.

At the same time, however, a large population means more people to consume those goods and services. So while a large population means a larger total output of goods and services, it need not mean a higher standard of living for the typical citizen. Indeed, both large and small nations are found at all levels of economic development.

Beyond these obvious effects of population size, population growth interacts with the other factors of production in ways that are more subtle and open to debate.

Stretching Natural Resources   Thomas Robert Malthus (1766–1834), an English minister and early economic thinker, is famous for his book called *An Essay on the Principle of Population as It Affects the Future Improvement of Society*. In it, he offered what may be history's most chilling forecast. Malthus argued that an ever-increasing population would continually strain society's ability to provide for itself. As a result, mankind was doomed to forever live in poverty.

Malthus's logic was simple. He began by noting that "food is necessary to the existence of man" and that "the passion between the sexes is necessary and will remain nearly in its present state." He concluded that "the power of population is infinitely greater than the power in the earth to produce subsistence for man." According to Malthus, the only check on population growth was "misery and vice." Attempts by charities or governments to alleviate poverty were counterproductive, he argued, because they merely allowed the poor to have more children, placing even greater strains on society's productive capabilities.

Malthus may have correctly described the world at the time when he lived, but fortunately, his dire forecast was far off the mark. The world population has increased about sixfold over the past two centuries, but living standards around the world are on average much higher. As a result of economic growth, chronic hunger and malnutrition are less common now than they were in Malthus's day. Modern famines occur from time to time but are more often the result of an unequal income distribution or political instability than inadequate food production.

Where did Malthus go wrong? As we discussed in a case study earlier in this chapter, growth in human ingenuity has offset the effects of a larger population. Pesticides, fertilizers, mechanized farm equipment, new crop varieties, and other technological advances that Malthus never imagined have allowed each farmer to feed ever greater numbers of people. Even with more mouths to feed, fewer farmers are necessary because each farmer is much more productive.

Diluting the Capital Stock   Whereas Malthus worried about the effects of population on the use of natural resources, some modern theories of economic

Thomas Robert Malthus

2002 ARPL / TOPHAM / THE IMAGEWORKS

growth emphasize its effects on capital accumulation. According to these theories, high population growth reduces GDP per worker because rapid growth in the number of workers forces the capital stock to be spread more thinly. In other words, when population growth is rapid, each worker is equipped with less capital. A smaller quantity of capital per worker leads to lower productivity and lower GDP per worker.

This problem is most apparent in the case of human capital. Countries with high population growth have large numbers of school-age children. This places a larger burden on the educational system. It is not surprising, therefore, that educational attainment tends to be low in countries with high population growth.

The differences in population growth around the world are large. In developed countries, such as the United States and those in Western Europe, the population has risen only about 1 percent per year in recent decades and is expected to rise even more slowly in the future. By contrast, in many poor African countries, population grows at about 3 percent per year. At this rate, the population doubles every 23 years. This rapid population growth makes it harder to provide workers with the tools and skills they need to achieve high levels of productivity.

Rapid population growth is not the main reason that less developed countries are poor, but some analysts believe that reducing the rate of population growth would help these countries raise their standards of living. In some countries, this goal is accomplished directly with laws that regulate the number of children families may have.

Another way in which a country can influence population growth is to apply one of the *Ten Principles of Economics*: People respond to incentives. Bearing a child, like any decision, has an opportunity cost. When the opportunity cost rises, people will choose to have smaller families. In particular, women with the opportunity to receive a good education and desirable employment tend to want fewer children than those with fewer opportunities outside the home. Hence, policies that foster equal treatment of women may be one way for less developed economies to reduce the rate of population growth and, perhaps, raise their standards of living.

Promoting Technological Progress   Rapid population growth may depress economic prosperity by reducing the amount of capital each worker has, but it may also have some benefits. Some economists have suggested that world population growth has been an engine of technological progress and economic prosperity. The mechanism is simple: If there are more people, then there are more scientists, inventors, and engineers to contribute to technological advance, which benefits everyone.

Economist Michael Kremer provided some support for this hypothesis in an article titled "Population Growth and Technological Change: One Million B.C. to 1990," which was published in the *Quarterly Journal of Economics* in 1993. Kremer began by noting that over the broad span of human history, world growth rates have increased with world population. For example, world growth was more rapid when the world population was 1 billion (which occurred around the year 1800) than when the population was only 100 million (around 500 B.C.). This fact is consistent with the hypothesis that a larger population induces more technological progress.

Kremer's second piece of evidence comes from comparing regions of the world. The melting of the polar icecaps at the end of the Ice Age around 10,000 B.C. flooded the land bridges and separated the world into several distinct regions that could not communicate with one another for thousands of years. If technological progress is more rapid when there are more people to discover things, then larger regions should have experienced more rapid growth.

According to Kremer, that is exactly what happened. The most successful region of the world in 1500 (when Columbus reestablished contact) comprised the "Old World" civilizations of the large Eurasia-Africa region. Next in technological development were the Aztec and Mayan civilizations in the Americas, followed by the hunter-gatherers of Australia, and then the primitive people of Tasmania, who lacked even fire-making and most stone and bone tools.

The smallest isolated region was Flinders Island, a tiny island between Tasmania and Australia. With the smallest population, Flinders Island had the fewest opportunities for technological advance and, indeed, seemed to regress.

IN THE NEWS

Using Experiments to Evaluate Aid

To figure out what policies work in developing nations, economists are increasingly turning to randomized controlled experiments.

What It Takes to Lift Families Out of Poverty

By Michaeleen Doucleff

Eighteen years ago, Dean Karlan was a fresh, bright-eyed graduate student in economics at the Massachusetts Institute of Technology. He wanted to answer what seemed like a simple question:

"Does global aid work?" Karlan says.

He was reading a bunch of studies on the topic. But none of them actually answered the question. "We were tearing our hair out reading these papers because it was frustrating," he says. "[We] never really felt like the papers were really satisfactory."

One problem was that no one was actually testing global aid programs—methodically— to see if they really changed people's lives permanently. "They haven't been taking the

scientific method to problems of poverty," he says.

Take, for instance, a charity that gives a family a cow. The charity might check on the family a year later and say, "Wow! The family is doing so much better with this cow. Cows must be the reason."

But maybe it wasn't the cow that improved the family's life. Maybe it had a bumper crop that year or property values went up in the neighborhood. Researchers really weren't doing those experiments, Karlan says.

So he and a bunch of his colleagues had a radical idea: Test aid with the same method doctors use to test drugs (that is, randomized control trials).

The idea is quite simple. Give some families aid but others nothing. Then follow both groups, and see if the aid actually made a difference in the long run.

Karlan, who's now a professor at Yale University, says many people were skeptical. "I have many conversations with people who say, 'You want to do what? Why would you want to do that?'"

One issue is that some families go home empty-handed, with no aid. So the idea seems unethical. But Karlan disagrees. "The whole point of this is to help more people," he says. "If we find out what works and what doesn't, in five years we can have a much bigger impact."

So Karlan and collaborators around the world, including those at the Abdul Latif Jameel Poverty Action Lab at MIT and the nonprofit Innovations for Poverty Action, decided to try out the idea with one of the toughest problems out there: helping families get out of extreme poverty.

An anti-poverty program in Bangladesh, called BRAC, looked like it was successful. It seemed to help nearly 400,000 families who were living off less than $1.25 each day. So Karlan and his colleagues wanted to test the program and see if it could work in other countries.

Around 3000 B.C., human society on Flinders Island died out completely. A large population, Kremer concluded, is a prerequisite for technological advance.

QuickQuiz *Describe three ways a government policymaker can try to raise the growth in living standards in a society. Are there any drawbacks to these policies?*

They teamed up with a network of researchers and nonprofits in six developing countries. They went to thousands of communities and found the poorest families.

Then they divided the families into two groups. They gave half the families nothing. And the other half a whole smorgasbord of aid for one to two years. They gave them:

1. Some livestock for making money, such as goats for milk, bees for honey, or guinea pigs for selling. "Depending on the site, there were different things specifically appropriate for that context," Karlan says.
2. Training about how to raise the livestock
3. Food or cash so they wouldn't eat the livestock
4. A savings account
5. Help with their health—both physical and mental

Karlan and his colleagues reported the results of the massive experiment in the journal *Science* this week.

So what did they find? Well, the strategy worked pretty well in five of the six countries they tried it in. Families who got the aid started making a little more money, and they had more food to eat.

"We see mental health go up. Happiness go up. We even saw things like female power increase," Karlan says.

But here's what sets this study apart from the rest: Families continued to make a bit more money even a year after the aid stopped.

"People were stuck. They give them this big push, and they seem to be on a sustained increased income level," says Justin Sandefur, an economist at the Center for Global Development in Washington, who wasn't involved in the study.

"What I found exciting and unique about this study is that the impact of the aid was durable and sustainable," he added.

The results suggest that the right kind of aid does help people in multiple places. It lifted the families up just a little bit so they could finally start inching out of extreme poverty.

But we shouldn't get too excited yet. These people are still very poor, says Sarah Baird, an economist at George Washington University.

The effect of the aid was actually quite small, she says. Families' incomes and food consumption together went up by only a small amount — about 5 percent, on average, when compared with the control group.

And it's still unknown how long this bump will last. The researchers looked at the change only a year after the aid stopped.

"Moving poverty is hard," Baird says. "The fact that they [Karlan and colleagues] were able to move it, and it was sustainable after a year, I think is important."

The findings are a leap forward, she says, because it shows charities and governments a basic strategy that often works.

And even a little bit of extra money can make a huge difference in these peoples' lives, she says. It can help them send their kids to school. Or even just give them a little more hope. ■

PER-ANDERS PETTERSSON/GETTY IMAGES NEWS/ GETTY IMAGES

25-4 Conclusion: The Importance of Long-Run Growth

In this chapter, we have discussed what determines the standard of living in a nation and how policymakers can endeavor to raise it through policies that promote economic growth. Most of this chapter is summarized in one of the *Ten Principles of Economics*: A country's standard of living depends on its ability to produce goods and services. Policymakers who want to encourage growth in living standards must aim to increase their nation's productive ability by encouraging rapid accumulation of the factors of production and ensuring that these factors are employed as effectively as possible.

Economists differ in their views on the role of government in promoting economic growth. At the very least, government can lend support to the invisible hand by maintaining property rights and political stability. More controversial is whether government should target and subsidize specific industries that might be especially important for technological progress. There is no doubt that these issues are among the most important in economics. The success of one generation's policymakers in learning and heeding the fundamental lessons about economic growth determines what kind of world the next generation will inherit.

CHAPTER QuickQuiz

1. Over the past century, real GDP per person in the United States has grown about _____ percent per year, which means it doubles about every _____ years.
   a. 2, 14
   b. 2, 35
   c. 5, 14
   d. 5, 35

2. The world's rich countries, such as the United States and Germany, have income per person that is about _____ times the income per person in the world's poor countries, such as Pakistan and India.
   a. 2
   b. 4
   c. 10
   d. 30

3. Most economists are _____ that natural resources will eventually limit economic growth. As evidence, they note that the prices of most natural resources, adjusted for overall inflation, have tended to _____ over time.
   a. concerned, rise
   b. concerned, fall
   c. not concerned, rise
   d. not concerned, fall

4. Because capital is subject to diminishing returns, higher saving and investment do not lead to higher
   a. income in the long run.
   b. income in the short run.
   c. growth in the long run.
   d. growth in the short run.

5. When the Japanese car maker Toyota expands one of its car factories in the United States, what is the likely impact of this event on the gross domestic product and gross national product of the United States?
   a. GDP rises and GNP falls.
   b. GNP rises and GDP falls.
   c. GDP shows a larger increase than GNP.
   d. GNP shows a larger increase than GDP.

6. Thomas Robert Malthus believed that population growth would
   a. put stress on the economy's ability to produce food, dooming humans to remain in poverty.
   b. spread the capital stock too thinly across the labor force, lowering each worker's productivity.
   c. promote technological progress, because there would be more scientists and inventors.
   d. eventually decline to sustainable levels, as birth control improved and people had smaller families.

SUMMARY

- Economic prosperity, as measured by GDP per person, varies substantially around the world. The average income in the world's richest countries is more than ten times that in the world's poorest countries. Because growth rates of real GDP also vary substantially, the relative positions of countries can change dramatically over time.

- The standard of living in an economy depends on the economy's ability to produce goods and services. Productivity, in turn, depends on the physical capital, human capital, natural resources, and technological knowledge available to workers.

- Government policies can try to influence the economy's growth rate in many ways: by encouraging saving and investment, encouraging investment from abroad, fostering education, promoting good health, maintaining property rights and political stability, allowing free trade, and promoting the research and development of new technologies.

- The accumulation of capital is subject to diminishing returns: The more capital an economy has, the less additional output the economy gets from an extra unit of capital. As a result, although higher saving leads to higher growth for a period of time, growth eventually slows down as capital, productivity, and income rise. Also because of diminishing returns, the return to capital is especially high in poor countries. Other things being equal, these countries can grow faster because of the catch-up effect.

- Population growth has a variety of effects on economic growth. On the one hand, more rapid population growth may lower productivity by stretching the supply of natural resources and by reducing the amount of capital available for each worker. On the other hand, a larger population may enhance the rate of technological progress because there are more scientists and engineers.

KEY CONCEPTS

productivity, p. 519
physical capital, p. 519
human capital, p. 522

natural resources, p. 522
technological knowledge, p. 523

diminishing returns, p. 525
catch-up effect, p. 526

QUESTIONS FOR REVIEW

1. What does the level of a nation's GDP measure? What does the growth rate of GDP measure? Would you rather live in a nation with a high level of GDP and a low growth rate or in a nation with a low level of GDP and a high growth rate?

2. List and describe four determinants of productivity.

3. In what way is a college degree a form of capital?

4. Explain how higher saving leads to a higher standard of living. What might deter a policymaker from trying to raise the rate of saving?

5. Does a higher rate of saving lead to higher growth temporarily or indefinitely?

6. Why would removing a trade restriction, such as a tariff, lead to more rapid economic growth?

7. How does the rate of population growth influence the level of GDP per person?

8. Describe two ways the U.S. government tries to encourage advances in technological knowledge.

PROBLEMS AND APPLICATIONS

1. Most countries, including the United States, import substantial amounts of goods and services from other countries. Yet the chapter says that a nation can enjoy a high standard of living only if it can produce a large quantity of goods and services itself. Can you reconcile these two facts?

2. Suppose that society decided to reduce consumption and increase investment.
   a. How would this change affect economic growth?
   b. What groups in society would benefit from this change? What groups might be hurt?

3. Societies choose what share of their resources to devote to consumption and what share to devote to investment. Some of these decisions involve private spending; others involve government spending.
   a. Describe some forms of private spending that represent consumption and some forms that represent investment. The national income accounts include tuition as a part of consumer spending. In your opinion, are the resources you devote to your education a form of consumption or a form of investment?
   b. Describe some forms of government spending that represent consumption and some forms that represent investment. In your opinion, should we view government spending on health programs as a form of consumption or investment? Would you distinguish between health programs for the young and health programs for the elderly?

4. What is the opportunity cost of investing in capital? Do you think a country can overinvest in capital? What is the opportunity cost of investing in human capital? Do you think a country can overinvest in human capital? Explain.

5. In the 1990s and the first decade of the 2000s, investors from the Asian economies of Japan and China made significant direct and portfolio investments in the United States. At the time, many Americans were unhappy that this investment was occurring.
   a. In what way was it better for the United States to receive this foreign investment than not to receive it?
   b. In what way would it have been better still for Americans to have made this investment?

6. In many developing nations, young women have lower enrollment rates in secondary school than do young men. Describe several ways in which greater educational opportunities for young women could lead to faster economic growth in these countries.

7. The International Property Right Index scores countries based on the legal and political environment and how well property rights are protected. Go online and find a recent ranking. Choose three countries with high scores and three countries with low scores. Then find estimates of GDP per person in each of these six countries. What pattern do you find? Give two possible interpretations of the pattern.

8. International data show a positive correlation between income per person and the health of the population.
   a. Explain how higher income might cause better health outcomes.
   b. Explain how better health outcomes might cause higher income.
   c. How might the relative importance of your two hypotheses be relevant for public policy?

9. The great 18th-century economist Adam Smith wrote, "Little else is requisite to carry a state to the highest degree of opulence from the lowest barbarism but peace, easy taxes, and a tolerable administration of justice: all the rest being brought about by the natural course of things." Explain how each of the three conditions Smith describes would promote economic growth.

To find additional study resources, visit cengagebrain.com, and search for "Mankiw."

Saving, Investment, and the Financial System

I magine that you have just graduated from college (with a degree in economics, of course) and you decide to start your own business—an economic forecasting firm. Before you make any money selling your forecasts, you have to incur substantial costs to set up your business. You have to buy computers with which to make your forecasts, as well as desks, chairs, and filing cabinets to furnish your new office. Each of these items is a type of capital that your firm will use to produce and sell its services.

How do you obtain the funds to invest in these capital goods? Perhaps you are able to pay for them out of your past savings. More likely, however, like most entrepreneurs, you do not have enough money of your own to finance the start of your business. As a result, you have to get the money you need from other sources.

There are various ways to finance these capital investments. You could borrow the money, perhaps from a bank or from a friend or relative. In this case, you would promise not only to return the money to the lender at a later date but also to pay the lender interest for the use of the money. Alternatively, you could convince someone to provide the money you need for your business in exchange for a share of your future profits, whatever they might happen to be. In either case, your investment in computers and office equipment is being financed by someone else's saving.

financial system
the group of institutions in the economy that help to match one person's saving with another person's investment

The **financial system** consists of the institutions that help to match one person's saving with another person's investment. As we discussed in the previous chapter, saving and investment are key ingredients to long-run economic growth: When a country saves a large portion of its GDP, more resources are available for investment in capital, and higher capital raises a country's productivity and living standard. The previous chapter, however, did not explain how the economy coordinates saving and investment. At any time, some people want to save some of their income for the future and others want to borrow to finance investments in new and growing businesses. What brings these two groups of people together? What ensures that the supply of funds from those who want to save balances the demand for funds from those who want to invest?

This chapter examines how the financial system works. First, we discuss the large variety of institutions that make up the financial system in our economy. Second, we examine the relationship between the financial system and some key macroeconomic variables—notably saving and investment. Third, we develop a model of the supply and demand for funds in financial markets. In the model, the interest rate is the price that adjusts to balance supply and demand. The model shows how various government policies affect the interest rate and, thereby, society's allocation of scarce resources.

26-1   Financial Institutions in the U.S. Economy

At the broadest level, the financial system moves the economy's scarce resources from savers (people who spend less than they earn) to borrowers (people who spend more than they earn). Savers save for various reasons—to put a child through college in several years or to retire comfortably in several decades. Similarly, borrowers borrow for various reasons—to buy a house in which to live or to start a business with which to make a living. Savers supply their money to the financial system with the expectation that they will get it back with interest at a later date. Borrowers demand money from the financial system with the knowledge that they will be required to pay it back with interest at a later date.

The financial system is made up of various financial institutions that help coordinate the actions of savers and borrowers. As a prelude to analyzing the economic forces that drive the financial system, let's discuss the most important of these institutions. Financial institutions can be grouped into two categories: financial markets and financial intermediaries. We consider each category in turn.

26-1a   Financial Markets

financial markets
financial institutions through which savers can directly provide funds to borrowers

Financial markets are the institutions through which a person who wants to save can directly supply funds to a person who wants to borrow. The two most important financial markets in our economy are the bond market and the stock market.

The Bond Market   When Intel, the giant maker of computer chips, wants to borrow to finance construction of a new factory, it can borrow directly from the public. It does this by selling bonds. A **bond** is a certificate of indebtedness that specifies the obligations of the borrower to the holder of the bond. Put simply, a bond is an IOU. It identifies the time at which the loan will be repaid, called the *date of maturity*, and the rate of interest that will be paid periodically until the loan matures. The buyer of a bond gives his money to Intel in exchange for this promise of interest and eventual repayment of the amount borrowed (called the *principal*). The buyer can hold the bond until maturity, or he can sell the bond at an earlier date to someone else.

bond
a certificate of indebtedness

There are millions of different bonds in the U.S. economy. When large corporations, the federal government, or state and local governments need to borrow to finance the purchase of a new factory, a new jet fighter, or a new school, they usually do so by issuing bonds. If you look at *The Wall Street Journal* or the business section of your local newspaper, you will find a listing of the prices and interest rates on some of the most important bond issues. These bonds differ according to three significant characteristics.

The first characteristic is a bond's *term*—the length of time until the bond matures. Some bonds have short terms, such as a few months, while others have terms as long as 30 years. (The British government has even issued a bond that never matures, called a *perpetuity*. This bond pays interest forever, but the principal is never repaid.) The interest rate on a bond depends, in part, on its term. Long-term bonds are riskier than short-term bonds because holders of long-term bonds have to wait longer for repayment of principal. If a holder of a long-term bond needs his money earlier than the distant date of maturity, he has no choice but to sell the bond to someone else, perhaps at a reduced price. To compensate for this risk, long-term bonds usually pay higher interest rates than short-term bonds.

The second important characteristic of a bond is its *credit risk*—the probability that the borrower will fail to pay some of the interest or principal. Such a failure to pay is called a *default*. Borrowers can (and sometimes do) default on their loans by declaring bankruptcy. When bond buyers perceive that the probability of default is high, they demand a higher interest rate as compensation for this risk. Because the U.S. government is considered a safe credit risk, government bonds tend to pay low interest rates. By contrast, financially shaky corporations raise money by issuing *junk bonds*, which pay very high interest rates. Buyers of bonds can judge credit risk by checking with various private agencies that evaluate the credit risk of different bonds. For example, Standard & Poor's rates bonds from AAA (the safest) to D (those already in default).

The third important characteristic of a bond is its *tax treatment*—the way the tax laws treat the interest earned on the bond. The interest on most bonds is taxable income; that is, the bond owner has to pay a portion of the interest he earns in income taxes. By contrast, when state and local governments issue bonds, called *municipal bonds*, the bond owners are not required to pay federal income tax on the interest income. Because of this tax advantage, bonds issued by state and local governments typically pay a lower interest rate than bonds issued by corporations or the federal government.

The Stock Market   Another way for Intel to raise funds to build a new semiconductor factory is to sell stock in the company. **Stock** represents ownership in a firm and is, therefore, a claim to the profits that the firm makes. For example, if Intel sells a total of 1,000,000 shares of stock, then each share represents ownership of 1/1,000,000 of the business.

stock
a claim to partial ownership in a firm

The sale of stock to raise money is called *equity finance*, whereas the sale of bonds is called *debt finance*. Although corporations use both equity and debt finance to raise money for new investments, stocks and bonds are very different. The owner of shares of Intel stock is a part owner of Intel, while the owner of an Intel bond is a creditor of the corporation. If Intel is very profitable, the stockholders enjoy the benefits of these profits, whereas the bondholders get only the interest on their bonds. And if Intel runs into financial difficulty, the bondholders are paid what they are due before stockholders receive anything at all. Compared to bonds, stocks offer the holder both higher risk and potentially higher return.

After a corporation issues stock by selling shares to the public, these shares trade among stockholders on organized stock exchanges. In these transactions, the corporation itself receives no money when its stock changes hands. The most important stock exchanges in the U.S. economy are the New York Stock Exchange and the NASDAQ (National Association of Securities Dealers Automated Quotations). Most of the world's countries have their own stock exchanges on which the shares of local companies trade.

The prices at which shares trade on stock exchanges are determined by the supply of and demand for the stock in these companies. Because stock represents ownership in a corporation, the demand for a stock (and thus its price) reflects people's perception of the corporation's future profitability. When people become optimistic about a company's future, they raise their demand for its stock and thereby bid up the price of a share of stock. Conversely, when people's expectations of a company's prospects decline, the price of a share falls.

Various stock indexes are available to monitor the overall level of stock prices. A *stock index* is computed as an average of a group of stock prices. The most famous stock index is the Dow Jones Industrial Average, which has been computed regularly since 1896. It is now based on the prices of the stocks of thirty major U.S. companies, such as General Electric, Microsoft, Coca-Cola, Boeing, Apple, and Wal-Mart. Another well-known stock index is the Standard & Poor's 500 Index, which is based on the prices of the stocks of 500 major companies. Because stock prices reflect expected profitability, these stock indexes are watched closely as possible indicators of future economic conditions.

26-1b Financial Intermediaries

financial intermediaries
financial institutions through which savers can indirectly provide funds to borrowers

Financial intermediaries are financial institutions through which savers can indirectly provide funds to borrowers. The term *intermediary* reflects the role of these institutions in standing between savers and borrowers. Here we consider two of the most important financial intermediaries: banks and mutual funds.

Banks   If the owner of a small grocery store wants to finance an expansion of his business, he probably takes a strategy quite different from that of Intel. Unlike Intel, a small grocer would find it difficult to raise funds in the bond and stock markets. Most buyers of stocks and bonds prefer to buy those issued by larger, more familiar companies. The small grocer, therefore, most likely finances his business expansion with a loan from a local bank.

Banks are the financial intermediaries with which people are most familiar. A primary job of banks is to take in deposits from people who want to save and use these deposits to make loans to people who want to borrow. Banks pay depositors interest on their deposits and charge borrowers slightly higher interest on their loans. The difference between these rates of interest covers the banks' costs and returns some profit to the owners of the banks.

Besides being financial intermediaries, banks play another important role in the economy: They facilitate purchases of goods and services by allowing people to write checks against their deposits and to access those deposits with debit cards. In other words, banks help create a special asset that people can use as a *medium of exchange*. A medium of exchange is an item that people can easily use to engage in transactions. A bank's role in providing a medium of exchange distinguishes it from many other financial institutions. Stocks and bonds, like bank deposits, are a possible *store of value* for the wealth that people have accumulated in past saving, but access to this wealth is not as easy, cheap, and immediate as just writing a check or swiping a debit card. For now, we ignore this second role of banks, but we will return to it when we discuss the monetary system later in the book.

Mutual Funds   A financial intermediary of increasing importance in the U.S. economy is the mutual fund. A **mutual fund** is an institution that sells shares to the public and uses the proceeds to buy a selection, or *portfolio*, of various types of stocks, bonds, or both stocks and bonds. The shareholder of the mutual fund accepts all the risk and return associated with the portfolio. If the value of the portfolio rises, the shareholder benefits; if the value of the portfolio falls, the shareholder suffers the loss.

mutual fund
an institution that sells shares to the public and uses the proceeds to buy a portfolio of stocks and bonds

The primary advantage of mutual funds is that they allow people with small amounts of money to diversify their holdings. Buyers of stocks and bonds are well advised to heed the adage: Don't put all your eggs in one basket. Because the value of any single stock or bond is tied to the fortunes of one company, holding a single kind of stock or bond is very risky. By contrast, people who hold a diverse portfolio of stocks and bonds face less risk because they have only a small stake in each company. Mutual funds make this diversification easy. With only a few hundred dollars, a person can buy shares in a mutual fund and, indirectly, become the part owner or creditor of hundreds of major companies. For this service, the company operating the mutual fund charges shareholders a fee, usually between 0.25 and 2.0 percent of assets each year.

A second advantage claimed by mutual fund companies is that mutual funds give ordinary people access to the skills of professional money managers. The managers of most mutual funds pay close attention to the developments and prospects of the companies in which they buy stock. These managers buy the stock of companies they view as having a profitable future and sell the stock of companies with less promising prospects. This professional management, it is argued, should increase the return that mutual fund depositors earn on their savings.

Financial economists, however, are often skeptical of this argument. With thousands of money managers paying close attention to each company's prospects, the price of a company's stock is usually a good reflection of the company's true value. As a result, it is hard to "beat the market" by buying good stocks and selling bad ones. In fact, mutual funds called *index funds*, which buy all the stocks in a given stock index, perform somewhat better on average than mutual funds that take advantage of active trading by professional money managers. The explanation for the superior performance of index funds is that they keep costs low by buying and selling very rarely and by not having to pay the salaries of professional money managers.

26-1c Summing Up

The U.S. economy contains a large variety of financial institutions. In addition to the bond market, the stock market, banks, and mutual funds, there are also pension funds, credit unions, insurance companies, and even the local loan shark. These institutions differ in many ways. When analyzing the macroeconomic role of the financial system, however, it is more important to keep in mind that, despite their differences, these financial institutions all serve the same goal: directing the resources of savers into the hands of borrowers.

QuickQuiz *What is a share of stock? What is a bond? Explain their differences and similarities.*

26-2 Saving and Investment in the National Income Accounts

Events that occur within the financial system are central to understanding developments in the overall economy. As we have just seen, the institutions that make up this system—the bond market, the stock market, banks, and mutual funds—have the role of coordinating the economy's saving and investment. And as we saw in the previous chapter, saving and investment are important determinants of long-run growth in GDP and living standards. As a result, macroeconomists need to understand how financial markets work and how various events and policies affect them.

As a starting point for analyzing financial markets, we discuss the key macroeconomic variables that measure activity in these markets. Our emphasis here is not on behavior but on accounting. *Accounting* refers to how various numbers are defined and added up. A personal accountant might help an individual add up his income and expenses. A national income accountant does the same thing for the economy as a whole. The national income accounts include, in particular, GDP and the many related statistics.

The rules of national income accounting include several important identities. Recall that an *identity* is an equation that must be true because of the way the variables in the equation are defined. Identities are useful to keep in mind, for they clarify how different variables are related to one another. Here we consider some accounting identities that shed light on the macroeconomic role of financial markets.

26-2a Some Important Identities

Recall that gross domestic product (GDP) is both total income in an economy and the total expenditure on the economy's output of goods and services. GDP (denoted as Y) is divided into four components of expenditure: consumption (C), investment (I), government purchases (G), and net exports (NX). We write

$$Y = C + I + G + NX.$$

This equation is an identity because every dollar of expenditure that shows up on the left side also shows up in one of the four components on the right side. Because of the way each of the variables is defined and measured, this equation must always hold.

In this chapter, we simplify our analysis by assuming that the economy we are examining is closed. A *closed economy* is one that does not interact with other economies. In particular, a closed economy does not engage in international trade in goods and services, nor does it engage in international borrowing and lending. Actual economies are *open economies*—that is, they interact with other economies around the world. Nonetheless, assuming a closed economy is a useful simplification with which we can learn some lessons that apply to all economies. Moreover, this assumption applies perfectly to the world economy (for interplanetary trade is not yet common).

Because a closed economy does not engage in international trade, imports and exports are exactly zero. Therefore, net exports (NX) are also zero. We can now simplify the identity as

$$Y = C + I + G.$$

This equation states that GDP is the sum of consumption, investment, and government purchases. Each unit of output sold in a closed economy is consumed, invested, or bought by the government.

To see what this identity can tell us about financial markets, subtract C and G from both sides of this equation. We then obtain

$$Y - C - G = I.$$

The left side of this equation ($Y - C - G$) is the total income in the economy that remains after paying for consumption and government purchases: This amount is called **national saving**, or just **saving**, and is denoted S. Substituting S for $Y - C - G$, we can write the last equation as

$$S = I.$$

This equation states that saving equals investment.

To understand the meaning of national saving, it is helpful to manipulate the definition a bit more. Let T denote the amount that the government collects from households in taxes minus the amount it pays back to households in the form of transfer payments (such as Social Security and welfare). We can then write national saving in either of two ways:

$$S = Y - C - G$$

or

$$S = (Y - T - C) + (T - G).$$

These equations are the same because the two T's in the second equation cancel each other, but each reveals a different way of thinking about national saving. In particular, the second equation separates national saving into two pieces: private saving ($Y - T - C$) and public saving ($T - G$).

Consider each of these two pieces. **Private saving** is the amount of income that households have left after paying their taxes and paying for their consumption. In particular, because households receive income of Y, pay taxes of T, and spend C on consumption, private saving is $Y - T - C$. **Public saving** is the amount of tax revenue that the government has left after paying for its spending. The government receives T in tax revenue and spends G on goods and services. If T exceeds G, the government runs a **budget surplus** because it receives more money than it spends. This surplus of $T - G$ represents public saving. If the government spends more than it receives in tax revenue, then G is larger than T. In this case, the government runs a **budget deficit**, and public saving ($T - G$) is a negative number.

Now consider how these accounting identities are related to financial markets. The equation $S = I$ reveals an important fact: *For the economy as a whole, saving must be equal to investment.* Yet this fact raises some important questions: What mechanisms lie behind this identity? What coordinates those people who are deciding how much to save and those people who are deciding how much to invest? The answer is the financial system. The bond market, the stock market, banks, mutual funds, and other financial markets and intermediaries stand between the two sides of the $S = I$ equation. They take in the nation's saving and direct it to the nation's investment.

national saving (saving)
the total income in the economy that remains after paying for consumption and government purchases

private saving
the income that households have left after paying for taxes and consumption

public saving
the tax revenue that the government has left after paying for its spending

budget surplus
an excess of tax revenue over government spending

budget deficit
a shortfall of tax revenue from government spending

26-2b The Meaning of Saving and Investment

The terms *saving* and *investment* can sometimes be confusing. Most people use these terms casually and sometimes interchangeably. By contrast, the macroeconomists who put together the national income accounts use these terms carefully and distinctly.

Consider an example. Suppose that Larry earns more than he spends and deposits his unspent income in a bank or uses it to buy some stock or a bond from a corporation. Because Larry's income exceeds his consumption, he adds to the nation's saving. Larry might think of himself as "investing" his money, but a macroeconomist would call Larry's act saving rather than investment.

In the language of macroeconomics, investment refers to the purchase of new capital, such as equipment or buildings. When Moe borrows from the bank to build himself a new house, he adds to the nation's investment. (Remember, the purchase of a new house is the one form of household spending that is investment rather than consumption.) Similarly, when the Curly Corporation sells some stock and uses the proceeds to build a new factory, it also adds to the nation's investment.

Although the accounting identity $S = I$ shows that saving and investment are equal for the economy as a whole, this does not have to be true for every individual household or firm. Larry's saving can be greater than his investment, and he can deposit the excess in a bank. Moe's saving can be less than his investment, and he can borrow the shortfall from a bank. Banks and other financial institutions make these individual differences between saving and investment possible by allowing one person's saving to finance another person's investment.

QuickQuiz *Define* private saving, public saving, national saving, *and* investment. *How are they related?*

26-3 The Market for Loanable Funds

Having discussed some of the important financial institutions in our economy and the macroeconomic role of these institutions, we are ready to build a model of financial markets. Our purpose in building this model is to explain how financial markets coordinate the economy's saving and investment. The model also gives us a tool with which we can analyze various government policies that influence saving and investment.

market for loanable funds
the market in which those who want to save supply funds and those who want to borrow to invest demand funds

To keep things simple, we assume that the economy has only one financial market, called the **market for loanable funds**. All savers go to this market to deposit their saving, and all borrowers go to this market to take out their loans. Thus, the term *loanable funds* refers to all income that people have chosen to save and lend out, rather than use for their own consumption, and to the amount that investors have chosen to borrow to fund new investment projects. In the market for loanable funds, there is one interest rate, which is both the return to saving and the cost of borrowing.

The assumption of a single financial market, of course, is not realistic. As we have seen, the economy has many types of financial institutions. But as we discussed in Chapter 2, the art in building an economic model is simplifying the world in order to explain it. For our purposes here, we can ignore the diversity of financial institutions and assume that the economy has a single financial market.

26-3a Supply and Demand for Loanable Funds

The economy's market for loanable funds, like other markets in the economy, is governed by supply and demand. To understand how the market for loanable funds operates, therefore, we first look at the sources of supply and demand in that market.

The supply of loanable funds comes from people who have some extra income they want to save and lend out. This lending can occur directly, such as when a household buys a bond from a firm, or it can occur indirectly, such as when a household makes a deposit in a bank, which then uses the funds to make loans. In both cases, *saving is the source of the supply of loanable funds.*

The demand for loanable funds comes from households and firms who wish to borrow to make investments. This demand includes families taking out mortgages to buy new homes. It also includes firms borrowing to buy new equipment or build factories. In both cases, *investment is the source of the demand for loanable funds.*

The interest rate is the price of a loan. It represents the amount that borrowers pay for loans and the amount that lenders receive on their saving. Because a high interest rate makes borrowing more expensive, the quantity of loanable funds demanded falls as the interest rate rises. Similarly, because a high interest rate makes saving more attractive, the quantity of loanable funds supplied rises as the interest rate rises. In other words, the demand curve for loanable funds slopes downward, and the supply curve for loanable funds slopes upward.

Figure 1 shows the interest rate that balances the supply and demand for loanable funds. In the equilibrium shown, the interest rate is 5 percent, and the quantity of loanable funds demanded and the quantity of loanable funds supplied both equal $1,200 billion.

The adjustment of the interest rate to the equilibrium level occurs for the usual reasons. If the interest rate were lower than the equilibrium level, the quantity of loanable funds supplied would be less than the quantity of loanable funds demanded. The resulting shortage of loanable funds would encourage lenders to

FIGURE 1

The Market for Loanable Funds
The interest rate in the economy adjusts to balance the supply and demand for loanable funds. The supply of loanable funds comes from national saving, including both private saving and public saving. The demand for loanable funds comes from firms and households that want to borrow for purposes of investment. Here the equilibrium interest rate is 5 percent, and $1,200 billion of loanable funds are supplied and demanded.

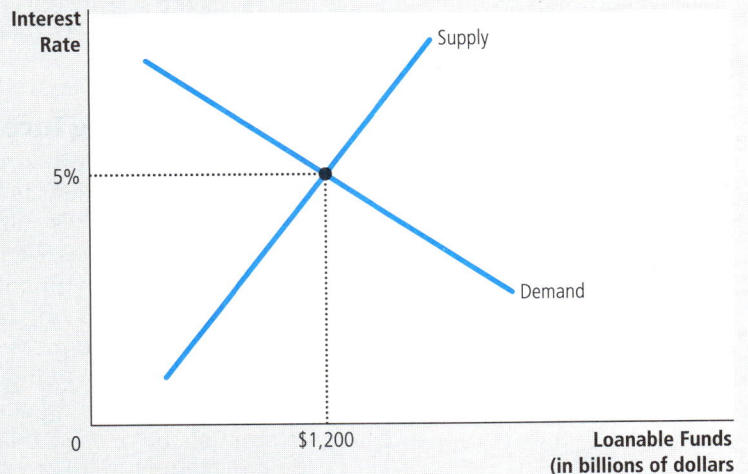

raise the interest rate they charge. A higher interest rate would encourage saving (thereby increasing the quantity of loanable funds supplied) and discourage borrowing for investment (thereby decreasing the quantity of loanable funds demanded). Conversely, if the interest rate were higher than the equilibrium level, the quantity of loanable funds supplied would exceed the quantity of loanable funds demanded. As lenders compete for the scarce borrowers, interest rates would be driven down. In this way, the interest rate approaches the equilibrium level at which the supply and demand for loanable funds exactly balance.

Recall that economists distinguish between the real interest rate and the nominal interest rate. The nominal interest rate is the monetary return to saving and the monetary cost of borrowing. It is the interest rate as usually reported. The real interest rate is the nominal interest rate corrected for inflation; it equals the nominal interest rate minus the inflation rate. Because inflation erodes the value of money over time, the real interest rate more accurately reflects the real return to saving and the real cost of borrowing. Therefore, the supply and demand for loanable funds depend on the real (rather than nominal) interest rate, and the equilibrium in Figure 1 should be interpreted as determining the real interest rate in the economy. For the rest of this chapter, when you see the term *interest rate*, you should remember that we are talking about the real interest rate.

This model of the supply and demand for loanable funds shows that financial markets work much like other markets in the economy. In the market for milk, for instance, the price of milk adjusts so that the quantity of milk supplied balances the quantity of milk demanded. In this way, the invisible hand coordinates the behavior of dairy farmers and the behavior of milk drinkers. Once we realize that saving represents the supply of loanable funds and investment represents the demand, we can see how the invisible hand coordinates saving and investment. When the interest rate adjusts to balance supply and demand in the market for loanable funds, it coordinates the behavior of people who want to save (the suppliers of loanable funds) and the behavior of people who want to invest (the demanders of loanable funds).

We can now use this analysis of the market for loanable funds to examine various government policies that affect the economy's saving and investment. Because this model is just supply and demand in a particular market, we analyze any policy using the three steps discussed in Chapter 4. First, we decide whether the policy shifts the supply curve or the demand curve. Second, we determine the direction of the shift. Third, we use the supply-and-demand diagram to see how the equilibrium changes.

26-3b Policy 1: Saving Incentives

Many economists and policymakers have advocated increases in how much people save. Their argument is simple. One of the *Ten Principles of Economics* in Chapter 1 is that a country's standard of living depends on its ability to produce goods and services. And as we discussed in the preceding chapter, saving is an important long-run determinant of a nation's productivity. If the United States could somehow raise its saving rate, more resources would be available for capital accumulation, GDP would grow more rapidly, and over time, U.S. citizens would enjoy a higher standard of living.

Another of the *Ten Principles of Economics* is that people respond to incentives. Many economists have used this principle to suggest that the low rate of saving is at least partly attributable to tax laws that discourage saving. The U.S. federal government, as well as many state governments, collects revenue by taxing income, including interest and dividend income. To see the effects of this policy, consider a 25-year-old who saves $1,000 and buys a 30-year bond that pays an interest rate of 9 percent. In the absence of taxes, the $1,000 grows to $13,268 when the individual reaches age 55. Yet if that interest is taxed at a rate of, say, 33 percent, the after-tax interest rate is only 6 percent. In this case, the $1,000 grows to only $5,743 over the 30 years. The tax on interest income substantially reduces the future payoff from current saving and, as a result, reduces the incentive for people to save.

In response to this problem, some economists and lawmakers have proposed reforming the tax code to encourage greater saving. For example, one proposal is to expand eligibility for special accounts, such as Individual Retirement Accounts, that allow people to shelter some of their saving from taxation. Let's consider the effect of such a saving incentive on the market for loanable funds, as illustrated in Figure 2. We analyze this policy following our three steps.

First, which curve would this policy affect? Because the tax change would alter the incentive for households to save *at any given interest rate*, it would affect the quantity of loanable funds supplied at each interest rate. Thus, the supply of loanable funds would shift. The demand for loanable funds would remain the same because the tax change would not directly affect the amount that borrowers want to borrow at any given interest rate.

Second, which way would the supply curve shift? Because saving would be taxed less heavily than under current law, households would increase their saving by consuming a smaller fraction of their income. Households would use this additional saving to increase their deposits in banks or to buy more bonds. The supply of loanable funds would increase, and the supply curve would shift to the right from S_1 to S_2, as shown in Figure 2.

Finally, we can compare the old and new equilibria. In the figure, the increased supply of loanable funds reduces the interest rate from 5 percent to 4 percent. The lower interest rate raises the quantity of loanable funds demanded from $1,200 billion to $1,600 billion. That is, the shift in the supply curve moves the market

---

FIGURE 2

Saving Incentives Increase the Supply of Loanable Funds

A change in the tax laws to encourage Americans to save more would shift the supply of loanable funds to the right from S_1 to S_2. As a result, the equilibrium interest rate would fall, and the lower interest rate would stimulate investment. Here the equilibrium interest rate falls from 5 percent to 4 percent, and the equilibrium quantity of loanable funds saved and invested rises from $1,200 billion to $1,600 billion.

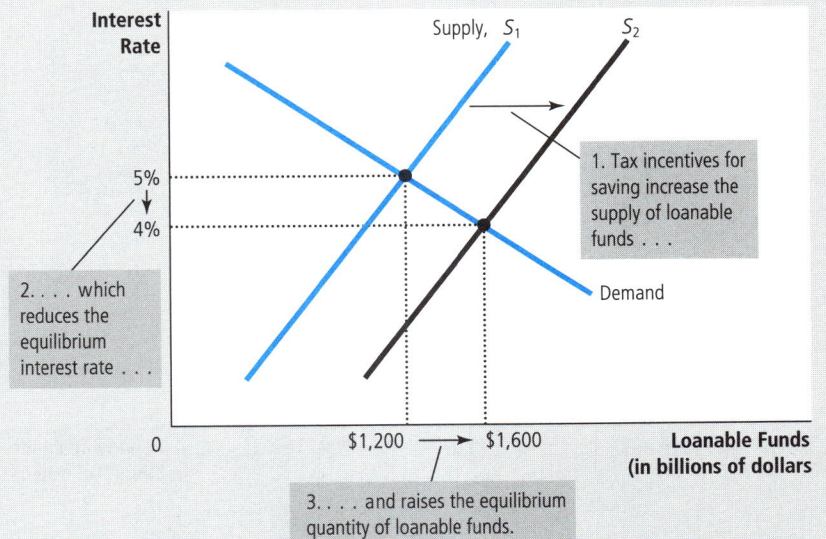

Interest Rate

Supply, S_1 S_2

5%

4%

1. Tax incentives for saving increase the supply of loanable funds . . .

Demand

2. . . . which reduces the equilibrium interest rate . . .

0          $1,200 ⟶ $1,600   **Loanable Funds (in billions of dollars**

3. . . . and raises the equilibrium quantity of loanable funds.

equilibrium along the demand curve. With a lower cost of borrowing, households and firms are motivated to borrow more to finance greater investment. Thus, *if a reform of the tax laws encouraged greater saving, the result would be lower interest rates and greater investment.*

This analysis of the effects of increased saving is widely accepted among economists, but there is less consensus about what kinds of tax changes should be enacted. Many economists endorse tax reform aimed at increasing saving to stimulate investment and growth. Yet others are skeptical that these tax changes would have much effect on national saving. These skeptics also doubt the equity of the proposed reforms. They argue that, in many cases, the benefits of the tax changes would accrue primarily to the wealthy, who are least in need of tax relief.

26-3c Policy 2: Investment Incentives

Suppose that Congress passed a tax reform aimed at making investment more attractive. In essence, this is what Congress does when it institutes an *investment tax credit*, which it does from time to time. An investment tax credit gives a tax advantage to any firm building a new factory or buying a new piece of equipment. Let's consider the effect of such a tax reform on the market for loanable funds, as illustrated in Figure 3.

First, would the law affect supply or demand? Because the tax credit would reward firms that borrow and invest in new capital, it would alter investment at any given interest rate and, thereby, change the demand for loanable funds. By contrast, because the tax credit would not affect the amount that households save at any given interest rate, it would not affect the supply of loanable funds.

Second, which way would the demand curve shift? Because firms would have an incentive to increase investment at any interest rate, the quantity of loanable funds demanded would be higher at any given interest rate. Thus, the demand curve for loanable funds would move to the right, as shown by the shift from D_1 to D_2 in the figure.

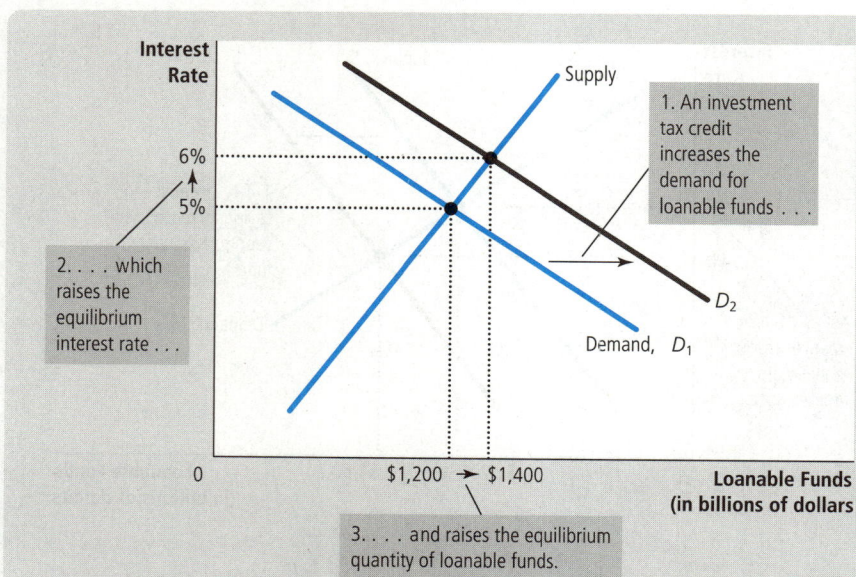

1. An investment tax credit increases the demand for loanable funds . . .

2. . . . which raises the equilibrium interest rate . . .

3. . . . and raises the equilibrium quantity of loanable funds.

FIGURE 3

Investment Incentives Increase the Demand for Loanable Funds

If the passage of an investment tax credit encouraged firms to invest more, the demand for loanable funds would increase. As a result, the equilibrium interest rate would rise, and the higher interest rate would stimulate saving. Here, when the demand curve shifts from D_1 to D_2, the equilibrium interest rate rises from 5 percent to 6 percent, and the equilibrium quantity of loanable funds saved and invested rises from $1,200 billion to $1,400 billion.

Third, consider how the equilibrium would change. In Figure 3, the increased demand for loanable funds raises the interest rate from 5 percent to 6 percent, and the higher interest rate in turn increases the quantity of loanable funds supplied from $1,200 billion to $1,400 billion, as households respond by increasing the amount they save. This change in household behavior is represented here as a movement along the supply curve. Thus, *if a reform of the tax laws encouraged greater investment, the result would be higher interest rates and greater saving.*

26-3d Policy 3: Government Budget Deficits and Surpluses

A perpetual topic of political debate is the status of the government budget. Recall that a *budget deficit* is an excess of government spending over tax revenue. Governments finance budget deficits by borrowing in the bond market, and the accumulation of past government borrowing is called the *government debt.* A *budget surplus*, an excess of tax revenue over government spending, can be used to repay some of the government debt. If government spending exactly equals tax revenue, the government is said to have a *balanced budget.*

Imagine that the government starts with a balanced budget and then, because of an increase in government spending, starts running a budget deficit. We can analyze the effects of the budget deficit by following our three steps in the market for loanable funds, as illustrated in Figure 4.

First, which curve shifts when the government starts running a budget deficit? Recall that national saving—the source of the supply of loanable funds— is composed of private saving and public saving. A change in the government budget balance represents a change in public saving and, therefore, in the supply of loanable funds. Because the budget deficit does not influence the amount that households and firms want to borrow to finance investment at any given interest rate, it does not alter the demand for loanable funds.

Second, which way does the supply curve shift? When the government runs a budget deficit, public saving is negative, and this reduces national saving. In other words, when the government borrows to finance its budget deficit, it reduces

FIGURE 4

The Effect of a Government Budget Deficit
When the government spends more than it receives in tax revenue, the resulting budget deficit lowers national saving. The supply of loanable funds decreases, and the equilibrium interest rate rises. Thus, when the government borrows to finance its budget deficit, it crowds out households and firms that otherwise would borrow to finance investment. Here, when the supply curve shifts from S_1 to S_2, the equilibrium interest rate rises from 5 percent to 6 percent, and the equilibrium quantity of loanable funds saved and invested falls from $1,200 billion to $800 billion.

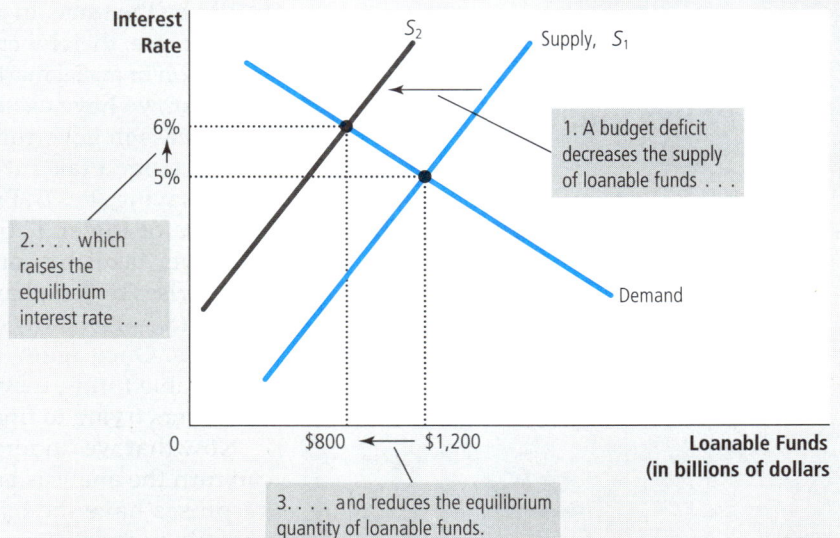

crowding out
a decrease in investment
that results from
government borrowing

the supply of loanable funds available to finance investment by households and firms. Thus, a budget deficit shifts the supply curve for loanable funds to the left from S_1 to S_2, as shown in Figure 4.

Third, we can compare the old and new equilibria. In the figure, when the budget deficit reduces the supply of loanable funds, the interest rate rises from 5 percent to 6 percent. This higher interest rate then alters the behavior of the households and firms that participate in the loan market. In particular, many demanders of loanable funds are discouraged by the higher interest rate. Fewer families buy new homes, and fewer firms choose to build new factories. The fall in investment because of government borrowing is called **crowding out** and is represented in Figure 4 by the movement along the demand curve from a quantity of $1,200 billion in loanable funds to a quantity of $800 billion. That is, when the government borrows to finance its budget deficit, it crowds out private borrowers who are trying to finance investment.

Thus, the most basic lesson about budget deficits follows directly from their effects on the supply and demand for loanable funds: *When the government reduces national saving by running a budget deficit, the interest rate rises and investment falls*. Because investment is important for long-run economic growth, government budget deficits reduce the economy's growth rate.

Why, you might ask, does a budget deficit affect the supply of loanable funds, rather than the demand for them? After all, the government finances a budget deficit by selling bonds, thereby borrowing from the private sector. Why does increased borrowing by the government shift the supply curve, whereas increased borrowing by private investors shifts the demand curve? To answer this question, we need to examine more precisely the meaning of "loanable funds." The model as presented here takes this term to mean the *flow of resources available to fund private investment*; thus, a government budget deficit reduces the supply of loanable funds. If, instead, we had defined the term "loanable funds" to mean the *flow of resources available from private saving*, then the government budget deficit would increase demand rather than reduce supply. Changing the interpretation of the term would cause a semantic change in how we described the model, but the bottom line from the analysis would be the same: In either case, a budget deficit increases the interest rate, thereby crowding out private borrowers who are relying on financial markets to fund private investment projects.

So far, we have examined a budget deficit that results from an increase in government spending, but a budget deficit that results from a tax cut has similar effects. A tax cut reduces public saving, $T - G$. Private saving, $Y - T - C$, might increase because of lower T, but as long as households respond to the lower taxes by consuming more, C increases, so private saving rises by less than public saving declines. Thus, national saving ($S = Y - C - G$), the sum of public and private saving, declines. Once again, the budget deficit reduces the supply of loanable funds, drives up the interest rate, and crowds out borrowers trying to finance capital investments.

Now that we understand the impact of budget deficits, we can turn the analysis around and see that government budget surpluses have the opposite effects. When the government collects more in tax revenue than it spends, it saves the difference by retiring some of the outstanding government

ASK THE EXPERTS

Fiscal Policy and Saving

"Sustained tax and spending policies that boost consumption in ways that reduce the saving rate are likely to lower long-run living standards."

What do economists say?

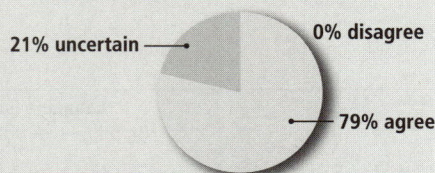

21% uncertain

0% disagree

79% agree

Source: IGM Economic Experts Panel, July 8, 2013.

debt. This budget surplus, or public saving, contributes to national saving. Thus, *a budget surplus increases the supply of loanable funds, reduces the interest rate, and stimulates investment.* Higher investment, in turn, means greater capital accumulation and more rapid economic growth.

CASE STUDY

THE HISTORY OF U.S. GOVERNMENT DEBT

How indebted is the U.S. government? The answer to this question varies substantially over time. Figure 5 shows the debt of the U.S. federal government expressed as a percentage of U.S. GDP. It shows that the government debt has fluctuated from zero in 1836 to 107 percent of GDP in 1945.

The behavior of the debt-to-GDP ratio is one gauge of what's happening with the government's finances. Because GDP is a rough measure of the government's tax base, a declining debt-to-GDP ratio indicates that the government indebtedness is shrinking relative to its ability to raise tax revenue. This suggests that the government is, in some sense, living within its means. By contrast, a rising debt-to-GDP ratio means that the government indebtedness is increasing relative to its ability to raise tax revenue. It is often interpreted as meaning that fiscal policy—government spending and taxes—cannot be sustained forever at current levels.

FIGURE 5

The U.S. Government Debt

The debt of the U.S. federal government, expressed here as a percentage of GDP, has varied throughout history. Wartime spending is typically associated with substantial increases in government debt.

Source: U.S. Department of Treasury; U.S. Department of Commerce; and T. S. Berry, "Production and Population since 1789," Bostwick Paper No. 6, Richmond, 1988.

Throughout history, the primary cause of fluctuations in government debt has been war. When wars occur, government spending on national defense rises substantially to pay for soldiers and military equipment. Taxes sometimes rise as well but typically by much less than the increase in spending. The result is a budget deficit and increasing government debt. When the war is over, government spending declines and the debt-to-GDP ratio starts declining as well.

There are two reasons to believe that debt financing of war is an appropriate policy. First, it allows the government to keep tax rates smooth over time. Without debt financing, tax rates would have to rise sharply during wars, and this would cause a substantial decline in economic efficiency. Second, debt financing of wars shifts part of the cost of wars to future generations, who will have to pay off the government debt. This is arguably a fair distribution of the burden, for future generations get some of the benefit when one generation fights a war to defend the nation against foreign aggressors.

One large increase in government debt that cannot be explained by war is the increase that occurred beginning around 1980. When President Ronald Reagan took office in 1981, he was committed to smaller government and lower taxes. Yet he found cutting government spending to be more difficult politically than cutting taxes. The result was the beginning of a period of large budget deficits that continued not only through Reagan's time in office but also for many years thereafter. As a result, government debt rose from 26 percent of GDP in 1980 to 48 percent of GDP in 1993.

Because government budget deficits reduce national saving, investment, and long-run economic growth, the rise in government debt during the 1980s troubled many economists and policymakers. When Bill Clinton moved into the Oval Office in 1993, deficit reduction was his first major goal. Similarly, when the Republicans took control of Congress in 1995, deficit reduction was high on their legislative agenda. Both of these efforts substantially reduced the size of the government budget deficit. In addition, a booming economy in the late 1990s brought in even more tax revenue. Eventually, the federal budget turned from deficit to surplus, and the debt-to-GDP ratio declined significantly for several years.

This fall in the debt-to-GDP ratio, however, stopped during the presidency of George W. Bush, as the budget surplus turned back into a budget deficit. There were three main reasons for this change. First, President Bush signed into law several major tax cuts, which he had promised during the 2000 presidential campaign. Second, in 2001, the economy experienced a *recession* (a reduction in economic activity), which automatically decreased tax revenue and increased government spending. Third, there were increases in government spending on homeland security following the September 11, 2001 attacks and on the subsequent wars in Iraq and Afghanistan.

Truly dramatic increases in the debt-to-GDP ratio started occurring in 2008, as the economy experienced a financial crisis and a deep recession. (The accompanying FYI box addresses this topic briefly, but we will study it more fully in coming chapters.) The recession automatically increased the budget deficit, and several policy measures enacted during the Bush and Obama administrations aimed at combating the recession reduced tax revenue and increased government spending even more. From 2009 to 2012, the federal government's budget deficit averaged about 9 percent of GDP, levels not seen since World War II. The borrowing to finance these deficits led to an increase in the debt-to-GDP ratio from 39 percent in 2008 to 70 percent in 2012. After 2012, as the economy recovered, the budget deficits shrank, and the increases in the debt-to-GDP ratio became smaller. ●

Quick**Quiz**   *If more Americans adopted a "live for today" approach to life, how would this affect saving, investment, and the interest rate?*

Financial Crises

In 2008 and 2009, the U.S. economy and many other major economies around the world experienced a financial crisis, which in turn led to a deep downturn in economic activity. We will examine these events in detail later in this book. But because this chapter introduces the financial system, let's discuss briefly the key elements of financial crises.

The first element of a financial crisis is a large decline in some asset prices. In 2008 and 2009, that asset was real estate. The price of housing, after experiencing a boom earlier in the decade, fell by about 30 percent over just a few years. Such a large decline in real estate prices had not been seen in the United States since the 1930s.

The second element of a financial crisis is widespread insolvencies at financial institutions. (A company is *insolvent* when its debts exceed the value of its assets.) In 2008 and 2009, many banks and other financial firms had in effect placed bets on real estate prices by holding mortgages backed by that real estate. When house prices fell, large numbers of homeowners stopped repaying their loans. These defaults pushed several major financial institutions toward bankruptcy.

The third element of a financial crisis is a decline in confidence in financial institutions. Although some deposits in banks are insured by government policies, not all are. As insolvencies mounted, every financial institution became a possible candidate for the next bankruptcy. Individuals and firms with uninsured deposits in those institutions pulled out their money. Facing a rash of withdrawals, banks started selling off assets (sometimes at reduced "fire-sale" prices) and cut back on new lending.

The fourth element of a financial crisis is a credit crunch. With many financial institutions facing difficulties, prospective borrowers had trouble getting loans, even if they had profitable investment projects. In essence, the financial system had trouble performing its normal function of directing the resources of savers into the hands of borrowers with the best investment opportunities.

The fifth element of a financial crisis is an economic downturn. With people unable to obtain financing for new investment projects, the overall demand for goods and services declined. As a result, for reasons we discuss more fully later in the book, national income fell and unemployment rose.

The sixth and final element of a financial crisis is a vicious circle. The economic downturn reduced the profitability of many companies and the value of many assets. Thus, we started over again at step one, and the problems in the financial system and the economic downturn reinforced each other.

Financial crises, such as the one of 2008 and 2009, can have severe consequences. Fortunately, they do end. Financial institutions eventually get back on their feet, perhaps with some help from government policy, and they return to their normal function of financial intermediation. ∎

26-4 Conclusion

"Neither a borrower nor a lender be," Polonius advises his son in Shakespeare's *Hamlet*. If everyone followed this advice, this chapter would have been unnecessary.

Few economists would agree with Polonius. In our economy, people borrow and lend often, and usually for good reason. You may borrow one day to start your own business or to buy a home. And people may lend to you in the hope that the interest you pay will allow them to enjoy a more prosperous retirement. The financial system's job is to coordinate all this borrowing and lending activity.

In many ways, financial markets are like other markets in the economy. The price of loanable funds—the interest rate—is governed by the forces of supply and demand, just as other prices in the economy are. And we can analyze shifts in supply or demand in financial markets as we do in other markets. One of the *Ten Principles of Economics* introduced in Chapter 1 is that markets are usually a good way to organize economic activity. This principle applies to financial markets as well. When financial markets bring the supply and demand for loanable funds into balance, they help allocate the economy's scarce resources to their most efficient uses.

In one way, however, financial markets are special. Financial markets, unlike most other markets, serve the important role of linking the present and the future. Those who supply loanable funds—savers—do so because they want to convert some of their current income into future purchasing power. Those who demand loanable funds—borrowers—do so because they want to invest today in order to have additional capital in the future to produce goods and services. Thus, well-functioning financial markets are important not only for current generations but also for future generations who will inherit many of the resulting benefits.

CHAPTER QuickQuiz

1. Elaine wants to buy and operate an ice-cream truck but doesn't have the financial resources to start the business. She borrows $10,000 from her friend George, to whom she promises an interest rate of 7 percent, and gets another $20,000 from her friend Jerry, to whom she promises a third of her profits. What best describes this situation?
   a. George is a stockholder, and Elaine is a bondholder.
   b. George is a stockholder, and Jerry is a bondholder.
   c. Jerry is a stockholder, and Elaine is a bondholder.
   d. Jerry is a stockholder, and George is a bondholder.

2. If the government collects more in tax revenue than it spends, and households consume more than they get in after-tax income, then
   a. private and public saving are both positive.
   b. private and public saving are both negative.
   c. private saving is positive, but public saving is negative.
   d. private saving is negative, but public saving is positive.

3. A closed economy has income of $1,000, government spending of $200, taxes of $150, and investment of $250. What is private saving?
   a. $100
   b. $200
   c. $300
   d. $400

4. If a popular TV show on personal finance convinces Americans to save more for retirement, the _____ curve for loanable funds would shift, driving the equilibrium interest rate _____.
   a. supply, up
   b. supply, down
   c. demand, up
   d. demand, down

5. If the business community becomes more optimistic about the profitability of capital, the _____ curve for loanable funds would shift, driving the equilibrium interest rate _____.
   a. supply, up
   b. supply, down
   c. demand, up
   d. demand, down

6. From 2008 to 2012, the ratio of government debt to GDP in the United States
   a. increased markedly.
   b. decreased markedly.
   c. was stable at a historically high level.
   d. was stable at a historically low level.

SUMMARY

- The U.S. financial system is made up of many types of financial institutions, such as the bond market, the stock market, banks, and mutual funds. All these institutions act to direct the resources of households that want to save some of their income into the hands of households and firms that want to borrow.
- National income accounting identities reveal some important relationships among macroeconomic

variables. In particular, for a closed economy, national saving must equal investment. Financial institutions are the mechanism through which the economy matches one person's saving with another person's investment.

- The interest rate is determined by the supply and demand for loanable funds. The supply of loanable funds comes from households that want to save some of their income and lend it out. The demand for loanable funds comes from households and firms that want to borrow for investment. To analyze how any policy or event affects the interest rate, one must consider how it affects the supply and demand for loanable funds.

• National saving equals private saving plus public saving. A government budget deficit represents negative public saving and, therefore, reduces national saving and the supply of loanable funds available to finance investment. When a government budget deficit crowds out investment, it reduces the growth of productivity and GDP.

KEY CONCEPTS

financial system, p. 542
financial markets, p. 542
bond, p. 543
stock, p. 543
financial intermediaries, p. 544

mutual fund, p. 545
national saving (saving), p. 548
private saving, p. 548
public saving, p. 548
budget surplus, p. 548

budget deficit, p. 548
market for loanable funds, p. 549
crowding out, p. 555

QUESTIONS FOR REVIEW

1. What is the role of the financial system? Name and describe two markets that are part of the financial system in the U.S. economy. Name and describe two financial intermediaries.

2. Why is it important for people who own stocks and bonds to diversify their holdings? What type of financial institution makes diversification easier?

3. What is national saving? What is private saving? What is public saving? How are these three variables related?

4. What is investment? How is it related to national saving in a closed economy?

5. Describe a change in the tax code that might increase private saving. If this policy were implemented, how would it affect the market for loanable funds?

6. What is a government budget deficit? How does it affect interest rates, investment, and economic growth?

PROBLEMS AND APPLICATIONS

1. For each of the following pairs, which bond would you expect to pay a higher interest rate? Explain.
   a. a bond of the U.S. government or a bond of an Eastern European government
   b. a bond that repays the principal in year 2020 or a bond that repays the principal in year 2040
   c. a bond from Coca-Cola or a bond from a software company you run in your garage
   d. a bond issued by the federal government or a bond issued by New York State

2. Many workers hold large amounts of stock issued by the firms at which they work. Why do you suppose companies encourage this behavior? Why might a

   person *not* want to hold stock in the company where he works?

3. Explain the difference between saving and investment as defined by a macroeconomist. Which of the following situations represent investment and which represent saving? Explain.
   a. Your family takes out a mortgage and buys a new house.
   b. You use your $200 paycheck to buy stock in AT&T.
   c. Your roommate earns $100 and deposits it in his account at a bank.
   d. You borrow $1,000 from a bank to buy a car to use in your pizza delivery business.

89

4. Suppose GDP is $8 trillion, taxes are $1.5 trillion, private saving is $0.5 trillion, and public saving is $0.2 trillion. Assuming this economy is closed, calculate consumption, government purchases, national saving, and investment.

5. Economists in Funlandia, a closed economy, have collected the following information about the economy for a particular year:

$Y = 10,000$

$C = 6,000$

$T = 1,500$

$G = 1,700$

The economists also estimate that the investment function is:

$$I = 3,300 - 100r,$$

where r is the country's real interest rate, expressed as a percentage. Calculate private saving, public saving, national saving, investment, and the equilibrium real interest rate.

6. Suppose that Intel is considering building a new chip-making factory.
   a. Assuming that Intel needs to borrow money in the bond market, why would an increase in interest rates affect Intel's decision about whether to build the factory?
   b. If Intel has enough of its own funds to finance the new factory without borrowing, would an increase in interest rates still affect Intel's decision about whether to build the factory? Explain.

7. Three students have each saved $1,000. Each has an investment opportunity in which he or she can invest up to $2,000. Here are the rates of return on the students' investment projects:

Harry	5 percent
Ron	8 percent
Hermione	20 percent

   a. If borrowing and lending are prohibited, so each student uses only personal saving to finance his or her own investment project, how much will each student have a year later when the project pays its return?
   b. Now suppose their school opens up a market for loanable funds in which students can borrow and lend among themselves at an interest rate r. What

would determine whether a student would choose to be a borrower or lender in this market?
   c. Among these three students, what would be the quantity of loanable funds supplied and quantity demanded at an interest rate of 7 percent? At 10 percent?
   d. At what interest rate would the loanable funds market among these three students be in equilibrium? At this interest rate, which student(s) would borrow and which student(s) would lend?
   e. At the equilibrium interest rate, how much does each student have a year later after the investment projects pay their return and loans have been repaid? Compare your answers to those you gave in part (a). Who benefits from the existence of the loanable funds market—the borrowers or the lenders? Is anyone worse off?

8. Suppose the government borrows $20 billion more next year than this year.
   a. Use a supply-and-demand diagram to analyze this policy. Does the interest rate rise or fall?
   b. What happens to investment? To private saving? To public saving? To national saving? Compare the size of the changes to the $20 billion of extra government borrowing.
   c. How does the elasticity of supply of loanable funds affect the size of these changes?
   d. How does the elasticity of demand for loanable funds affect the size of these changes?
   e. Suppose households believe that greater government borrowing today implies higher taxes to pay off the government debt in the future. What does this belief do to private saving and the supply of loanable funds today? Does it increase or decrease the effects you discussed in parts (a) and (b)?

9. This chapter explains that investment can be increased both by reducing taxes on private saving and by reducing the government budget deficit.
   a. Why is it difficult to implement both of these policies at the same time?
   b. What would you need to know about private saving to judge which of these two policies would be a more effective way to raise investment?

To find additional study resources, visit cengagebrain.com, and search for "Mankiw."

PART X

Money and Prices in the Long Run

The Monetary System

When you walk into a restaurant to buy a meal, you get something of value—a full stomach. To pay for this service, you might hand the restaurateur several worn-out pieces of greenish paper decorated with strange symbols, government buildings, and the portraits of famous dead Americans. Or you might hand her a single piece of paper with the name of a bank and your signature. Or you might show her a plastic card and sign a paper slip. Whether you pay by cash, check, or debit card, the restaurateur is happy to work hard to satisfy your gastronomical desires in exchange for these pieces of paper, which, in and of themselves, are worthless.

Anyone who has lived in a modern economy is familiar with this social custom. Even though paper money has no intrinsic value, the restaurateur is confident

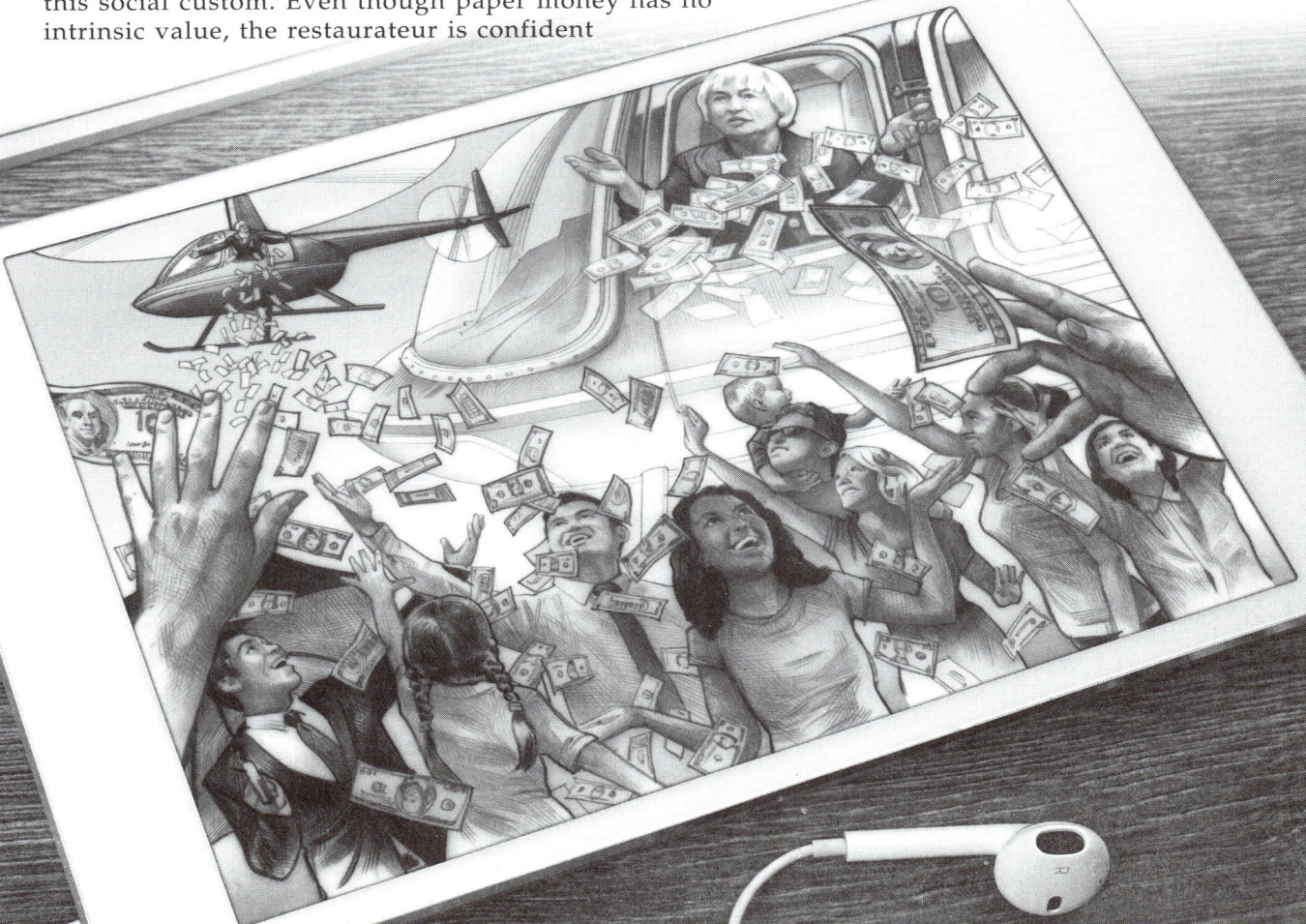

that, in the future, some third person will accept it in exchange for something that the restaurateur does value. And that third person is confident that some fourth person will accept the money, with the knowledge that yet a fifth person will accept the money . . . and so on. To the restaurateur and to other people in our society, your cash, check, or debit card receipt represents a claim to goods and services in the future.

The social custom of using money for transactions is extraordinarily useful in a large, complex society. Imagine, for a moment, that there was no item in the economy widely accepted in exchange for goods and services. People would have to rely on *barter*—the exchange of one good or service for another—to obtain the things they need. To get your restaurant meal, for instance, you would have to offer the restaurateur something of immediate value. You could offer to wash some dishes, mow her lawn, or give her your family's secret recipe for meat loaf. An economy that relies on barter will have trouble allocating its scarce resources efficiently. In such an economy, trade is said to require the *double coincidence of wants*—the unlikely occurrence that two people each have a good or service that the other wants.

The existence of money makes trade easier. The restaurateur does not care whether you can produce a valuable good or service for her. She is happy to accept your money, knowing that other people will do the same for her. Such a convention allows trade to be roundabout. The restaurateur accepts your money and uses it to pay her chef; the chef uses her paycheck to send her child to day care; the day care center uses this tuition to pay a teacher; and the teacher hires you to mow her lawn. As money flows from person to person in the economy, it facilitates production and trade, thereby allowing each person to specialize in what she does best and raising everyone's standard of living.

In this chapter, we begin to examine the role of money in the economy. We discuss what money is, the various forms that money takes, how the banking system helps create money, and how the government controls the quantity of money in circulation. Because money is so important in the economy, we devote much effort in the rest of this book to learning how changes in the quantity of money affect various economic variables, including inflation, interest rates, production, and employment. Consistent with our long-run focus in the previous four chapters, in the next chapter we examine the long-run effects of changes in the quantity of money. The short-run effects of monetary changes are a more complex topic, which we take up later in the book. This chapter provides the background for all of this further analysis.

29-1 The Meaning of Money

What is money? This might seem like an odd question. When you read that billionaire Mark Zuckerberg has a lot of money, you know what that means: He is so rich that he can buy almost anything he wants. In this sense, the term *money* is used to mean *wealth*.

money
the set of assets in an economy that people regularly use to buy goods and services from other people

Economists, however, use the word in a more specific sense: **Money** is the set of assets in the economy that people regularly use to buy goods and services from each other. The cash in your wallet is money because you can use it to buy a meal at a restaurant or a shirt at a store. By contrast, if you happened to own a large share of Facebook, as Mark Zuckerberg does, you would be wealthy, but this asset is not considered a form of money. You could not buy a meal or a shirt with this wealth without first obtaining some cash. According to the economist's definition, money includes only those few types of wealth that are regularly accepted by sellers in exchange for goods and services.

29-1a The Functions of Money

Money has three functions in the economy: It is a *medium of exchange*, a *unit of account*, and a *store of value*. These three functions together distinguish money from other assets in the economy, such as stocks, bonds, real estate, art, and even baseball cards. Let's examine each of these functions of money.

A **medium of exchange** is an item that buyers give to sellers when they purchase goods and services. When you go to a store to buy a shirt, the store gives you the shirt and you give the store your money. This transfer of money from buyer to seller allows the transaction to take place. When you walk into a store, you are confident that the store will accept your money for the items it is selling because money is the commonly accepted medium of exchange.

A **unit of account** is the yardstick people use to post prices and record debts. When you go shopping, you might observe that a shirt costs $50 and a hamburger costs $5. Even though it would be accurate to say that the price of a shirt is 10 hamburgers and the price of a hamburger is of a shirt, prices are never quoted in this way. Similarly, if you take out a loan from a bank, the size of your future loan repayments will be measured in dollars, not in a quantity of goods and services. When we want to measure and record economic value, we use money as the unit of account.

A **store of value** is an item that people can use to transfer purchasing power from the present to the future. When a seller accepts money today in exchange for a good or service, that seller can hold the money and become a buyer of another good or service at another time. Money is not the only store of value in the economy: A person can also transfer purchasing power from the present to the future by holding nonmonetary assets such as stocks and bonds. The term *wealth* is used to refer to the total of all stores of value, including both money and nonmonetary assets.

Economists use the term **liquidity** to describe the ease with which an asset can be converted into the economy's medium of exchange. Because money is the economy's medium of exchange, it is the most liquid asset available. Other assets vary widely in their liquidity. Most stocks and bonds can be sold easily with small cost, so they are relatively liquid assets. By contrast, selling a house, a Rembrandt painting, or a 1948 Joe DiMaggio baseball card requires more time and effort, so these assets are less liquid.

When people decide how to allocate their wealth, they have to balance the liquidity of each possible asset against the asset's usefulness as a store of value. Money is the most liquid asset, but it is far from perfect as a store of value. When prices rise, the value of money falls. In other words, when goods and services become more expensive, each dollar in your wallet can buy less. This link between the price level and the value of money is key to understanding how money affects the economy, a topic we start to explore in the next chapter.

29-1b The Kinds of Money

When money takes the form of a commodity with intrinsic value, it is called **commodity money**. The term *intrinsic value* means that the item would have value even if it were not used as money. One example of commodity money is gold. Gold has intrinsic value because it is used in industry and in the making of jewelry. Although today we no longer use gold as money, historically gold was a common form of money because it is relatively easy to carry, measure, and verify for impurities. When an economy uses gold as money (or uses paper money that is convertible into gold on demand), it is said to be operating under a *gold standard*.

medium of exchange an item that buyers give to sellers when they want to purchase goods and services

unit of account the yardstick people use to post prices and record debts

store of value an item that people can use to transfer purchasing power from the present to the future

liquidity the ease with which an asset can be converted into the economy's medium of exchange

commodity money money that takes the form of a commodity with intrinsic value

Another example of commodity money is cigarettes. In prisoner-of-war camps during World War II, prisoners traded goods and services with one another using cigarettes as the store of value, unit of account, and medium of exchange. Similarly, as the Soviet Union was breaking up in the late 1980s, cigarettes started replacing the ruble as the preferred currency in Moscow. In both cases, even nonsmokers were happy to accept cigarettes in an exchange, knowing that they could use the cigarettes to buy other goods and services.

fiat money
money without intrinsic value that is used as money by government decree

Money without intrinsic value is called **fiat money**. A *fiat* is an order or decree, and fiat money is established as money by government decree. For example, compare the paper dollars in your wallet (printed by the U.S. government) and the paper dollars from a game of Monopoly (printed by the Parker Brothers game company). Why can you use the first to pay your bill at a restaurant but not the second? The answer is that the U.S. government has decreed its dollars to be valid money. Each paper dollar in your wallet reads: "This note is legal tender for all debts, public and private."

Although the government is central to establishing and regulating a system of fiat money (by prosecuting counterfeiters, for example), other factors are also required for the success of such a monetary system. To a large extent, the acceptance of fiat money depends as much on expectations and social convention as on government decree. The Soviet government in the 1980s never abandoned the ruble as the official currency. Yet the people of Moscow preferred to accept cigarettes (or even American dollars) in exchange for goods and services because they were more confident that these alternative monies would be accepted by others in the future.

IN THE NEWS

Why Gold?

For many centuries, when societies have used a form of commodity money, the most common choice has been the gold standard. This outcome may have a sound scientific basis.

A Chemist Explains Why Gold Beat Out Lithium, Osmium, Einsteinium...

By Jacob Goldstein and David Kestenbaum

The periodic table lists 118 different chemical elements. And yet, for thousands of years, humans have really, really liked one of them in particular: gold. Gold has been used as money for millennia, and its price has been going through the roof.

Why gold? Why not osmium, lithium, or ruthenium?

We went to an expert to find out: Sanat Kumar, a chemical engineer at Columbia University. We asked him to take the periodic table, and start eliminating anything that wouldn't work as money.

The periodic table looks kind of like a bingo card. Each square has a different element in it—one for carbon, another for gold, and so on.

Sanat starts with the far-right column of the table. The elements there have a really appealing characteristic: They're not going to change. They're chemically stable.

But there's also a big drawback: They're gases. You could put all your gaseous money in a jar, but if you opened the jar, you'd be broke. So Sanat crosses out the right-hand column.

Then he swings over to the far left-hand column, and points to one of the elements there: Lithium

"If you expose lithium to air, it will cause a huge fire that can burn through concrete walls," he says.

Money that spontaneously bursts into flames is clearly a bad idea. In fact, you don't want your money undergoing any kind of spontaneous chemical reactions. And it turns out that a lot of the elements in the periodic table are pretty reactive.

Not all of them burst into flames. But sometimes they corrode, start to fall apart.

So Sanat crosses out another 38 elements, because they're too reactive.

Then we ask him about those two weird rows at the bottom of the table. They're always

29-1c Money in the U.S. Economy

As we will see, the quantity of money circulating in the economy, called the *money stock*, has a powerful influence on many economic variables. But before we consider why that is true, we need to ask a preliminary question: What is the quantity of money? In particular, suppose you were given the task of measuring how much money there is in the U.S. economy. What would you include in your measure?

The most obvious asset to include is **currency**—the paper bills and coins in the hands of the public. Currency is clearly the most widely accepted medium of exchange in our economy. There is no doubt that it is part of the money stock.

Yet currency is not the only asset that you can use to buy goods and services. Many stores also accept personal checks. Wealth held in your checking account is almost as convenient for buying things as wealth held in your wallet. To measure the money stock, therefore, you might want to include **demand deposits**—balances in bank accounts that depositors can access on demand simply by writing a check or swiping a debit card at a store.

Once you start to consider balances in checking accounts as part of the money stock, you are led to consider the large variety of other accounts that people hold at banks and other financial institutions. Bank depositors usually cannot write checks against the balances in their savings accounts, but they can easily transfer funds from savings into checking accounts. In addition, depositors in money market mutual funds can often write checks against their balances. Thus, these other accounts should plausibly be part of the U.S. money stock.

currency
the paper bills and coins in the hands of the public

demand deposits
balances in bank accounts that depositors can access on demand by writing a check

---

broken out separately from the main table, and they have some great names—promethium, einsteinium.

But it turns out they're radioactive—put some einsteinium in your pocket, and a year later, you'll be dead.

So we're down from 118 elements to 30, and we've come up with a list of three key requirements:

1. Not a gas.
2. Doesn't corrode or burst into flames.
3. Doesn't kill you.

Now Sanat adds a new requirement: You want the thing you pick to be rare. This lets him cross off a lot of the boxes near the top of the table, because the elements clustered there tend to be more abundant.

At the same time, you don't want to pick an element that's too rare. So osmium—which apparently comes to earth via meteorites—gets the axe.

That leaves us with just five elements: rhodium, palladium, silver, platinum and gold. And

In Gold We Trust

FIKMIK/SHUTTERSTOCK

all of them, as it happens, are considered precious metals.

But even here we can cross things out. Silver has been widely used as money, of course. But it's reactive—it tarnishes. So Sanat says it's not the best choice.

Early civilizations couldn't have used rhodium or palladium, because they weren't discovered until the early 1800s.

That leaves platinum and gold, both of which can be found in rivers and streams.

But if you were in the ancient world and wanted to make platinum coins, you would have needed some sort of magic furnace from the future. The melting point for platinum is over 3,000 degrees Fahrenheit.

Gold happens to melt at a much lower temperature, which made it much easier for pre-industrial people to work with.

So we ask Sanat: If we could run the clock back and start history again, could things go a different way, or would gold emerge again as the element of choice?

"For the earth, with every parameter we have, gold is the sweet spot," he says. "It would come out no other way." ■

Source: ©2010 National Public Radio, Inc. NPR news report titled "A Chemist Explains Why Gold Beat Out Lithium, Osmium, Einsteinium ..." by Jacob Goldstein and David Kestenbaum was originally published on NPR.org on November 19, 2010, and is used with the permission of NPR. Any unauthorized duplication is strictly prohibited.

FIGURE 1

Two Measures of the Money Stock for the U.S. Economy

The two most widely followed measures of the money stock are M1 and M2. This figure shows the size of each measure in January 2016.

Source: Federal Reserve.

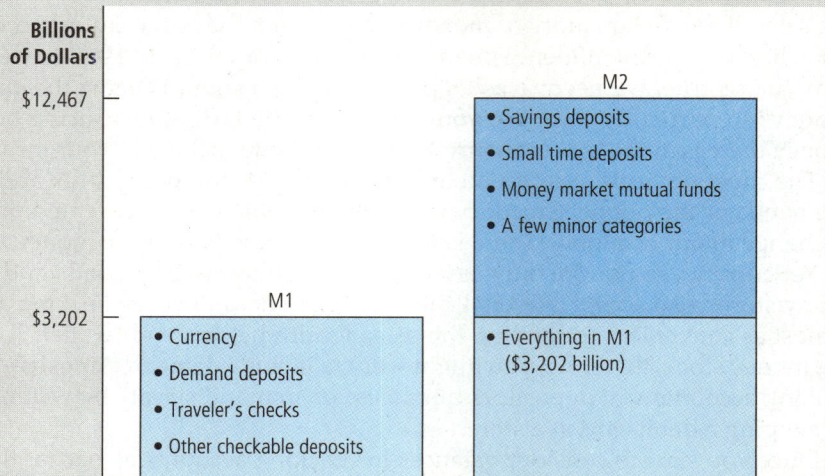

Billions of Dollars

$12,467

$3,202

M2
- Savings deposits
- Small time deposits
- Money market mutual funds
- A few minor categories
- Everything in M1 ($3,202 billion)

M1
- Currency
- Demand deposits
- Traveler's checks
- Other checkable deposits

In a complex economy such as ours, it is not easy to draw a line between assets that can be called "money" and assets that cannot. The coins in your pocket clearly are part of the money stock, and the Empire State Building clearly is not, but there are many assets in between these extremes for which the choice is less clear. Because different analysts can reasonably disagree about where to draw the dividing line between monetary and nonmonetary assets, various measures of the money stock are available for the U.S. economy. Figure 1 shows the two most commonly used, designated M1 and M2. M2 includes more assets in its measure of money than does M1.

For our purposes in this book, we need not dwell on the differences between the various measures of money. None of our discussion will hinge on the distinction between M1 and M2. The important point is that the money stock for the U.S. economy includes not only currency but also deposits in banks and other financial institutions that can be readily accessed and used to buy goods and services.

CASE STUDY

WHERE IS ALL THE CURRENCY?

One puzzle about the money stock of the U.S. economy concerns the amount of currency. In January 2016, there was $1.4 trillion of currency outstanding. To put this number in perspective, we can divide it by 252 million, the number of adults (age 16 and older) in the United States. This calculation implies that the average adult holds over $5,500 of currency. Most people are surprised to learn that our economy has so much currency because they carry far less than this in their wallets.

Who is holding all this currency? No one knows for sure, but there are two plausible explanations.

The first explanation is that much of the currency is held abroad. In foreign countries without a stable monetary system, people often prefer U.S. dollars to domestic assets. Estimates suggest that over half of U.S. dollars circulate outside the United States.

The second explanation is that much of the currency is held by drug dealers, tax evaders, and other criminals. For most people in the U.S. economy, currency is not a particularly good way to hold wealth. Not only can currency be lost or stolen

Why Credit Cards Aren't Money

It might seem natural to include credit cards as part of the economy's stock of money. After all, people use credit cards to make many of their purchases. Aren't credit cards, therefore, a medium of exchange?

At first this argument may seem persuasive, but credit cards are excluded from all measures of the quantity of money. The reason is that credit cards are not really a method of payment but rather a method of *deferring* payment. When you buy a meal with a credit card, the bank that issued the card pays the restaurant what it is due. At a later date, you will have to repay the bank (perhaps with interest). When the time comes to pay your credit card bill, you will probably do so by writing a check against your checking account. The balance in this checking account is part of the economy's stock of money.

Notice that credit cards are different from debit cards, which automatically withdraw funds from a bank account to pay for items bought. Rather than allowing the user to postpone payment for a purchase, a debit card gives the user immediate access to deposits in a bank account. In this sense, a debit card is more similar to a check than to a credit card. The account balances that lie behind debit cards are included in measures of the quantity of money.

Even though credit cards are not considered a form of money, they are nonetheless important for analyzing the monetary system. People who have credit cards can pay many of their bills together at the end of the month, rather than sporadically as they make purchases. As a result, people who have credit cards probably hold less money on average than people who do not have credit cards. Thus, the introduction and increased popularity of credit cards may reduce the amount of money that people choose to hold. ■

but it also does not earn interest, whereas a bank deposit does. Thus, most people hold only small amounts of currency. By contrast, criminals may avoid putting their wealth in banks because a bank deposit gives police a paper trail that they can use to trace illegal activities. For criminals, currency may be the best store of value available. ●

QuickQuiz *List and describe the three functions of money.*

29-2 The Federal Reserve System

Whenever an economy uses a system of fiat money, as the U.S. economy does, some agency must be responsible for regulating the system. In the United States, that agency is the **Federal Reserve**, often simply called the **Fed**. If you look at the top of a dollar bill, you will see that it is called a "Federal Reserve Note." The Fed is an example of a **central bank**—an institution designed to oversee the banking system and regulate the quantity of money in the economy. Other major central banks around the world include the Bank of England, the Bank of Japan, and the European Central Bank.

29-2a The Fed's Organization

The Federal Reserve was created in 1913 after a series of bank failures in 1907 convinced Congress that the United States needed a central bank to ensure the health of the nation's banking system. Today, the Fed is run by its board of governors, which has seven members appointed by the president and confirmed by the Senate. The governors have 14-year terms. Just as federal judges are given

Federal Reserve (Fed)
the central bank of the United States

central bank
an institution designed to oversee the banking system and regulate the quantity of money in the economy

lifetime appointments to insulate them from politics, Fed governors are given long terms to give them independence from short-term political pressures when they formulate monetary policy.

Among the seven members of the board of governors, the most important is the chair. The chair directs the Fed staff, presides over board meetings, and testifies regularly about Fed policy in front of congressional committees. The president appoints the chair to a 4-year term. As this book was going to press, the chair of the Fed was Janet Yellen, a former economics professor who was appointed to the Fed job by President Barack Obama in 2014.

The Federal Reserve System is made up of the Federal Reserve Board in Washington, D.C., and twelve regional Federal Reserve Banks located in major cities around the country. The presidents of the regional banks are chosen by each bank's board of directors, whose members are typically drawn from the region's banking and business community.

The Fed has two related jobs. The first is to regulate banks and ensure the health of the banking system. This task is largely the responsibility of the regional Federal Reserve Banks. In particular, the Fed monitors each bank's financial condition and facilitates bank transactions by clearing checks. It also acts as a bank's bank. That is, the Fed makes loans to banks when banks themselves want to borrow. When financially troubled banks find themselves short of cash, the Fed acts as a *lender of last resort*—a lender to those who cannot borrow anywhere else—to maintain stability in the overall banking system.

money supply
the quantity of money available in the economy

monetary policy
the setting of the money supply by policymakers in the central bank

The Fed's second and more important job is to control the quantity of money that is made available in the economy, called the **money supply**. Decisions by policymakers concerning the money supply constitute **monetary policy**. At the Federal Reserve, monetary policy is made by the Federal Open Market Committee (FOMC). The FOMC meets about every six weeks in Washington, D.C., to discuss the condition of the economy and consider changes in monetary policy.

29-2b The Federal Open Market Committee

The Federal Open Market Committee is made up of the seven members of the board of governors and five of the twelve regional bank presidents. All twelve regional presidents attend each FOMC meeting, but only five get to vote. Voting rights rotate among the twelve regional presidents over time. The president of the New York Fed always gets a vote, however, because New York is the traditional financial center of the U.S. economy and because all Fed purchases and sales of government bonds are conducted at the New York Fed's trading desk.

Through the decisions of the FOMC, the Fed has the power to increase or decrease the number of dollars in the economy. In simple metaphorical terms, you can imagine the Fed printing dollar bills and dropping them around the country by helicopter. Similarly, you can imagine the Fed using a giant vacuum cleaner to suck dollar bills out of people's wallets. Although in practice the Fed's methods for changing the money supply are more complex and subtle than this, the helicopter-vacuum metaphor is a good first step to understanding the meaning of monetary policy.

Later in this chapter, we discuss how the Fed actually changes the money supply, but it is worth noting here that the Fed's primary tool is the *open-market operation*—the purchase and sale of U.S. government bonds. (Recall that a U.S.

government bond is a certificate of indebtedness of the federal government.) If the FOMC decides to increase the money supply, the Fed creates dollars and uses them to buy government bonds from the public in the nation's bond markets. After the purchase, these dollars are in the hands of the public. Thus, an open-market purchase of bonds by the Fed increases the money supply. Conversely, if the FOMC decides to decrease the money supply, the Fed sells government bonds from its portfolio to the public in the nation's bond markets. After the sale, the dollars the Fed receives for the bonds are out of the hands of the public. Thus, an open-market sale of bonds by the Fed decreases the money supply.

Central banks are important institutions because changes in the money supply can profoundly affect the economy. One of the *Ten Principles of Economics* introduced in Chapter 1 is that prices rise when the government prints too much money. Another of the *Ten Principles of Economics* is that society faces a short-run trade-off between inflation and unemployment. The power of the Fed rests on these principles. For reasons we discuss more fully in the coming chapters, the Fed's policy decisions are key determinants of the economy's rate of inflation in the long run and the economy's employment and production in the short run. Indeed, the Fed's chair has been called the second most powerful person in the United States.

QuickQuiz *What are the primary responsibilities of the Federal Reserve? If the Fed wants to increase the supply of money, how does it usually do so?*

29-3 Banks and the Money Supply

So far, we have introduced the concept of "money" and discussed how the Federal Reserve controls the supply of money by buying and selling government bonds in open-market operations. This explanation of the money supply is correct, but it is not complete. In particular, it omits the key role that banks play in the monetary system.

Recall that the amount of money you hold includes both currency (the bills in your wallet and coins in your pocket) and demand deposits (the balance in your checking account). Because demand deposits are held in banks, the behavior of banks can influence the quantity of demand deposits in the economy and, therefore, the money supply. This section examines how banks affect the money supply and, in doing so, how they complicate the Fed's job of controlling the money supply.

"I've heard a lot about money, and now I'd like to try some."

29-3a The Simple Case of 100-Percent-Reserve Banking

To see how banks influence the money supply, let's first imagine a world without any banks at all. In this simple world, currency is the only form of money. To be concrete, let's suppose that the total quantity of currency is $100. The supply of money is, therefore, $100.

Now suppose that someone opens a bank, appropriately called First National Bank. First National Bank is only a depository institution—that is, it accepts deposits but does not make loans. The purpose of the bank is to give depositors a safe place to keep their money. Whenever a person deposits some money,

reserves
deposits that banks have received but have not loaned out

the bank keeps the money in its vault until the depositor withdraws it, writes a check, or uses a debit card to access her balance. Deposits that banks have received but have not loaned out are called **reserves**. In this imaginary economy, all deposits are held as reserves, so this system is called *100-percent-reserve banking*.

We can express the financial position of First National Bank with a *T-account*, which is a simplified accounting statement that shows changes in a bank's assets and liabilities. Here is the T-account for First National Bank if the economy's entire $100 of money is deposited in the bank:

First National Bank

Assets		Liabilities	
Reserves	$100.00	Deposits	$100.00

On the left side of the T-account are the bank's assets of $100 (the reserves it holds in its vaults). On the right side are the bank's liabilities of $100 (the amount it owes to its depositors). Because the assets and liabilities exactly balance, this accounting statement is called a *balance sheet*.

Now consider the money supply in this imaginary economy. Before First National Bank opens, the money supply is the $100 of currency that people are holding. After the bank opens and people deposit their currency, the money supply is the $100 of demand deposits. (There is no longer any currency outstanding, since it is all in the bank vault.) Each deposit in the bank reduces currency and raises demand deposits by exactly the same amount, leaving the money supply unchanged. Thus, *if banks hold all deposits in reserve, banks do not influence the supply of money.*

29-3b Money Creation with Fractional-Reserve Banking

Eventually, the bankers at First National Bank may start to reconsider their policy of 100-percent-reserve banking. Leaving all that money idle in their vaults seems unnecessary. Why not lend some of it out and earn a profit by charging interest on the loans? Families buying houses, firms building new factories, and students paying for college would all be happy to pay interest to borrow some of that money for a while. First National Bank has to keep some reserves so that currency is available if depositors want to make withdrawals. But if the flow of new deposits is roughly the same as the flow of withdrawals, First National needs to keep only a fraction of its deposits in reserve. Thus, First National adopts a system called **fractional-reserve banking**.

fractional-reserve banking
a banking system in which banks hold only a fraction of deposits as reserves

reserve ratio
the fraction of deposits that banks hold as reserves

The fraction of total deposits that a bank holds as reserves is called the **reserve ratio**. This ratio is influenced by both government regulation and bank policy. As we discuss more fully later in the chapter, the Fed sets a minimum amount of reserves that banks must hold, called a *reserve requirement*. In addition, banks may hold reserves above the legal minimum, called *excess reserves*, so they can be more confident that they will not run short of cash. For our purpose here, we take the reserve ratio as given to examine how fractional-reserve banking influences the money supply.

Let's suppose that First National has a reserve ratio of 1/10, or 10 percent. This means that it keeps 10 percent of its deposits in reserve and loans out the rest. Now let's look again at the bank's T-account:

First National Bank

Assets		Liabilities	
Reserves	$10.00	Deposits	$100.00
Loans	90.00		

First National still has $100 in liabilities because making the loans did not alter the bank's obligation to its depositors. But now the bank has two kinds of assets: It has $10 of reserves in its vault, and it has loans of $90. (These loans are liabilities of the people borrowing from First National, but they are assets of the bank because the borrowers will later repay the loans.) In total, First National's assets still equal its liabilities.

Once again consider the supply of money in the economy. Before First National makes any loans, the money supply is the $100 of deposits. Yet when First National lends out some of these deposits, the money supply increases. The depositors still have demand deposits totaling $100, but now the borrowers hold $90 in currency. The money supply (which equals currency plus demand deposits) equals $190. Thus, *when banks hold only a fraction of deposits in reserve, the banking system creates money.*

At first, this creation of money by fractional-reserve banking may seem too good to be true: It appears that the bank has created money out of thin air. To make this feat seem less miraculous, note that when First National Bank loans out some of its reserves and creates money, it does not create any wealth. Loans from First National give the borrowers some currency and thus the ability to buy goods and services. Yet the borrowers are also taking on debts, so the loans do not make them any richer. In other words, as a bank creates the asset of money, it also creates a corresponding liability for those who borrowed the created money. At the end of this process of money creation, the economy is more liquid in the sense that there is more of the medium of exchange, but the economy is no wealthier than before.

29-3c The Money Multiplier

The creation of money does not stop with First National Bank. Suppose the borrower from First National uses the $90 to buy something from someone who then deposits the currency in Second National Bank. Here is the T-account for Second National Bank:

Second National Bank

Assets		Liabilities	
Reserves	$ 9.00	Deposits	$90.00
Loans	81.00		

After the deposit, this bank has liabilities of $90. If Second National also has a reserve ratio of 10 percent, it keeps assets of $9 in reserve and makes $81 in loans. In this way, Second National Bank creates an additional $81 of money. If this $81 is eventually deposited in Third National Bank, which also has a reserve ratio of

10 percent, this bank keeps $8.10 in reserve and makes $72.90 in loans. Here is the T-account for Third National Bank:

Third National Bank

Assets		Liabilities	
Reserves	$ 8.10	Deposits	$81.00
Loans	72.90		

The process goes on and on. Each time that money is deposited and a bank loan is made, more money is created.

How much money is eventually created in this economy? Let's add it up:

Original deposit	= $100.00
First National lending	= $ 90.00 (= .9 × $100.00)
Second National lending	= $ 81.00 (= .9 × $90.00)
Third National lending	= $ 72.90 (= .9 × $81.00)
•	•
•	•
•	•
Total money supply	= $1,000.00

It turns out that even though this process of money creation can continue forever, it does not create an infinite amount of money. If you laboriously add the infinite sequence of numbers in the preceding example, you find that the $100 of reserves generates $1,000 of money. The amount of money the banking system generates with each dollar of reserves is called the **money multiplier**. In this imaginary economy, where the $100 of reserves generates $1,000 of money, the money multiplier is 10.

What determines the size of the money multiplier? It turns out that the answer is simple: *The money multiplier is the reciprocal of the reserve ratio.* If R is the reserve ratio for all banks in the economy, then each dollar of reserves generates $1/R$ dollars of money. In our example, $R = 1/10$, so the money multiplier is 10.

This reciprocal formula for the money multiplier makes sense. If a bank holds $1,000 in deposits, then a reserve ratio of $1/10$ (10 percent) means that the bank must hold $100 in reserves. The money multiplier just turns this idea around: If the banking system as a whole holds a total of $100 in reserves, it can have only $1,000 in deposits. In other words, if R is the ratio of reserves to deposits at each bank (that is, the reserve ratio), then the ratio of deposits to reserves in the banking system (that is, the money multiplier) must be $1/R$.

This formula shows how the amount of money banks create depends on the reserve ratio. If the reserve ratio were only $1/20$ (5 percent), then the banking system would have 20 times as much in deposits as in reserves, implying a money multiplier of 20. Each dollar of reserves would generate $20 of money. Similarly, if the reserve ratio were $1/4$ (25 percent), deposits would be 4 times reserves, the money multiplier would be 4, and each dollar of reserves would generate $4 of money. Thus, *the higher the reserve ratio, the less of each deposit banks loan out, and the smaller the money multiplier.* In the special case of 100-percent-reserve banking, the reserve ratio is 1, the money multiplier is 1, and banks do not make loans or create money.

money multiplier
the amount of money the banking system generates with each dollar of reserves

29-3d Bank Capital, Leverage, and the Financial Crisis of 2008–2009

In the previous sections, we have seen a simplified explanation of how banks work. But the reality of modern banking is a bit more complicated, and these complications played a key role in the financial crisis of 2008 and 2009. Before looking at that crisis, we need to learn a bit more about how banks actually function.

In the bank balance sheets you have seen so far, a bank accepts deposits and either uses those deposits to make loans or holds them as reserves. More realistically, a bank gets financial resources not only from accepting deposits but also, like other companies, from issuing equity and debt. The resources that a bank obtains from issuing equity to its owners are called **bank capital**. A bank uses these financial resources in various ways to generate profit for its owners. It not only makes loans and holds reserves but also buys financial securities, such as stocks and bonds.

Here is a more realistic example of a bank's balance sheet:

bank capital
the resources a bank's owners have put into the institution

More Realistic National Bank

Assets		Liabilities and Owners' Equity	
Reserves	$200	Deposits	$800
Loans	700	Debt	150
Securities	100	Capital (owners' equity)	50

On the right side of this balance sheet are the bank's liabilities and capital (also called *owners' equity*). This bank obtained $50 of resources from its owners. It also took in $800 of deposits and issued $150 of debt. The total of $1,000 was put to use in three ways; these are listed on the left side of the balance sheet, which shows the bank's assets. This bank held $200 in reserves, made $700 in bank loans, and used $100 to buy financial securities, such as government or corporate bonds. The bank decides how to allocate its resources among asset classes based on their risk and return, as well as on any regulations (such as reserve requirements) that restrict the bank's choices.

By the rules of accounting, the reserves, loans, and securities on the left side of the balance sheet must always equal, in total, the deposits, debt, and capital on the right side of the balance sheet. There is no magic in this equality. It occurs because the value of the owners' equity is, by definition, the value of the bank's assets (reserves, loans, and securities) minus the value of its liabilities (deposits and debt). Therefore, the left and right sides of the balance sheet always sum to the same total.

Many businesses in the economy rely on **leverage**, the use of borrowed money to supplement existing funds for investment purposes. Indeed, whenever anyone uses debt to finance an investment project, she is applying leverage. Leverage is particularly important for banks, however, because borrowing and lending are at the heart of what they do. To fully understand banking, therefore, it is crucial to understand how leverage works.

leverage
the use of borrowed money to supplement existing funds for purposes of investment

The **leverage ratio** is the ratio of the bank's total assets to bank capital. In this example, the leverage ratio is $1,000/$50, or 20. A leverage ratio of 20 means that for every dollar of capital that the bank owners have contributed, the bank has

leverage ratio
the ratio of assets to bank capital

$20 of assets. Of the $20 of assets, $19 are financed with borrowed money—either by taking in deposits or issuing debt.

You may have learned in a science class that a lever can amplify a force: A boulder that you cannot move with your arms alone will move more easily if you use a lever. A similar result occurs with bank leverage. To see how this amplification works, let's continue with this numerical example. Suppose that the bank's assets were to rise in value by 5 percent because, say, some of the securities the bank was holding rose in price. Then the $1,000 of assets would now be worth $1,050. Because the depositors and debt holders are still owed $950, the bank capital rises from $50 to $100. Thus, when the leverage rate is 20, a 5-percent increase in the value of assets increases the owners' equity by 100 percent.

The same principle works on the downside, but with troubling consequences. Suppose that some people who borrowed from the bank default on their loans, reducing the value of the bank's assets by 5 percent, to $950. Because the depositors and debt holders have the legal right to be paid before the bank owners, the value of the owners' equity falls to zero. Thus, when the leverage ratio is 20, a 5-percent fall in the value of the bank's assets leads to a 100-percent fall in bank capital. If the value of assets were to fall by more than 5 percent, the bank's assets would fall below its liabilities. In this case, the bank would be *insolvent*, and it would be unable to pay off its debt holders and depositors in full.

capital requirement
a government regulation specifying a minimum amount of bank capital

Bank regulators require banks to hold a certain amount of capital. The goal of such a **capital requirement** is to ensure that banks will be able to pay off their depositors (without having to resort to government-provided deposit insurance funds). The amount of capital required depends on the kind of assets a bank holds. If the bank holds safe assets such as government bonds, regulators require less capital than if the bank holds risky assets such as loans to borrowers whose credit is of dubious quality.

Economic turmoil can result when banks find themselves with too little capital to satisfy capital requirements. An example of this phenomenon occurred in 2008 and 2009, when many banks realized they had incurred sizable losses on some of their assets—specifically, mortgage loans and securities backed by mortgage loans. The shortage of capital induced the banks to reduce lending, a phenomenon called a *credit crunch*, which in turn contributed to a severe downturn in economic activity. (This event is discussed more fully in Chapter 33.) To address this problem, the U.S. Treasury, working together with the Federal Reserve, put many billions of dollars of public funds into the banking system to increase the amount of bank capital. As a result, it temporarily made the U.S. taxpayer a part owner of many banks. The goal of this unusual policy was to recapitalize the banking system so that bank lending could return to a more normal level, which in fact occurred by late 2009.

QuickQuiz   *Describe how banks create money.*

29-4 The Fed's Tools of Monetary Control

As we have already discussed, the Federal Reserve is responsible for controlling the supply of money in the economy. Now that we understand how banking works, we are in a better position to understand how the Fed carries out this job. Because banks create money in a system of fractional-reserve banking, the Fed's control of the money supply is indirect. When the Fed decides to change the money supply, it must consider how its actions will work through the banking system.

The Fed has various tools in its monetary toolbox. We can group the tools into two groups: those that influence the quantity of reserves and those that influence the reserve ratio and thereby the money multiplier.

29-4a How the Fed Influences the Quantity of Reserves

The first way the Fed can change the money supply is by changing the quantity of reserves. The Fed alters the quantity of reserves in the economy either by buying or selling bonds in open-market operations or by making loans to banks (or by some combination of the two). Let's consider each of these in turn.

Open-Market Operations As we noted earlier, the Fed conducts **open-market operations** when it buys or sells government bonds. To increase the money supply, the Fed instructs its bond traders at the New York Fed to buy bonds from the public in the nation's bond markets. The dollars the Fed pays for the bonds increase the number of dollars in the economy. Some of these new dollars are held as currency, and some are deposited in banks. Each new dollar held as currency increases the money supply by exactly $1. Each new dollar deposited in a bank increases the money supply by more than a dollar because it increases reserves and, thereby, the amount of money that the banking system can create.

To reduce the money supply, the Fed does just the opposite: It sells government bonds to the public in the nation's bond markets. The public pays for these bonds with its holdings of currency and bank deposits, directly reducing the amount of money in circulation. In addition, as people make withdrawals from banks to buy these bonds from the Fed, banks find themselves with a smaller quantity of reserves. In response, banks reduce the amount of lending, and the process of money creation reverses itself.

Open-market operations are easy to conduct. In fact, the Fed's purchases and sales of government bonds in the nation's bond markets are similar to the transactions that any individual might undertake for her own portfolio. (Of course, when two individuals engage in a purchase or sale with each other, money changes hands, but the amount of money in circulation remains the same.) In addition, the Fed can use open-market operations to change the money supply by a small or large amount on any day without major changes in laws or bank regulations. Therefore, open-market operations are the tool of monetary policy that the Fed uses most often.

Fed Lending to Banks The Fed can also increase the quantity of reserves in the economy by lending reserves to banks. Banks borrow from the Fed when they feel they do not have enough reserves on hand, either to satisfy bank regulators, meet depositor withdrawals, make new loans, or for some other business reason.

There are various ways banks can borrow from the Fed. Traditionally, banks borrow from the Fed's *discount window* and pay an interest rate on that loan called the **discount rate**. When the Fed makes such a loan to a bank, the banking system has more reserves than it otherwise would, and these additional reserves allow the banking system to create more money.

The Fed can alter the money supply by changing the discount rate. A higher discount rate discourages banks from borrowing reserves from the Fed. Thus, an increase in the discount rate reduces the quantity of reserves in the banking system, which in turn reduces the money supply. Conversely, a lower discount rate encourages banks to borrow from the Fed, increasing the quantity of reserves and the money supply.

open-market operations
the purchase and sale of U.S. government bonds by the Fed

discount rate
the interest rate on the loans that the Fed makes to banks

At times, the Fed has set up other mechanisms for banks to borrow from it. For example, from 2007 to 2010, under the *Term Auction Facility*, the Fed set a quantity of funds it wanted to lend to banks, and eligible banks then bid to borrow those funds. The loans went to the highest eligible bidders—that is, to the banks that had acceptable collateral and offered to pay the highest interest rate. Unlike at the discount window, where the Fed sets the price of a loan and the banks determine the quantity of borrowing, at the Term Auction Facility the Fed set the quantity of borrowing and competitive bidding among banks determined the price. The more funds the Fed made available, the greater the quantity of reserves and the larger the money supply.

The Fed lends to banks not only to control the money supply but also to help financial institutions when they are in trouble. For example, when the stock market crashed by 22 percent on October 19, 1987, many Wall Street brokerage firms found themselves temporarily in need of funds to finance the high volume of stock trading. The next morning, before the stock market opened, Fed Chair Alan Greenspan announced the Fed's "readiness to serve as a source of liquidity to support the economic and financial system." Many economists believe that Greenspan's reaction to the stock crash was an important reason it had few repercussions.

Similarly, in 2008 and 2009, a fall in housing prices throughout the United States led to a sharp rise in the number of homeowners defaulting on their mortgage loans, and many financial institutions holding those mortgages ran into trouble. In an attempt to prevent these events from having broader economic ramifications, the Fed provided many billions of dollars in loans to financial institutions in distress.

29-4b How the Fed Influences the Reserve Ratio

In addition to influencing the quantity of reserves, the Fed changes the money supply by influencing the reserve ratio and thereby the money multiplier. The Fed can influence the reserve ratio either through regulating the quantity of reserves banks must hold or through the interest rate that the Fed pays banks on their reserves. Again, let's consider each of these policy tools in turn.

Reserve Requirements   One way the Fed can influence the reserve ratio is by altering **reserve requirements**, the regulations that set the minimum amount of reserves that banks must hold against their deposits. Reserve requirements influence how much money the banking system can create with each dollar of reserves. An increase in reserve requirements means that banks must hold more reserves and, therefore, can loan out less of each dollar that is deposited. As a result, an increase in reserve requirements raises the reserve ratio, lowers the money multiplier, and decreases the money supply. Conversely, a decrease in reserve requirements lowers the reserve ratio, raises the money multiplier, and increases the money supply.

reserve requirements
regulations on the minimum amount of reserves that banks must hold against deposits

The Fed changes reserve requirements only rarely because such changes disrupt the business of banking. When the Fed increases reserve requirements, for instance, some banks find themselves short of reserves, even though they have seen no change in deposits. As a result, they have to curtail lending until they build their level of reserves to the new required level. Moreover, in recent years, this particular tool has become less effective because many banks hold excess reserves (that is, more reserves than are required).

Paying Interest on Reserves   Traditionally, banks did not earn any interest on the reserves they held. In October 2008, however, the Fed began paying *interest on reserves*. That is, when a bank holds reserves on deposit at the Fed, the Fed now pays the bank interest on those deposits. This change gives the Fed another tool with which to influence the economy. The higher the interest rate on reserves, the more reserves banks will choose to hold. Thus, an increase in the interest rate on reserves will tend to increase the reserve ratio, lower the money multiplier, and lower the money supply.

29-4c **Problems in Controlling the Money Supply**

The Fed's various tools—open-market operations, bank lending, reserve requirements, and interest on reserves—have powerful effects on the money supply. Yet the Fed's control of the money supply is not precise. The Fed must wrestle with two problems, each of which arises because much of the money supply is created by our system of fractional-reserve banking.

The first problem is that the Fed does not control the amount of money that households choose to hold as deposits in banks. The more money households deposit, the more reserves banks have, and the more money the banking system can create. The less money households deposit, the less reserves banks have, and the less money the banking system can create. To see why this is a problem, suppose that one day people lose confidence in the banking system and withdraw some of their deposits to hold more currency. When this happens, the banking system loses reserves and creates less money. The money supply falls, even without any Fed action.

The second problem of monetary control is that the Fed does not control the amount that bankers choose to lend. When money is deposited in a bank, it creates more money only when the bank loans it out. Because banks can choose to hold excess reserves instead, the Fed cannot be sure how much money the banking system will create. For instance, suppose that one day bankers become more cautious about economic conditions and decide to make fewer loans and hold greater reserves. In this case, the banking system creates less money than it otherwise would. Because of the bankers' decision, the money supply falls.

Hence, in a system of fractional-reserve banking, the amount of money in the economy depends in part on the behavior of depositors and bankers. Because the Fed cannot control or perfectly predict this behavior, it cannot perfectly control the money supply. Yet if the Fed is vigilant, these problems need not be large. The Fed collects data on deposits and reserves from banks every week, so it quickly becomes aware of any changes in depositor or banker behavior. It can, therefore, respond to these changes and keep the money supply close to whatever level it chooses.

CASE STUDY

BANK RUNS AND THE MONEY SUPPLY

Most likely you have never witnessed a bank run in real life, but you may have seen one depicted in movies such as *Mary Poppins* or *It's a Wonderful Life*. A bank run occurs when depositors fear that a bank may be having financial troubles and "run" to the bank to withdraw their deposits. The United States has not seen a major bank run in recent history, but in the United Kingdom, a bank called Northern Rock experienced a run in 2007 and, as a result, was eventually taken over by the government.

Bank runs are a problem for banks under fractional-reserve banking. Because a bank holds only a fraction of its deposits in reserve, it cannot satisfy withdrawal

A not-so-wonderful bank run

requests from all depositors. Even if the bank is *solvent* (meaning that its assets exceed its liabilities), it will not have enough cash on hand to allow all depositors immediate access to all of their money. When a run occurs, the bank is forced to close its doors until some bank loans are repaid or until some lender of last resort (such as the Fed) provides it with the currency it needs to satisfy depositors.

Bank runs complicate the control of the money supply. An important example of this problem occurred during the Great Depression in the early 1930s. After a wave of bank runs and bank closings, households and bankers became more cautious. Households withdrew their deposits from banks, preferring to hold their money in the form of currency. This decision reversed the process of money creation, as bankers responded to falling reserves by reducing bank loans. At the same time, bankers increased their reserve ratios so that they would have enough cash on hand to meet their depositors' demands in any future bank runs. The higher reserve ratio reduced the money multiplier, which further reduced the money supply. From 1929 to 1933, the money supply fell by 28 percent, without the Federal Reserve taking any deliberate contractionary action. Many economists point to this massive fall in the money supply to explain the high unemployment and falling prices that prevailed during this period. (In future chapters, we examine the mechanisms by which changes in the money supply affect unemployment and prices.)

IN THE NEWS

A Trip to Jekyll Island

Here's the story of how the Federal Reserve came into being.

The Stranger-Than-Fiction Story of How the Fed Was Created

By Roger Lowenstein

According to opinion surveys, no institution save the Internal Revenue Service is held in lower regard than the Federal Reserve. It's also a font of conspiracy theories stoked by radical libertarians, who insist the Fed is debauching the currency and will ultimately bankrupt the country.

The Fed's unpopularity would make sense if it had, say, failed to intervene and save the system during the 2008 financial crisis. But, in fact, the Fed did rescue the economy....

Nonetheless, dissatisfaction is alive in Congress, where various bills would strip the Fed's autonomy and subject sensitive monetary decisions to the scrutiny of elected politicians. Some bills would go even further and explore a return to the gold standard.

For central bank watchers, this dynamic — effective policy rewarded with populist scorn — is nothing new. In America, it has always been thus.

At Alexander Hamilton's urging, Congress first chartered a national bank — the ur-Fed — in 1791. However, Thomas Jefferson, who famously mistrusted banks (he thought agriculture more virtuous), and who was fearful of a strong central government, opposed this development. After 20 years, the Jeffersonians won and Congress let the charter expire.

This decision led to disaster: ruinous inflation. So Congress chartered a Second Bank of the United States, which began in 1817, providing the growing country with a better, more uniform currency and improved its public finances. But success couldn't save it. Andrew Jackson despised the Second Bank as a tool of East Coast elites, and it too was abolished.

For most of the 19th century, the U.S., unlike most nations in Europe, did not have a lender of last resort. Frequent panics and credit shortages were the result. Yet some of the very people who could have benefited most from a central bank, such as farmers who were starved for credit, preferred the status quo. Like Jackson and Jefferson before them, they were fearful that a government bank would tyrannize the people, perhaps in cahoots with Wall Street.

After a financial panic in 1907 virtually shut down the banking system, reformers began to press once more for a central bank. But popular mistrust remained so pronounced that they were afraid to go public.

This is the point — 105 years ago — when the story seems to have been hijacked by a future Hollywood scriptwriter.

On a November evening in 1910, a powerful senator, Rhode Island Republican Nelson W. Aldrich, boarded his private rail car near

Today, bank runs are not a major problem for the U.S. banking system or the Fed. The federal government now guarantees the safety of deposits at most banks, primarily through the Federal Deposit Insurance Corporation (FDIC). Depositors do not make runs on their banks because they are confident that, even if their bank goes bankrupt, the FDIC will make good on the deposits. The policy of government deposit insurance has costs: Bankers whose deposits are guaranteed may have too little incentive to avoid bad risks when making loans. But one benefit of deposit insurance is a more stable banking system. As a result, most people see bank runs only in the movies. ●

29-4d The Federal Funds Rate

If you read about U.S. monetary policy in the newspaper, you will find much discussion of the federal funds rate. This raises several questions:

Q: What is the federal funds rate?

A: The **federal funds rate** is the short-term interest rate that banks charge one another for loans. If one bank finds itself short of reserves while another bank has excess reserves, the second bank can lend some reserves to the first. The loans are temporary—typically overnight. The price of the loan is the federal funds rate.

federal funds rate
the interest rate at which banks make overnight loans to one another

New York. A light snow was falling, muting the hushed, conspiratorial tones of his guests, which is exactly how Aldrich wanted it.

The reform-minded banker Paul Warburg, one of his guests, was toting a hunting rifle, but he had no interest in hunting. The party also included a member of the powerful Morgan bank, as well as an assistant U.S. Treasury secretary, and Frank Vanderlip, head of the country's largest bank, National City.

"On what sort of errand are we going?" Vanderlip inquired.

"It may be a wild-goose chase; it may the biggest thing you and I ever did," Warburg replied.

Masquerading as duck hunters, they disembarked in Brunswick, Ga., and traveled by launch to Jekyll Island, home of an exclusive club surrounded by pine and palmetto groves. Over the course of a week, Aldrich and his bankers mapped out a draft of what was to become the Federal Reserve Act, changing the U.S. economy forever.

Congress was never told that Aldrich's bill had been drafted by Wall Street moguls. His bill did not pass, but it was the basis of a successor bill, the Federal Reserve Act, which Woodrow Wilson signed in 1913. Years later, when the Jekyll trip was revealed to the public, extremists seized on this stranger-than-fiction episode to bolster their claim that the Fed was a bankers' plot against the American people. For conspiracy theorists, the bankers' conclave on Jekyll became a metaphor for the Fed itself. The obvious irony is that, fearing Americans' irrational suspicion of central banking, Aldrich and his crew resorted to a plot that, ultimately, deepened the country's paranoia.

Despite their clandestine tactics, the financiers' motives were actually patriotic. Aldrich had visited Europe and studied its central banks. He wanted expert help to draft an American equivalent. And in between sumptuous meals featuring wild turkey and freshly scalloped oysters, his group of wealthy bankers earnestly wrestled with issues that still provoke us today: How should power over the economy be apportioned between Washington and localities? How should the central bank set interest rates and the money supply?

The Federal Reserve today is not perfect. But it is more transparent than ever, thanks to reforms instituted by the previous chairman, Ben S. Bernanke, and it is no less necessary than was a central bank in 1791. Americans' paranoia is unjustified, just as it has always been. ■

Roger Lowenstein is the author of "America's Bank: The Epic Struggle to Create the Federal Reserve."

Source: *Los Angeles Times*, November 2, 2015.

Senator Nelson Aldrich

LIBRARY OF CONGRESS PRINTS AND PHOTOGRAPHS DIVISION WASHINGTON

Q: How is the federal funds rate different from the discount rate?

A: The discount rate is the interest rate banks pay to borrow directly from the Federal Reserve through the discount window. Borrowing reserves from another bank in the federal funds market is an alternative to borrowing reserves from the Fed, and a bank short of reserves will typically do whichever is cheaper. In practice, the discount rate and the federal funds rate move closely together.

Q: Does the federal funds rate matter only for banks?

A: Not at all. Although only banks borrow directly in the federal funds market, the economic impact of this market is much broader. Because different parts of the financial system are highly interconnected, interest rates on different kinds of loans are strongly correlated with one another. So when the federal funds rate rises or falls, other interest rates often move in the same direction.

Q: What does the Federal Reserve have to do with the federal funds rate?

A: In recent years, the Federal Reserve has set a target goal for the federal funds rate. When the Federal Open Market Committee meets approximately every 6 weeks, it decides whether to raise or lower that target.

Q: How can the Fed make the federal funds rate hit the target it sets?

A: Although the actual federal funds rate is set by supply and demand in the market for loans among banks, the Fed can use open-market operations to influence that market. For example, when the Fed buys bonds in open-market operations, it injects reserves into the banking system. With more reserves in the system, fewer banks find themselves in need of borrowing reserves to meet reserve requirements. The fall in demand for borrowing reserves decreases the price of such borrowing, which is the federal funds rate. Conversely, when the Fed sells bonds and withdraws reserves from the banking system, more banks find themselves short of reserves, and they bid up the price of borrowing reserves. Thus, open-market purchases lower the federal funds rate, and open-market sales raise the federal funds rate.

Q: But don't these open-market operations affect the money supply?

A: Yes, absolutely. When the Fed announces a change in the federal funds rate, it is committing itself to the open-market operations necessary to make that change happen, and these open-market operations will alter the supply of money. Decisions by the FOMC to change the target for the federal funds rate are also decisions to change the money supply. They are two sides of the same coin. Other things being equal, a decrease in the target for the federal funds rate means an expansion in the money supply, and an increase in the target for the federal funds rate means a contraction in the money supply.

Quick Quiz   *If the Fed wanted to use all of its policy tools to decrease the money supply, what would it do?*

29-5 Conclusion

Some years ago, a book made the best-seller list with the title *Secrets of the Temple: How the Federal Reserve Runs the Country*. Though no doubt an exaggeration, this title did highlight the important role of the monetary system in our daily lives. Whenever we buy or sell anything, we are relying on the extraordinarily useful social convention called "money." Now that we know what money is and what determines its supply, we can discuss how changes in the quantity of money affect the economy. We begin to address that topic in the next chapter.

CHAPTER QuickQuiz

1. The money supply includes all of the following EXCEPT
   a. metal coins.
   b. paper currency.
   c. lines of credit accessible with credit cards.
   d. bank balances accessible with debit cards.

2. Chloe takes $100 of currency from her wallet and deposits it into her checking account. If the bank adds the entire $100 to reserves, the money supply _____, but if the bank lends out some of the $100, the money supply _____.
   a. increases, increases even more
   b. increases, increases by less
   c. is unchanged, increases
   d. decreases, decreases by less

3. If the reserve ratio is ¼ and the central bank increases the quantity of reserves in the banking system by $120, the money supply increases by
   a. $90.
   b. $150.
   c. $160.
   d. $480.

4. A bank has capital of $200 and a leverage ratio of 5. If the value of the bank's assets declines by 10 percent, then its capital will be reduced to
   a. $100.
   b. $150.
   c. $180.
   d. $185.

5. Which of the following actions by the Fed would reduce the money supply?
   a. an open-market purchase of government bonds
   b. a reduction in banks' reserve requirements
   c. an increase in the interest rate paid on reserves
   d. a decrease in the discount rate on Fed lending

6. In a system of fractional-reserve banking, even without any action by the central bank, the money supply declines if households choose to hold _____ currency or if banks choose to hold _____ excess reserves.
   a. more, more
   b. more, less
   c. less, more
   d. less, less

SUMMARY

- The term *money* refers to assets that people regularly use to buy goods and services.
- Money serves three functions. As a medium of exchange, it is the item used to make transactions. As a unit of account, it provides the way to record prices and other economic values. As a store of value, it offers a way to transfer purchasing power from the present to the future.
- Commodity money, such as gold, is money that has intrinsic value: It would be valued even if it were not used as money. Fiat money, such as paper dollars, is money without intrinsic value: It would be worthless if it were not used as money.
- In the U.S. economy, money takes the form of currency and various types of bank deposits, such as checking accounts.
- The Federal Reserve, the central bank of the United States, is responsible for regulating the U.S. monetary system. The Fed chair is appointed by the president and confirmed by Congress every 4 years. The chair is the head of the Federal Open Market Committee, which meets about every 6 weeks to consider changes in monetary policy.
- Bank depositors provide resources to banks by depositing their funds into bank accounts. These deposits are part of a bank's liabilities. Bank owners also provide resources (called bank capital) for the bank. Because of leverage (the use of borrowed funds for investment), a small change in the value of a bank's assets can lead to a large change in the value of the bank's capital. To protect depositors, bank regulators require banks to hold a certain minimum amount of capital.
- The Fed controls the money supply primarily through open-market operations: The purchase of government bonds increases the money supply, and the sale of government bonds decreases the money supply. The Fed also uses other tools to control the money supply. It can expand the money supply by decreasing the discount rate, increasing its lending to banks, lowering reserve requirements, or decreasing the interest rate on reserves. It can contract the money supply by increasing the discount rate, decreasing its lending to banks, raising reserve requirements, or increasing the interest rate on reserves.
- When individuals deposit money in banks and banks loan out some of these deposits, the quantity of money in the economy increases. Because the banking system influences the money supply in this way, the Fed's control of the money supply is imperfect.

- The Federal Reserve has in recent years set monetary policy by choosing a target for the federal funds rate, a short-term interest rate at which banks make loans to one another. As the Fed achieves its target, it adjusts the money supply.

KEY CONCEPTS

money, p. 604
medium of exchange, p. 605
unit of account, p. 605
store of value, p. 605
liquidity, p. 605
commodity money, p. 605
fiat money, p. 606
currency, p. 607
demand deposits, p. 607

Federal Reserve (Fed), p. 609
central bank, p. 609
money supply, p. 610
monetary policy, p. 610
reserves, p. 612
fractional-reserve banking, p. 612
reserve ratio, p. 612
money multiplier, p. 614
bank capital, p. 615

leverage, p. 615
leverage ratio, p. 615
capital requirement, p. 616
open-market operations, p. 617
discount rate, p. 617
reserve requirements, p. 618
federal funds rate, p. 621

QUESTIONS FOR REVIEW

1. What distinguishes money from other assets in the economy?

2. What is commodity money? What is fiat money? Which kind do we use?

3. What are demand deposits and why should they be included in the stock of money?

4. Who is responsible for setting monetary policy in the United States? How is this group chosen?

5. If the Fed wants to increase the money supply with open-market operations, what does it do?

6. Why don't banks hold 100-percent reserves? How is the amount of reserves banks hold related to the amount of money the banking system creates?

7. Bank A has a leverage ratio of 10, while Bank B has a leverage ratio of 20. Similar losses on bank loans at the two banks cause the value of their assets to fall by 7 percent. Which bank shows a larger change in bank capital? Does either bank remain solvent? Explain.

8. What is the discount rate? What happens to the money supply when the Fed raises the discount rate?

9. What are reserve requirements? What happens to the money supply when the Fed raises reserve requirements?

10. Why can't the Fed control the money supply perfectly?

PROBLEMS AND APPLICATIONS

1. Which of the following are considered money in the U.S. economy? Which are not? Explain your answers by discussing each of the three functions of money.
   a. a U.S. penny
   b. a Mexican peso
   c. a Picasso painting
   d. a plastic credit card

2. Explain whether each of the following events increases or decreases the money supply.
   a. The Fed buys bonds in open-market operations.
   b. The Fed reduces the reserve requirement.
   c. The Fed increases the interest rate it pays on reserves.
   d. Citibank repays a loan it had previously taken from the Fed.
   e. After a rash of pickpocketing, people decide to hold less currency.
   f. Fearful of bank runs, bankers decide to hold more excess reserves.
   g. The FOMC increases its target for the federal funds rate.

3. Your uncle repays a $100 loan from Tenth National Bank (TNB) by writing a $100 check from his TNB checking account. Use T-accounts to show the effect of this transaction on your uncle and on TNB. Has your uncle's wealth changed? Explain.

4. Beleaguered State Bank (BSB) holds $250 million in deposits and maintains a reserve ratio of 10 percent.
   a. Show a T-account for BSB.
   b. Now suppose that BSB's largest depositor withdraws $10 million in cash from her account. If BSB decides to restore its reserve ratio by reducing the amount of loans outstanding, show its new T-account.
   c. Explain what effect BSB's action will have on other banks.
   d. Why might it be difficult for BSB to take the action described in part (b)? Discuss another way for BSB to return to its original reserve ratio.

5. You take $100 you had kept under your mattress and deposit it in your bank account. If this $100 stays in the banking system as reserves and if banks hold reserves equal to 10 percent of deposits, by how much does the total amount of deposits in the banking system increase? By how much does the money supply increase?

6. Happy Bank starts with $200 in bank capital. It then accepts $800 in deposits. It keeps 12.5 percent (1/8th) of deposits in reserve. It uses the rest of its assets to make bank loans.
   a. Show the balance sheet of Happy Bank.
   b. What is Happy Bank's leverage ratio?
   c. Suppose that 10 percent of the borrowers from Happy Bank default and these bank loans become worthless. Show the bank's new balance sheet.
   d. By what percentage do the bank's total assets decline? By what percentage does the bank's capital decline? Which change is larger? Why?

7. The Fed conducts a $10 million open-market purchase of government bonds. If the required reserve ratio is 10 percent, what are the largest and smallest possible increases in the money supply that could result? Explain.

8. Assume that the reserve requirement is 5 percent. All other things being equal, will the money supply expand more if the Fed buys $2,000 worth of bonds or if someone deposits in a bank $2,000 that she had been hiding in her cookie jar? If one creates more, how much more does it create? Support your thinking.

9. Suppose that the reserve requirement for checking deposits is 10 percent and that banks do not hold any excess reserves.
   a. If the Fed sells $1 million of government bonds, what is the effect on the economy's reserves and money supply?
   b. Now suppose the Fed lowers the reserve requirement to 5 percent, but banks choose to hold another 5 percent of deposits as excess reserves. Why might banks do so? What is the overall change in the money multiplier and the money supply as a result of these actions?

10. Assume that the banking system has total reserves of $100 billion. Assume also that required reserves are 10 percent of checking deposits and that banks hold no excess reserves and households hold no currency.
    a. What is the money multiplier? What is the money supply?
    b. If the Fed now raises required reserves to 20 percent of deposits, what are the change in reserves and the change in the money supply?

11. Assume that the reserve requirement is 20 percent. Also assume that banks do not hold excess reserves and there is no cash held by the public. The Fed decides that it wants to expand the money supply by $40 million.
    a. If the Fed is using open-market operations, will it buy or sell bonds?
    b. What quantity of bonds does the Fed need to buy or sell to accomplish the goal? Explain your reasoning.

12. The economy of Elmendyn contains 2,000 $1 bills.
    a. If people hold all money as currency, what is the quantity of money?
    b. If people hold all money as demand deposits and banks maintain 100 percent reserves, what is the quantity of money?
    c. If people hold equal amounts of currency and demand deposits and banks maintain 100 percent reserves, what is the quantity of money?
    d. If people hold all money as demand deposits and banks maintain a reserve ratio of 10 percent, what is the quantity of money?
    e. If people hold equal amounts of currency and demand deposits and banks maintain a reserve ratio of 10 percent, what is the quantity of money?

To find additional study resources, visit cengagebrain.com, and search for "Mankiw."

Money Growth and Inflation

Today, if you want to buy an ice-cream cone, you need at least a couple of dollars, but that has not always been the case. In the 1930s, my grandmother ran a sweet shop in Trenton, New Jersey, where she sold ice-cream cones in two sizes. A cone with a small scoop of ice cream cost 3 cents. Hungry customers could buy a large scoop for a nickel.

You may not be surprised at the increase in the price of ice cream. In most modern economies, most prices tend to rise over time. This increase in the overall level of prices is called *inflation*. Earlier in the book, we examined how economists

measure the inflation rate as the percentage change in the consumer price index (CPI), the GDP deflator, or some other index of the overall price level. These price indexes show that, in the United States over the past 80 years, prices have risen on average 3.6 percent per year. Accumulated over so many years, a 3.6 percent annual inflation rate leads to a seventeenfold increase in the price level.

Inflation may seem natural and inevitable to a person who grew up in the United States during recent decades, but in fact, it is not inevitable at all. There were long periods in the 19th century during which most prices fell—a phenomenon called *deflation*. The average level of prices in the U.S. economy was 23 percent lower in 1896 than in 1880, and this deflation was a major issue in the presidential election of 1896. Farmers, who had accumulated large debts, suffered when declines in crop prices reduced their incomes and thus their ability to pay off their debts. They advocated government policies to reverse the deflation.

Although inflation has been the norm in more recent history, there has been substantial variation in the rate at which prices rise. From 2005 to 2015, prices rose at an average rate of 1.2 percent per year. By contrast, in the 1970s, prices rose by 7.8 percent per year, which meant the price level more than doubled over the decade. The public often views such high rates of inflation as a major economic problem. In fact, when President Jimmy Carter ran for reelection in 1980, challenger Ronald Reagan pointed to high inflation as one of the failures of Carter's economic policy.

International data show an even broader range of inflation experiences. In 2015, while the inflation rate in the United States was a mere 0.1 percent, it was 1.5 percent in China, 4.9 percent in India, 15 percent in Russia, and 84 percent in Venezuela. And even the high inflation rates in Russia and Venezuela are moderate by some standards. In February 2008, the central bank of Zimbabwe announced the inflation rate in its economy had reached 24,000 percent; some independent estimates put the figure even higher. An extraordinarily high rate of inflation such as this is called *hyperinflation*.

What determines whether an economy experiences inflation and, if so, how much? This chapter answers this question by developing the *quantity theory of money*. Chapter 1 summarized this theory as one of the *Ten Principles of Economics*: Prices rise when the government prints too much money. This insight has a long and venerable tradition among economists. The quantity theory was discussed by the famous 18th-century philosopher and economist David Hume and was advocated more recently by the prominent economist Milton Friedman. This theory can explain moderate inflations, such as those we have experienced in the United States, as well as hyperinflations.

After developing a theory of inflation, we turn to a related question: Why is inflation a problem? At first glance, the answer to this question may seem obvious: Inflation is a problem because people don't like it. In the 1970s, when the United States experienced a relatively high rate of inflation, opinion polls placed inflation as the most important issue facing the nation. President Ford echoed this sentiment in 1974 when he called inflation "public enemy number one." Ford wore a "WIN" button on his lapel—for Whip Inflation Now.

But what, exactly, are the costs that inflation imposes on a society? The answer may surprise you. Identifying the various costs of inflation is not as straightforward as it first appears. As a result, although all economists decry hyperinflation, some economists argue that the costs of moderate inflation are not nearly as large as the public believes.

30-1   The Classical Theory of Inflation

We begin our study of inflation by developing the quantity theory of money. This theory is often called "classical" because it was developed by some of the earliest economic thinkers. Most economists today rely on this theory to explain the long-run determinants of the price level and the inflation rate.

30-1a   The Level of Prices and the Value of Money

Suppose we observe that over some period of time the price of an ice-cream cone rises from a nickel to a dollar. What conclusion should we draw from the fact that people are willing to give up so much more money in exchange for a cone? It is possible that people have come to enjoy ice cream more (perhaps because some chemist has developed a miraculous new flavor). But that is probably not the case. It is more likely that people's enjoyment of ice cream has stayed roughly the same and that, over time, the money used to buy ice cream has become less valuable. Indeed, the first insight about inflation is that it is more about the value of money than about the value of goods.

This insight helps point the way toward a theory of inflation. When the consumer price index and other measures of the price level rise, commentators are often tempted to look at the many individual prices that make up these price indexes: "The CPI rose by 3 percent last month, led by a 20 percent rise in the price of coffee and a 30 percent rise in the price of heating oil." Although this approach does contain some interesting information about what's happening in the economy, it also misses a key point: Inflation is an economy-wide phenomenon that concerns, first and foremost, the value of the economy's medium of exchange.

The economy's overall price level can be viewed in two ways. So far, we have viewed the price level as the price of a basket of goods and services. When the price level rises, people have to pay more for the goods and services they buy. Alternatively, we can view the price level as a measure of the value of money. A rise in the price level means a lower value of money because each dollar in your wallet now buys a smaller quantity of goods and services.

It may help to express these ideas mathematically. Suppose P is the price level as measured by the consumer price index or the GDP deflator. Then P measures the number of dollars needed to buy a basket of goods and services. Now turn this idea around: The quantity of goods and services that can be bought with \$1 equals $1/P$. In other words, if P is the price of goods and services measured in terms of money, $1/P$ is the value of money measured in terms of goods and services.

"So what's it going to be? The same size as last year or the same price as last year?"

This mathematics is simplest to understand in an economy that produces only a single good, say, ice-cream cones. In that case, P would be the price of a cone. When the price of a cone (P) is \$2, then the value of a dollar ($1/P$) is half a cone. When the price (P) rises to \$3, the value of a dollar ($1/P$) falls to a third of a cone. The actual economy produces thousands of goods and services, so we use a price index rather than the price of a single good. But the logic remains the same: When the overall price level rises, the value of money falls.

30-1b Money Supply, Money Demand, and Monetary Equilibrium

What determines the value of money? The answer to this question, like many in economics, is supply and demand. Just as the supply and demand for bananas determines the price of bananas, the supply and demand for money determines the value of money. Thus, our next step in developing the quantity theory of money is to consider the determinants of money supply and money demand.

First consider money supply. In the preceding chapter, we discussed how the Federal Reserve, together with the banking system, determines the supply of money. When the Fed sells bonds in open-market operations, it receives dollars in exchange and contracts the money supply. When the Fed buys government bonds, it pays out dollars and expands the money supply. In addition, if any of these dollars are deposited in banks, which hold some as reserves and loan out the rest, the money multiplier swings into action, and these open-market operations can have an even greater effect on the money supply. For our purposes in this chapter, we ignore the complications introduced by the banking system and simply take the quantity of money supplied as a policy variable that the Fed controls.

Now consider money demand. Most fundamentally, the demand for money reflects how much wealth people want to hold in liquid form. Many factors influence the quantity of money demanded. The amount of currency that people hold in their wallets, for instance, depends on how much they rely on credit cards and on whether an automatic teller machine is easy to find. And as we will emphasize in Chapter 34, the quantity of money demanded depends on the interest rate that a person could earn by using the money to buy an interest-bearing bond rather than leaving it in his wallet or low-interest checking account.

Although many variables affect the demand for money, one variable stands out in importance: the average level of prices in the economy. People hold money because it is the medium of exchange. Unlike other assets, such as bonds or stocks, people can use money to buy the goods and services on their shopping lists. How much money they choose to hold for this purpose depends on the prices of those goods and services. The higher prices are, the more money the typical transaction requires, and the more money people will choose to hold in their wallets and checking accounts. That is, a higher price level (a lower value of money) increases the quantity of money demanded.

What ensures that the quantity of money the Fed supplies balances the quantity of money people demand? The answer depends on the time horizon being considered. Later in this book, we examine the short-run answer and learn that interest rates play a key role. The long-run answer, however, is much simpler. *In the long run, money supply and money demand are brought into equilibrium by the overall level of prices.* If the price level is above the equilibrium level, people will want to hold more money than the Fed has created, so the price level must fall to balance supply and demand. If the price level is below the equilibrium level, people will want to hold less money than the Fed has created, and the price level must rise to balance supply and demand. At the equilibrium price level, the quantity of money that people want to hold exactly balances the quantity of money supplied by the Fed.

Figure 1 illustrates these ideas. The horizontal axis of this graph shows the quantity of money. The left vertical axis shows the value of money $1/P$, and the right vertical axis shows the price level P. Notice that the price-level axis on the right is inverted: A low price level is shown near the top of this axis, and a high price level is shown near the bottom. This inverted axis illustrates that when the value of money is high (as shown near the top of the left axis), the price level is low (as shown near the top of the right axis).

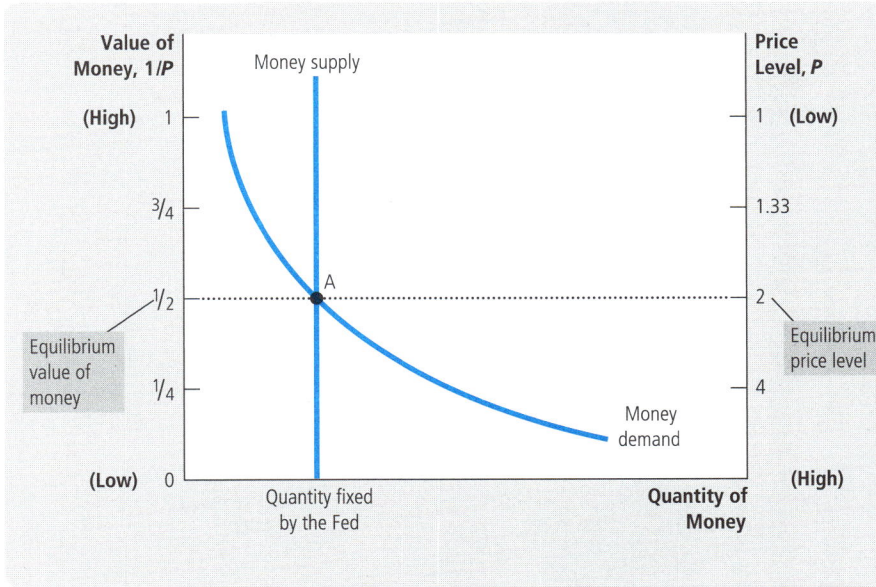

FIGURE 1

How the Supply and Demand for Money Determine the Equilibrium Price Level
The horizontal axis shows the quantity of money. The left vertical axis shows the value of money, and the right vertical axis shows the price level. The supply curve for money is vertical because the quantity of money supplied is fixed by the Fed. The demand curve for money slopes downward because people want to hold a larger quantity of money when each dollar buys less. At the equilibrium, point A, the value of money (on the left axis) and the price level (on the right axis) have adjusted to bring the quantity of money supplied and the quantity of money demanded into balance.

The two curves in this figure are the supply and demand curves for money. The supply curve is vertical because the Fed has fixed the quantity of money available. The demand curve for money slopes downward, indicating that when the value of money is low (and the price level is high), people demand a larger quantity of it to buy goods and services. At the equilibrium, shown in the figure as point A, the quantity of money demanded balances the quantity of money supplied. This equilibrium of money supply and money demand determines the value of money and the price level.

30-1c The Effects of a Monetary Injection

Let's now consider the effects of a change in monetary policy. To do so, imagine that the economy is in equilibrium and then, suddenly, the Fed doubles the supply of money by printing some dollar bills and dropping them around the country from helicopters. (Or, less dramatically and more realistically, the Fed could inject money into the economy by buying some government bonds from the public in open-market operations.) What happens after such a monetary injection? How does the new equilibrium compare to the old one?

Figure 2 shows what happens. The monetary injection shifts the supply curve to the right from MS_1 to MS_2, and the equilibrium moves from point A to point B. As a result, the value of money (shown on the left axis) decreases from to , and the equilibrium price level (shown on the right axis) increases from 2 to 4. In other words, when an increase in the money supply makes dollars more plentiful, the result is an increase in the price level that makes each dollar less valuable.

This explanation of how the price level is determined and why it might change over time is called the **quantity theory of money**. According to the quantity theory, the quantity of money available in an economy determines the value of money, and growth in the quantity of money is the primary cause of inflation. As economist Milton Friedman once put it, "Inflation is always and everywhere a monetary phenomenon."

quantity theory of money
a theory asserting that the quantity of money available determines the price level and that the growth rate in the quantity of money available determines the inflation rate

121

FIGURE 2

An Increase in the Money Supply

When the Fed increases the supply of money, the money supply curve shifts from MS_1 to MS_2. The value of money (on the left axis) and the price level (on the right axis) adjust to bring supply and demand back into balance. The equilibrium moves from point A to point B. Thus, when an increase in the money supply makes dollars more plentiful, the price level increases, making each dollar less valuable.

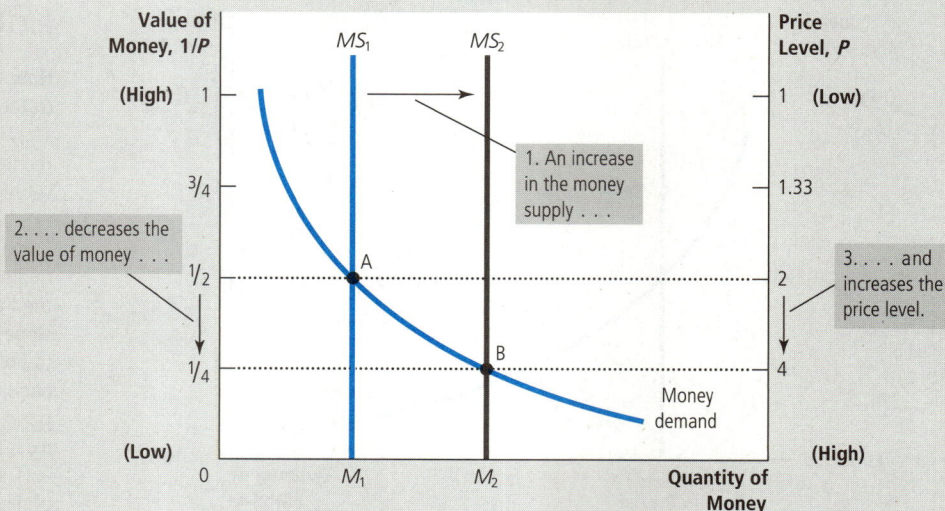

Value of Money, $1/P$

(High)   1

$3/4$

2. . . . decreases the value of money . . .

$1/2$ A

$1/4$ B

(Low)

0   M_1 M_2

MS_1 MS_2

1. An increase in the money supply . . .

Money demand

Price Level, P

1   (Low)

1.33

3. . . . and increases the price level.

2

4

(High)

Quantity of Money

30-1d   A Brief Look at the Adjustment Process

So far, we have compared the old equilibrium and the new equilibrium after an injection of money. How does the economy move from the old to the new equilibrium? A complete answer to this question requires an understanding of short-run fluctuations in the economy, which we examine later in this book. Here, we briefly consider the adjustment process that occurs after a change in the money supply.

The immediate effect of a monetary injection is to create an excess supply of money. Before the injection, the economy was in equilibrium (point A in Figure 2). At the prevailing price level, people had exactly as much money as they wanted. But after the helicopters drop the new money and people pick it up off the streets, people have more dollars in their wallets than they want. At the prevailing price level, the quantity of money supplied now exceeds the quantity demanded.

People try to get rid of this excess supply of money in various ways. They might use it to buy goods and services. Or they might use this excess money to make loans to others by buying bonds or by depositing the money in a bank savings account. These loans allow other people to buy goods and services. In either case, the injection of money increases the demand for goods and services.

The economy's ability to supply goods and services, however, has not changed. As we saw in the chapter on production and growth, the economy's output of goods and services is determined by the available labor, physical capital, human capital, natural resources, and technological knowledge. None of these is altered by the injection of money.

Thus, the greater demand for goods and services causes the prices of goods and services to increase. The increase in the price level, in turn, increases the quantity of money demanded because people are using more dollars for every transaction. Eventually, the economy reaches a new equilibrium (point B in Figure 2) at which the quantity of money demanded again equals the quantity of money supplied.

In this way, the overall price level for goods and services adjusts to bring money supply and money demand into balance.

30-1e The Classical Dichotomy and Monetary Neutrality

We have seen how changes in the money supply lead to changes in the average level of prices of goods and services. How do monetary changes affect other economic variables, such as production, employment, real wages, and real interest rates? This question has long intrigued economists, including David Hume in the 18th century.

Hume and his contemporaries suggested that economic variables should be divided into two groups. The first group consists of **nominal variables**—variables measured in monetary units. The second group consists of **real variables**—variables measured in physical units. For example, the income of corn farmers is a nominal variable because it is measured in dollars, whereas the quantity of corn they produce is a real variable because it is measured in bushels. Nominal GDP is a nominal variable because it measures the dollar value of the economy's output of goods and services; real GDP is a real variable because it measures the total quantity of goods and services produced and is not influenced by the current prices of those goods and services. The separation of real and nominal variables is now called the **classical dichotomy**. (A *dichotomy* is a division into two groups, and *classical* refers to the earlier economic thinkers.)

Applying the classical dichotomy is tricky when we turn to prices. Most prices are quoted in units of money and, therefore, are nominal variables. When we say that the price of corn is $2 a bushel or that the price of wheat is $1 a bushel, both prices are nominal variables. But what about a *relative* price—the price of one thing compared to another? In our example, we could say that the price of a bushel of corn is 2 bushels of wheat. This relative price is not measured in terms of money. When comparing the prices of any two goods, the dollar signs cancel, and the resulting number is measured in physical units. Thus, while dollar prices are nominal variables, relative prices are real variables.

This lesson has many applications. For instance, the real wage (the dollar wage adjusted for inflation) is a real variable because it measures the rate at which people exchange goods and services for a unit of labor. Similarly, the real interest rate (the nominal interest rate adjusted for inflation) is a real variable because it measures the rate at which people exchange goods and services today for goods and services in the future.

Why separate variables into these groups? The classical dichotomy is useful because different forces influence real and nominal variables. According to classical analysis, nominal variables are influenced by developments in the economy's monetary system, whereas money is largely irrelevant for explaining real variables.

This idea was implicit in our discussion of the real economy in the long run. In previous chapters, we examined how real GDP, saving, investment, real interest rates, and unemployment are determined without mentioning the existence of money. In that analysis, the economy's production of goods and services depends on technology and factor supplies, the real interest rate balances the supply and demand for loanable funds, the real wage balances the supply and demand for labor, and unemployment results when the real wage is kept above the equilibrium level. These conclusions have nothing to do with the quantity of money supplied.

Changes in the supply of money, according to classical analysis, affect nominal variables but not real ones. When the central bank doubles the money supply, the

nominal variables
variables measured in monetary units

real variables
variables measured in physical units

classical dichotomy
the theoretical separation of nominal and real variables

monetary neutrality
the proposition that
changes in the money
supply do not affect real
variables

price level doubles, the dollar wage doubles, and all other dollar values double. Real variables, such as production, employment, real wages, and real interest rates, are unchanged. The irrelevance of monetary changes for real variables is called **monetary neutrality**.

An analogy helps explain monetary neutrality. As the unit of account, money is the yardstick we use to measure economic transactions. When a central bank doubles the money supply, all prices double, and the value of the unit of account falls by half. A similar change would occur if the government were to reduce the length of the yard from 36 to 18 inches: With the new, shorter yardstick, all *measured* distances (nominal variables) would double, but the *actual* distances (real variables) would remain the same. The dollar, like the yard, is merely a unit of measurement, so a change in its value should not have real effects.

Is monetary neutrality realistic? Not completely. A change in the length of the yard from 36 to 18 inches would not matter in the long run, but in the short run, it would lead to confusion and mistakes. Similarly, most economists today believe that over short periods of time—within the span of a year or two—monetary changes affect real variables. Hume himself also doubted that monetary neutrality would apply in the short run. (We will study short-run non-neutrality later in the book, and this topic will help explain why the Fed changes the money supply over time.)

Yet classical analysis is right about the economy in the long run. Over the course of a decade, monetary changes have significant effects on nominal variables (such as the price level) but only negligible effects on real variables (such as real GDP). When studying long-run changes in the economy, the neutrality of money offers a good description of how the world works.

30-1f Velocity and the Quantity Equation

We can obtain another perspective on the quantity theory of money by considering the following question: How many times per year is the typical dollar bill used to pay for a newly produced good or service? The answer to this question is given by a variable called the **velocity of money**. In physics, the term *velocity* refers to the speed at which an object travels. In economics, the velocity of money refers to the speed at which the typical dollar bill travels around the economy from wallet to wallet.

velocity of money
the rate at which money
changes hands

To calculate the velocity of money, we divide the nominal value of output (nominal GDP) by the quantity of money. If P is the price level (the GDP deflator), Y the quantity of output (real GDP), and M the quantity of money, then velocity is

$$V = (P \times Y)/M.$$

To see why this makes sense, imagine a simple economy that produces only pizza. Suppose that the economy produces 100 pizzas in a year, that a pizza sells for $10, and that the quantity of money in the economy is $50. Then the velocity of money is

$$V = (\$10 \times 100)/\$50$$
$$= 20.$$

In this economy, people spend a total of $1,000 per year on pizza. For this $1,000 of spending to take place with only $50 of money, each dollar bill must change hands on average 20 times per year.

With slight algebraic rearrangement, this equation can be rewritten as

$$M \times V = P \times Y.$$

This equation states that the quantity of money (M) times the velocity of money (V) equals the price of output (P) times the amount of output (Y). It is called the **quantity equation** because it relates the quantity of money (M) to the nominal value of output ($P \times Y$). The quantity equation shows that an increase in the quantity of money in an economy must be reflected in one of the other three variables: The price level must rise, the quantity of output must rise, or the velocity of money must fall.

In many cases, it turns out that the velocity of money is relatively stable. For example, Figure 3 shows nominal GDP, the quantity of money (as measured by M2), and the velocity of money for the U.S. economy since 1960. During this period, the money supply and nominal GDP both increased more than thirtyfold. By contrast, the velocity of money, although not exactly constant, has not changed

quantity equation
the equation $M \times V = P \times Y$, which relates the quantity of money, the velocity of money, and the dollar value of the economy's output of goods and services

This figure shows the nominal value of output as measured by nominal GDP, the quantity of money as measured by M2, and the velocity of money as measured by their ratio. For comparability, all three series have been scaled to equal 100 in 1960. Notice that nominal GDP and the quantity of money have grown dramatically over this period, while velocity has been relatively stable.

Source: U.S. Department of Commerce; Federal Reserve Board.

FIGURE 3

Nominal GDP, the Quantity of Money, and the Velocity of Money

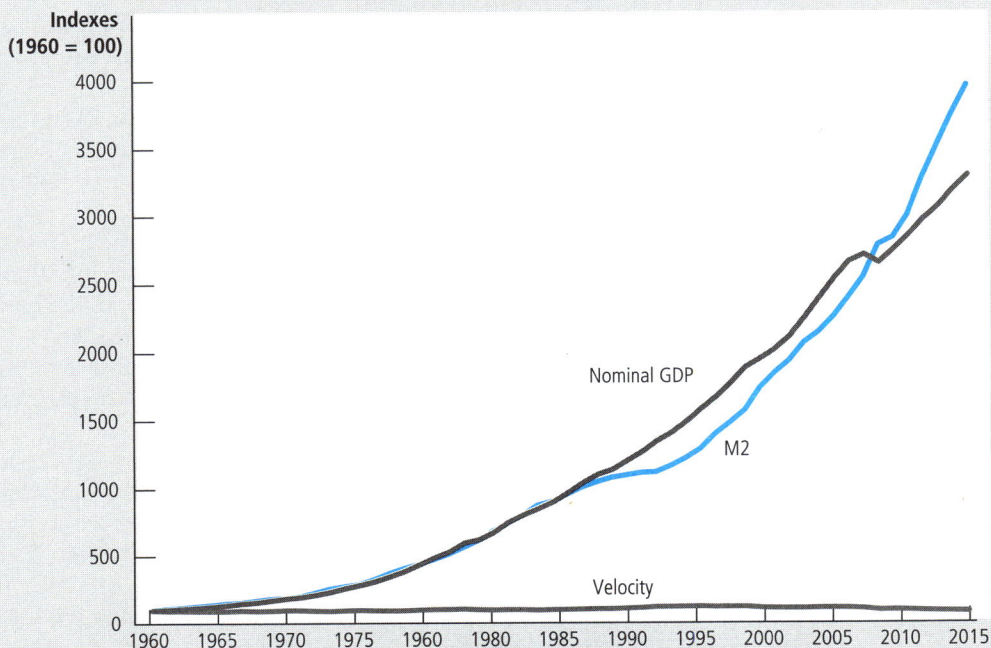

dramatically. Thus, for some purposes, the assumption of constant velocity is a good approximation.

We now have all the elements necessary to explain the equilibrium price level and inflation rate. They are as follows:

1. The velocity of money is relatively stable over time.
2. Because velocity is stable, when the central bank changes the quantity of money (M), it causes proportionate changes in the nominal value of output ($P \times Y$).
3. The economy's output of goods and services (Y) is primarily determined by factor supplies (labor, physical capital, human capital, and natural resources) and the available production technology. In particular, because money is neutral, money does not affect output.
4. With output (Y) determined by factor supplies and technology, when the central bank alters the money supply (M) and induces proportional changes in the nominal value of output ($P \times Y$), these changes are reflected in changes in the price level (P).
5. Therefore, when the central bank increases the money supply rapidly, the result is a high rate of inflation.

These five steps are the essence of the quantity theory of money.

CASE STUDY   **MONEY AND PRICES DURING FOUR HYPERINFLATIONS**
Although earthquakes can wreak havoc on a society, they have the beneficial by-product of providing much useful data for seismologists. These data can shed light on alternative theories and, thereby, help society predict and deal with future threats. Similarly, hyperinflations offer monetary economists a natural experiment they can use to study the effects of money on the economy.

Hyperinflations are interesting in part because the changes in the money supply and price level are so large. Indeed, hyperinflation is generally defined as inflation that exceeds 50 percent *per month*. This means that the price level increases more than 100-fold over the course of a year.

The data on hyperinflation show a clear link between the quantity of money and the price level. Figure 4 graphs data from four classic hyperinflations that occurred during the 1920s in Austria, Hungary, Germany, and Poland. Each graph shows the quantity of money in the economy and an index of the price level. The slope of the money line represents the rate at which the quantity of money was growing, and the slope of the price line represents the inflation rate. The steeper the lines, the higher the rates of money growth or inflation.

Notice that in each graph the quantity of money and the price level are almost parallel. In each instance, growth in the quantity of money is moderate at first and so is inflation. But over time, the quantity of money in the economy starts growing faster and faster. At about the same time, inflation also takes off. Then when the quantity of money stabilizes, the price level stabilizes as well. These episodes illustrate well one of the *Ten Principles of Economics*: Prices rise when the government prints too much money. ●

This figure shows the quantity of money and the price level during four hyperinflations. (Note that these variables are graphed on *logarithmic* scales. This means that equal vertical distances on the graph represent equal *percentage* changes in the variable.) In each case, the quantity of money and the price level move closely together. The strong association between these two variables is consistent with the quantity theory of money, which states that growth in the money supply is the primary cause of inflation.

Source: Adapted from Thomas J. Sargent, "The End of Four Big Inflations," in Robert Hall, ed., *Inflation* (Chicago: University of Chicago Press, 1983), pp. 41–93.

FIGURE 4

Money and Prices during Four Hyperinflations

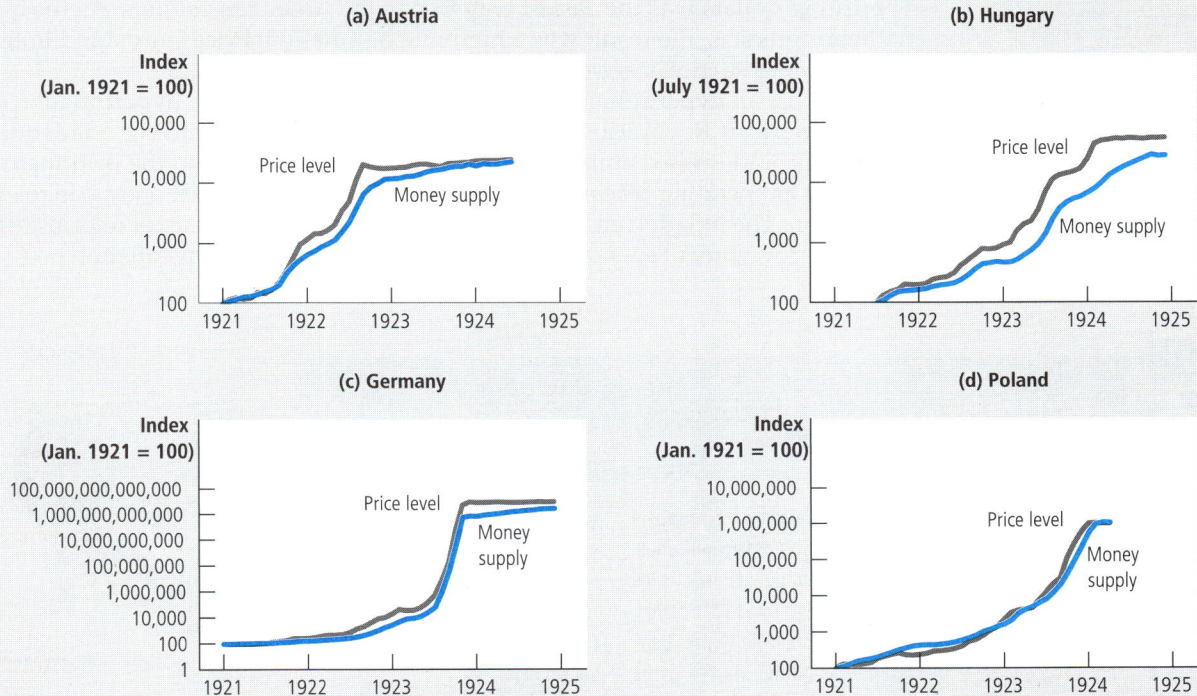

(a) Austria

(b) Hungary

(c) Germany

(d) Poland

30-1g The Inflation Tax

If inflation is so easy to explain, why do countries experience hyperinflation? That is, why do the central banks of these countries choose to print so much money that its value is certain to fall rapidly over time?

The answer is that the governments of these countries are using money creation as a way to pay for their spending. When the government wants to build roads, pay salaries to its soldiers, or give transfer payments to the poor or elderly, it first has to raise the necessary funds. Normally, the government does this by levying taxes, such as income and sales taxes, and by borrowing from the public by selling government bonds. Yet the government can also pay for spending simply by printing the money it needs.

When the government raises revenue by printing money, it is said to levy an **inflation tax**. The inflation tax is not exactly like other taxes, however, because no one receives a bill from the government for this tax. Instead, the inflation tax is

inflation tax
the revenue the government raises by creating money

subtler. When the government prints money, the price level rises, and the dollars in your wallet become less valuable. Thus, *the inflation tax is like a tax on everyone who holds money*.

The importance of the inflation tax varies from country to country and over time. In the United States in recent years, the inflation tax has been a trivial source of revenue: It has accounted for less than 3 percent of government revenue. During the 1770s, however, the Continental Congress of the fledgling United States relied heavily on the inflation tax to pay for military spending. Because the new government had a limited ability to raise funds through regular taxes or borrowing, printing dollars was the easiest way to pay the American soldiers. As the quantity theory predicts, the result was a high rate of inflation: Prices measured in terms of the continental dollar rose more than a 100-fold over a few years.

Almost all hyperinflations follow the same pattern as the hyperinflation during the American Revolution. The government has high spending, inadequate tax revenue, and limited ability to borrow. As a result, it turns to the printing press to pay for its spending. The massive increases in the quantity of money lead to massive inflation. The inflation ends when the government institutes fiscal reforms—such as cuts in government spending—that eliminate the need for the inflation tax.

FYI

Hyperinflation in Zimbabwe

During the first decade of the 2000s, the nation of Zimbabwe experienced one of history's most extreme examples of hyperinflation. In many ways, the story is common: Large government budget deficits led to the creation of large quantities of money and high rates of inflation. The hyperinflation ended in April 2009 when the Zimbabwe central bank stopped printing the Zimbabwe dollar and the nation started using foreign currencies such as the U.S. dollar and the South African rand as the medium of exchange.

Estimates vary about how high inflation in Zimbabwe got, but the magnitude of the problem is well documented by the denomination of the notes being issued by the central bank. Before the hyperinflation started, the Zimbabwe dollar was worth a bit more than one U.S. dollar, so the denominations of the paper currency were similar to those one would find in the United States. A person might carry, for example, a 10-dollar note in his wallet. In January 2008, however, after years of high inflation, the Reserve Bank of Zimbabwe issued notes worth 10 million Zimbabwe dollars, which was then equivalent to about 4 U.S. dollars. But even that did not prove to be large enough. A year later, the central bank announced it would issue notes worth 10 trillion Zimbabwe dollars, then worth about 3 U.S. dollars.

As prices rose and the central bank printed ever-larger denominations of money, the older, smaller-denomination currency lost value and became almost worthless. One indication of this phenomenon can be found on this sign from a public restroom in Zimbabwe, shown below. ∎

TOILET PAPER ONLY
TO BE USED IN THIS TOILET
- NO CARDBOARD
- NO CLOTH
- NO ZIM DOLLARS
- NO NEWSPAPER

ISTOCK/GETTY IMAGES

30-1h The Fisher Effect

According to the principle of monetary neutrality, an increase in the rate of money growth raises the rate of inflation but does not affect any real variable. An important application of this principle concerns the effect of money on interest rates. Interest rates are important variables for macroeconomists to understand because they link the economy of the present and the economy of the future through their effects on saving and investment.

To understand the relationship between money, inflation, and interest rates, recall the distinction between the nominal interest rate and the real interest rate. The *nominal interest rate* is the interest rate you hear about at your bank. If you have a savings account, for instance, the nominal interest rate tells you how fast the number of dollars in your account will rise over time. The *real interest rate* corrects the nominal interest rate for the effect of inflation to tell you how fast the purchasing power of your savings account will rise over time. The real interest rate is the nominal interest rate minus the inflation rate:

$$\text{Real interest rate} = \text{Nominal interest rate} - \text{Inflation rate}.$$

For example, if the bank posts a nominal interest rate of 7 percent per year and the inflation rate is 3 percent per year, then the real value of the deposits grows by 4 percent per year.

We can rewrite this equation to show that the nominal interest rate is the sum of the real interest rate and the inflation rate:

$$\text{Nominal interest rate} = \text{Real interest rate} + \text{Inflation rate}.$$

This way of looking at the nominal interest rate is useful because different economic forces determine each of the two terms on the right side of this equation. As we discussed earlier in the book, the supply and demand for loanable funds determine the real interest rate. And according to the quantity theory of money, growth in the money supply determines the inflation rate.

Let's now consider how growth in the money supply affects interest rates. In the long run over which money is neutral, a change in money growth should not affect the real interest rate. The real interest rate is, after all, a real variable. For the real interest rate not to be affected, the nominal interest rate must adjust one-for-one to changes in the inflation rate. Thus, *when the Fed increases the rate of money growth, the long-run result is both a higher inflation rate and a higher nominal interest rate*. This adjustment of the nominal interest rate to the inflation rate is called the **Fisher effect**, after Irving Fisher (1867–1947), the economist who first studied it.

Keep in mind that our analysis of the Fisher effect has maintained a long-run perspective. The Fisher effect need not hold in the short run because inflation may be unanticipated. A nominal interest rate is a payment on a loan, and it is typically set when the loan is first made. If a jump in inflation catches the borrower and lender by surprise, the nominal interest rate they agreed on will fail to reflect the higher inflation. But if inflation remains high, people will eventually come to expect it, and loan agreements will reflect this expectation. To be precise, therefore, the Fisher effect states that the nominal interest rate adjusts to expected inflation. Expected inflation moves with actual inflation in the long run, but that is not necessarily true in the short run.

The Fisher effect is crucial for understanding changes over time in the nominal interest rate. Figure 5 shows the nominal interest rate and the inflation rate in

Fisher effect

the one-for-one adjustment of the nominal interest rate to the inflation rate

FIGURE 5

The Nominal Interest Rate and the Inflation Rate

This figure uses annual data since 1960 to show the nominal interest rate on three-month Treasury bills and the inflation rate as measured by the consumer price index. The close association between these two variables is evidence for the Fisher effect: When the inflation rate rises, so does the nominal interest rate.

Source: U.S. Department of Treasury; U.S. Department of Labor.

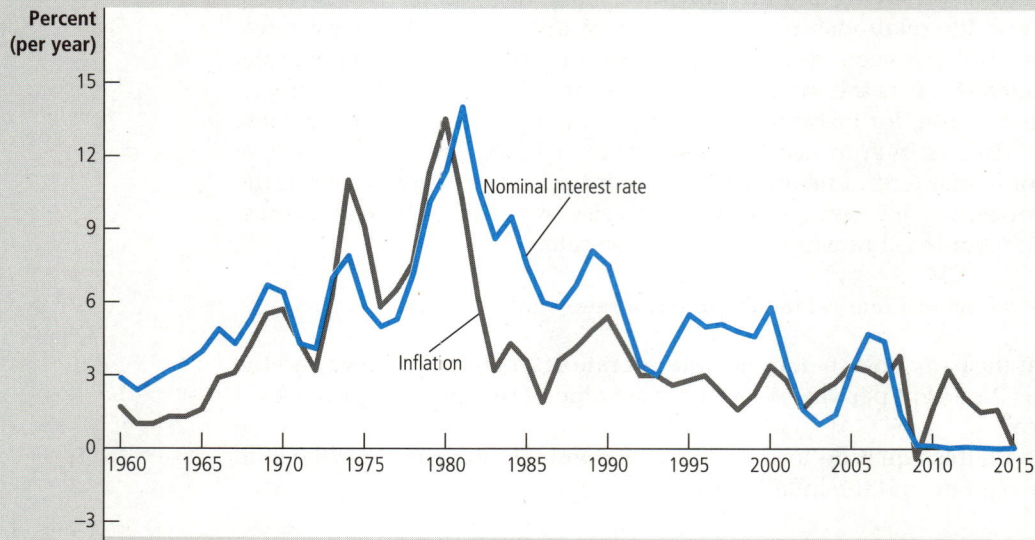

the U.S. economy since 1960. The close association between these two variables is clear. The nominal interest rate rose from the early 1960s through the 1970s because inflation was also rising during this time. Similarly, the nominal interest rate fell from the early 1980s through the 1990s because the Fed got inflation under control. In recent years, both the nominal interest rate and the inflation rate have been low by historical standards.

QuickQuiz *The government of a country increases the growth rate of the money supply from 5 percent per year to 50 percent per year. What happens to prices? What happens to nominal interest rates? Why might the government be doing this?*

30-2 The Costs of Inflation

In the late 1970s, when the U.S. inflation rate reached about 10 percent per year, inflation dominated debates over economic policy. And even though inflation has been low over the past 20 years, it remains a closely watched macroeconomic variable. One study found that *inflation* is the economic term mentioned most often in U.S. newspapers (ahead of second-place finisher *unemployment* and third-place finisher *productivity*).

Inflation is closely watched and widely discussed because it is thought to be a serious economic problem. But is that true? And if so, why?

30-2a A Fall in Purchasing Power? The Inflation Fallacy

If you ask the typical person why inflation is bad, he will tell you that the answer is obvious: Inflation robs him of the purchasing power of his hard-earned dollars. When prices rise, each dollar of income buys fewer goods and services. Thus, it might seem that inflation directly lowers living standards.

Yet further thought reveals a fallacy in this answer. When prices rise, buyers of goods and services pay more for what they buy. At the same time, however, sellers of goods and services get more for what they sell. Because most people earn their incomes by selling their services, such as their labor, inflation in incomes goes hand in hand with inflation in prices. Thus, *inflation does not in itself reduce people's real purchasing power*.

People believe the inflation fallacy because they do not appreciate the principle of monetary neutrality. A worker who receives an annual raise of 10 percent tends to view that raise as a reward for his own talent and effort. When an inflation rate of 6 percent reduces the real value of that raise to only 4 percent, the worker might feel that he has been cheated of what is rightfully his due. In fact, as we discussed in the chapter on production and growth, real incomes are determined by real variables, such as physical capital, human capital, natural resources, and the available production technology. Nominal incomes are determined by those factors and the overall price level. If the Fed were to lower the inflation rate from 6 percent to zero, our worker's annual raise would fall from 10 percent to 4 percent. He might feel less robbed by inflation, but his real income would not rise more quickly.

If nominal incomes tend to keep pace with rising prices, why then is inflation a problem? It turns out that there is no single answer to this question. Instead, economists have identified several costs of inflation. Each of these costs shows some way in which persistent growth in the money supply does, in fact, have some adverse effect on real variables.

30-2b Shoeleather Costs

As we have discussed, inflation is like a tax on the holders of money. The tax itself is not a cost to society: It is only a transfer of resources from households to the government. Yet most taxes give people an incentive to alter their behavior to avoid paying the tax, and this distortion of incentives causes deadweight losses for society as a whole. Like other taxes, the inflation tax also causes deadweight losses because people waste scarce resources trying to avoid it.

How can a person avoid paying the inflation tax? Because inflation erodes the real value of the money in your wallet, you can avoid the inflation tax by holding less money. One way to do this is to go to the bank more often. For example, rather than withdrawing $200 every four weeks, you might withdraw $50 once a week. By making more frequent trips to the bank, you can keep more of your wealth in your interest-bearing savings account and less in your wallet, where inflation erodes its value.

The cost of reducing your money holdings is called the **shoeleather cost** of inflation because making more frequent trips to the bank causes your shoes to wear out more quickly. Of course, this term is not to be taken literally: The actual cost of reducing your money holdings is not the wear and tear on your shoes but the time and convenience you must sacrifice to keep less money on hand than you would if there were no inflation.

The shoeleather costs of inflation may seem trivial. Indeed, they are in the U.S. economy, which has had only moderate inflation in recent years. But this cost is magnified in countries experiencing hyperinflation. Here is a description of one

shoeleather costs
the resources wasted when inflation encourages people to reduce their money holdings

person's experience in Bolivia during its hyperinflation (as reported in the August 13, 1985, issue of *The Wall Street Journal*):

> When Edgar Miranda gets his monthly teacher's pay of 25 million pesos, he hasn't a moment to lose. Every hour, pesos drop in value. So, while his wife rushes to market to lay in a month's supply of rice and noodles, he is off with the rest of the pesos to change them into black-market dollars.
>
> Mr. Miranda is practicing the First Rule of Survival amid the most out-of-control inflation in the world today. Bolivia is a case study of how runaway inflation undermines a society. Price increases are so huge that the figures build up almost beyond comprehension. In one six-month period, for example, prices soared at an annual rate of 38,000 percent. By official count, however, last year's inflation reached 2,000 percent, and this year's is expected to hit 8,000 percent—though other estimates range many times higher. In any event, Bolivia's rate dwarfs Israel's 370 percent and Argentina's 1,100 percent—two other cases of severe inflation.
>
> It is easier to comprehend what happens to the thirty-eight-year-old Mr. Miranda's pay if he doesn't quickly change it into dollars. The day he was paid 25 million pesos, a dollar cost 500,000 pesos. So he received $50. Just days later, with the rate at 900,000 pesos, he would have received $27.

As this story shows, the shoeleather costs of inflation can be substantial. With the high inflation rate, Mr. Miranda does not have the luxury of holding the local money as a store of value. Instead, he is forced to convert his pesos quickly into goods or into U.S. dollars, which offer a more stable store of value. The time and effort that Mr. Miranda expends to reduce his money holdings are a waste of resources. If the monetary authority pursued a low-inflation policy, Mr. Miranda would be happy to hold pesos, and he could put his time and effort to more productive use. In fact, shortly after this article was written, the Bolivian inflation rate was reduced substantially with a more restrictive monetary policy.

30-2c   Menu Costs

Most firms do not change the prices of their products every day. Instead, firms often announce prices and leave them unchanged for weeks, months, or even years. One survey found that the typical U.S. firm changes its prices about once a year.

menu costs
the costs of changing prices

Firms change prices infrequently because there are costs to changing prices. Costs of price adjustment are called **menu costs**, a term derived from a restaurant's cost of printing a new menu. Menu costs include the costs of deciding on new prices, printing new price lists and catalogs, sending these new price lists and catalogs to dealers and customers, advertising the new prices, and even dealing with customer annoyance over price changes.

Inflation increases the menu costs that firms must bear. In the current U.S. economy, with its low inflation rate, annual price adjustment is an appropriate business strategy for many firms. But when high inflation makes firms' costs rise rapidly, annual price adjustment is impractical. During hyperinflations, for example, firms must change their prices daily or even more often just to keep up with all the other prices in the economy.

30-2d   Relative-Price Variability and the Misallocation of Resources

Suppose that the Eatabit Eatery prints a new menu with new prices every January and then leaves its prices unchanged for the rest of the year. If there is no inflation, Eatabit's relative prices—the prices of its meals compared to other prices in the economy—would be constant over the course of the year. By contrast, if the inflation rate is 12 percent per year, Eatabit's relative prices will automatically fall by 1 percent each month. The restaurant's relative prices will be high in the early months of the year, just after it has printed a new menu, and low in the later months. And the higher the inflation rate, the greater is this automatic variability. Thus, because prices change only once in a while, inflation causes relative prices to vary more than they otherwise would.

Why does this matter? The reason is that market economies rely on relative prices to allocate scarce resources. Consumers decide what to buy by comparing the quality and prices of various goods and services. Through these decisions, they determine how the scarce factors of production are allocated among industries and firms. When inflation distorts relative prices, consumer decisions are distorted and markets are less able to allocate resources to their best use.

30-2e Inflation-Induced Tax Distortions

Almost all taxes distort incentives, cause people to alter their behavior, and lead to a less efficient allocation of the economy's resources. Many taxes, however, become even more problematic in the presence of inflation. The reason is that lawmakers often fail to take inflation into account when writing the tax laws. Economists who have studied the tax code conclude that inflation tends to raise the tax burden on income earned from savings.

One example of how inflation discourages saving is the tax treatment of *capital gains*—the profits made by selling an asset for more than its purchase price. Suppose that in 1988 you used some of your savings to buy stock in IBM for $30 and that in 2016 you sold the stock for $130. According to the tax law, you have earned a capital gain of $100, which you must include in your income when computing how much income tax you owe. But because the overall price level doubled from 1988 to 2016, the $30 you invested in 1988 is equivalent (in terms of purchasing power) to $60 in 2016. When you sell your stock for $130, you have a real gain (an increase in purchasing power) of only $70. The tax code, however, does not take account of inflation and assesses you a tax on a gain of $100. Thus, inflation exaggerates the size of capital gains and inadvertently increases the tax burden on this type of income.

Another example is the tax treatment of interest income. The income tax treats the *nominal* interest earned on savings as income, even though part of the nominal interest rate merely compensates for inflation. To see the effects of this policy, consider the numerical example in Table 1. The table compares two economies, both of which tax interest income at a rate of 25 percent. In Economy A, inflation is zero and the nominal and real interest rates are both 4 percent. In this case, the 25 percent tax on interest income reduces the real interest rate from 4 percent to 3 percent. In Economy B, the real interest rate is again 4 percent but the inflation rate is 8 percent. As a result of the Fisher effect, the nominal interest rate is 12 percent. Because the income tax treats this entire 12 percent interest as income, the government takes 25 percent of it, leaving an after-tax nominal interest rate of only 9 percent and an after-tax real interest rate of only 1 percent. In this case, the 25 percent tax on interest income reduces the real interest rate from 4 percent to 1 percent. Because the after-tax real interest rate provides the incentive to save, saving is much less attractive in the economy with inflation (Economy B) than in the economy with stable prices (Economy A).

The taxes on nominal capital gains and on nominal interest income are two examples of how the tax code interacts with inflation. There are many others. Because of these inflation-induced tax changes, higher inflation tends to

TABLE 1

How Inflation Raises the Tax Burden on Saving
In the presence of zero inflation, a 25 percent tax on interest income reduces the real interest rate from 4 percent to 3 percent. In the presence of 8 percent inflation, the same tax reduces the real interest rate from 4 percent to 1 percent.

	Economy A (price stability)	Economy B (inflation)
Real interest rate	4%	4%
Inflation rate	0	8
Nominal interest rate (real interest rate + inflation rate)	4	12
Reduced interest due to 25 percent tax (0.25 × nominal interest rate)	1	3
After-tax nominal interest rate (0.75 × nominal interest rate)	3	9
After-tax real interest rate (after-tax nominal interest rate − inflation rate)	3	1

discourage people from saving. Recall that the economy's saving provides the resources for investment, which in turn is a key ingredient to long-run economic growth. Thus, when inflation raises the tax burden on saving, it tends to depress the economy's long-run growth rate. There is, however, no consensus among economists about the size of this effect.

One solution to this problem, other than eliminating inflation, is to index the tax system. That is, the tax laws could be rewritten to take account of the effects of inflation. In the case of capital gains, for example, the tax code could adjust the purchase price using a price index and assess the tax only on the real gain. In the case of interest income, the government could tax only real interest income by excluding that portion of the interest income that merely compensates for inflation. To some extent, the tax laws have moved in the direction of indexation. For example, the income levels at which income tax rates change are adjusted automatically each year based on changes in the consumer price index. Yet many other aspects of the tax laws—such as the tax treatment of capital gains and interest income—are not indexed.

In an ideal world, the tax laws would be written so that inflation would not alter anyone's real tax liability. In the real world, however, tax laws are far from perfect. More complete indexation would probably be desirable, but it would further complicate a tax code that many people already consider too complex.

30-2f Confusion and Inconvenience

Imagine that we took a poll and asked people the following question: "This year the yard is 36 inches. How long do you think it should be next year?" Assuming we could get people to take us seriously, they would tell us that the yard should stay the same length—36 inches. Anything else would just complicate life needlessly.

What does this finding have to do with inflation? Recall that money, as the economy's unit of account, is what we use to quote prices and record debts. In other words, money is the yardstick with which we measure economic transactions. The job of the Federal Reserve is a bit like the job of the Bureau of

Standards—to ensure the reliability of a commonly used unit of measurement. When the Fed increases the money supply and creates inflation, it erodes the real value of the unit of account.

It is difficult to judge the costs of the confusion and inconvenience that arise from inflation. Earlier, we discussed how the tax code incorrectly measures real incomes in the presence of inflation. Similarly, accountants incorrectly measure firms' earnings when prices are rising over time. Because inflation causes dollars at different times to have different real values, computing a firm's profit—the difference between its revenue and costs—is more complicated in an economy with inflation. Therefore, to some extent, inflation makes investors less able to sort successful from unsuccessful firms, which in turn impedes financial markets in their role of allocating the economy's saving to alternative types of investment.

30-2g A Special Cost of Unexpected Inflation: Arbitrary Redistributions of Wealth

So far, the costs of inflation we have discussed occur even if inflation is steady and predictable. Inflation has an additional cost, however, when it comes as a surprise. Unexpected inflation redistributes wealth among the population in a way that has nothing to do with either merit or need. These redistributions occur because many loans in the economy are specified in terms of the unit of account—money.

Consider an example. Suppose that Sam Student takes out a $20,000 loan at a 7 percent interest rate from Bigbank to attend college. In 10 years, the loan will come due. After his debt has compounded for 10 years at 7 percent, Sam will owe Bigbank $40,000. The real value of this debt will depend on inflation over the decade. If Sam is lucky, the economy will have a hyperinflation. In this case, wages and prices will rise so high that Sam will be able to pay the $40,000 debt out of pocket change. By contrast, if the economy goes through a major deflation, then wages and prices will fall, and Sam will find the $40,000 debt a greater burden than he anticipated.

This example shows that unexpected changes in prices redistribute wealth among debtors and creditors. A hyperinflation enriches Sam at the expense of Bigbank because it diminishes the real value of the debt; Sam can repay the loan in dollars that are less valuable than he anticipated. Deflation enriches Bigbank at Sam's expense because it increases the real value of the debt; in this case, Sam has to repay the loan in dollars that are more valuable than he anticipated. If inflation were predictable, then Bigbank and Sam could take inflation into account when setting the nominal interest rate. (Recall the Fisher effect.) But if inflation is hard to predict, it imposes risk on Sam and Bigbank that both would prefer to avoid.

This cost of unexpected inflation is important to consider together with another fact: Inflation is especially volatile and uncertain when the average rate of inflation is high. This is seen most simply by examining the experience of different countries. Countries with low average inflation, such as Germany in the late 20th century, tend to have stable inflation. Countries with high average inflation, such as many countries in Latin America, tend to have unstable inflation. There are no known examples of economies with high, stable inflation. This relationship between the level and volatility of inflation points to another cost of inflation. If a country pursues a high-inflation monetary policy, it will have to bear not only the costs of high expected inflation but also the arbitrary redistributions of wealth associated with unexpected inflation.

30-2h Inflation Is Bad, but Deflation May Be Worse

In recent U.S. history, inflation has been the norm. But the level of prices has fallen at times, such as during the late 19th century and early 1930s. From 1998 to 2012, Japan experienced a 4-percent decline in its overall price level. So as we conclude our discussion of the costs of inflation, we should briefly consider the costs of deflation as well.

Some economists have suggested that a small and predictable amount of deflation may be desirable. Milton Friedman pointed out that deflation would lower the nominal interest rate (via the Fisher effect) and that a lower nominal interest rate would reduce the cost of holding money. The shoeleather costs of holding money would, he argued, be minimized by a nominal interest rate close to zero, which in turn would require deflation equal to the real interest rate. This prescription for moderate deflation is called the *Friedman rule*.

Yet there are also costs of deflation. Some of these mirror the costs of inflation. For example, just as a rising price level induces menu costs and relative-price variability, so does a falling price level. Moreover, in practice, deflation is rarely as steady and predictable as Friedman recommended. More often, it comes as a surprise, resulting in the redistribution of wealth toward creditors and away from debtors. Because debtors are often poorer, these redistributions in wealth are particularly painful.

Perhaps most important, deflation often arises because of broader macroeconomic difficulties. As we will see in future chapters, falling prices result when some event, such as a monetary contraction, reduces the overall demand for goods and services in the economy. This fall in aggregate demand can lead to falling incomes and rising unemployment. In other words, deflation is often a symptom of deeper economic problems.

CASE STUDY

THE WIZARD OF OZ AND THE FREE-SILVER DEBATE

As a child, you probably saw the movie *The Wizard of Oz*, based on a children's book written in 1900. The movie and book tell the story of a young girl, Dorothy, who finds herself lost in a strange land far from home. You probably did not know, however, that some scholars believe that the story is actually an allegory about U.S. monetary policy in the late 19th century.

From 1880 to 1896, the price level in the U.S. economy fell by 23 percent. Because this event was unanticipated, it led to a major redistribution of wealth. Most farmers in the western part of the country were debtors. Their creditors were the bankers in the east. When the price level fell, it caused the real value of these debts to rise, which enriched the banks at the expense of the farmers.

According to Populist politicians of the time, the solution to the farmers' problem was the free coinage of silver. During this period, the United States was operating with a gold standard. The quantity of gold determined the money supply and, thereby, the price level. The free-silver advocates wanted silver, as well as gold, to be used as money. If adopted, this proposal would have increased the money supply, pushed up the price level, and reduced the real burden of the farmers' debts.

The debate over silver was heated, and it was central to the politics of the 1890s. A common election slogan of the Populists was "We Are Mortgaged. All but Our Votes." One prominent advocate of free silver was William Jennings Bryan, the Democratic nominee for president in 1896. He is remembered in part for a speech at the Democratic Party's nominating convention in which he said, "You shall not press down upon the brow of labor this crown of thorns. You shall not crucify mankind upon a cross of gold." Rarely since then have politicians waxed so poetic about alternative approaches to monetary policy. Nonetheless, Bryan lost the election to Republican William McKinley, and the United States remained on the gold standard.

L. Frank Baum, author of the book *The Wonderful Wizard of Oz*, was a midwestern journalist. When he sat down to write a story for children, he made the characters represent protagonists in the major political battle of his time. Here is how economic historian Hugh Rockoff, writing in the *Journal of Political Economy* in 1990, interprets the story:

DOROTHY:	Traditional American values
TOTO:	Prohibitionist party, also called the Teetotalers
SCARECROW:	Farmers
TIN WOODSMAN:	Industrial workers
COWARDLY LION:	William Jennings Bryan
MUNCHKINS:	Citizens of the East
WICKED WITCH OF THE EAST:	Grover Cleveland
WICKED WITCH OF THE WEST:	William McKinley
WIZARD:	Marcus Alonzo Hanna, chairman of the Republican Party
OZ:	Abbreviation for ounce of gold
YELLOW BRICK ROAD:	Gold standard

At the end of Baum's story, Dorothy does find her way home, but it is not by just following the yellow brick road. After a long and perilous journey, she learns that the wizard is incapable of helping her or her friends. Instead, Dorothy finally discovers the magical power of her *silver* slippers. (When the book was made into a movie in 1939, Dorothy's slippers were changed from silver to ruby. The Hollywood filmmakers were more interested in showing off the new technology of Technicolor than in telling a story about 19th-century monetary policy.)

The Populists lost the debate over the free coinage of silver, but they eventually got the monetary expansion and inflation that they wanted. In 1898, prospectors discovered gold near the Klondike River in the Canadian Yukon. Increased supplies of gold also arrived from the mines of South Africa. As a result, the money supply and the price level started to rise in the United States and in other countries operating on the gold standard. Within 15 years, prices in the United States were back to the levels that had prevailed in the 1880s, and farmers were better able to handle their debts. ●

An early debate over monetary policy

QuickQuiz   *List and describe six costs of inflation.*

30-3 Conclusion

This chapter discussed the causes and costs of inflation. The primary cause of inflation is growth in the quantity of money. When the central bank creates money in large quantities, the value of money falls quickly. To maintain stable prices, the central bank must maintain strict control over the money supply.

The costs of inflation are more subtle. They include shoeleather costs, menu costs, increased variability of relative prices, unintended changes in tax liabilities, confusion and inconvenience, and arbitrary redistributions of wealth. Are these costs, in total, large or small? All economists agree that they become huge during hyperinflation. But during periods of moderate inflation—when prices rise by less than 10 percent per year—the size of these costs is more open to debate.

This chapter presented many of the most important lessons about inflation, but the analysis is incomplete. When the central bank reduces the rate of money growth, prices rise less rapidly, as the quantity theory suggests. Yet as the economy makes the transition to the lower inflation rate, the change in monetary policy will likely disrupt production and employment. That is, even though monetary policy is neutral in the long run, it has profound effects on real variables in the short run. Later in this book we will examine the reasons for short-run monetary non-neutrality to enhance our understanding of the causes and effects of inflation.

CHAPTER QuickQuiz

1. The classical principle of monetary neutrality states that changes in the money supply do not influence _____ variables and is thought most applicable in the _____ run.
   a. nominal, short
   b. nominal, long
   c. real, short
   d. real, long

2. If nominal GDP is $400, real GDP is $200, and the money supply is $100, then
   a. the price level is ½, and velocity is 2.
   b. the price level is ½, and velocity is 4.
   c. the price level is 2, and velocity is 2.
   d. the price level is 2, and velocity is 4.

3. According to the quantity theory of money, which variable in the quantity equation is most stable over long periods of time?
   a. money
   b. velocity
   c. price level
   d. output

4. Hyperinflations occur when the government runs a large budget _____, which the central bank finances with a substantial monetary _____.
   a. deficit, contraction
   b. deficit, expansion
   c. surplus, contraction
   d. surplus, expansion

5. According to the quantity theory of money and the Fisher effect, if the central bank increases the rate of money growth,
   a. inflation and the nominal interest rate both increase.
   b. inflation and the real interest rate both increase.
   c. the nominal interest rate and the real interest rate both increase.
   d. inflation, the real interest rate, and the nominal interest rate all increase.

6. If an economy always has inflation of 10 percent per year, which of the following costs of inflation will it NOT suffer?
   a. shoeleather costs from reduced holdings of money
   b. menu costs from more frequent price adjustment
   c. distortions from the taxation of nominal capital gains
   d. arbitrary redistributions between debtors and creditors

SUMMARY

- The overall level of prices in an economy adjusts to bring money supply and money demand into balance. When the central bank increases the supply of money, it causes the price level to rise. Persistent growth in the quantity of money supplied leads to continuing inflation.

- The principle of monetary neutrality asserts that changes in the quantity of money influence nominal variables but not real variables. Most economists believe that monetary neutrality approximately describes the behavior of the economy in the long run.

- A government can pay for some of its spending simply by printing money. When countries rely heavily on this "inflation tax," the result is hyperinflation.

- One application of the principle of monetary neutrality is the Fisher effect. According to the Fisher effect, when the inflation rate rises, the nominal interest rate rises by the same amount so that the real interest rate remains the same.

- Many people think that inflation makes them poorer because it raises the cost of what they buy. This view is a fallacy, however, because inflation also raises nominal incomes.

- Economists have identified six costs of inflation: shoeleather costs associated with reduced money holdings, menu costs associated with more frequent adjustment of prices, increased variability of relative prices, unintended changes in tax liabilities due to nonindexation of the tax code, confusion and inconvenience resulting from a changing unit of account, and arbitrary redistributions of wealth between debtors and creditors. Many of these costs are large during hyperinflation, but the size of these costs for moderate inflation is less clear.

KEY CONCEPTS

quantity theory of money, p. 631
nominal variables, p. 633
real variables, p. 633
classical dichotomy, p. 633

monetary neutrality, p. 634
velocity of money, p. 634
quantity equation, p. 635
inflation tax, p. 637

Fisher effect, p. 639
shoeleather costs, p. 641
menu costs, p. 642

QUESTIONS FOR REVIEW

1. Explain how an increase in the price level affects the real value of money.

2. According to the quantity theory of money, what is the effect of an increase in the quantity of money?

3. Explain the difference between nominal and real variables and give two examples of each. According to the principle of monetary neutrality, which variables are affected by changes in the quantity of money?

4. In what sense is inflation like a tax? How does thinking about inflation as a tax help explain hyperinflation?

5. According to the Fisher effect, how does an increase in the inflation rate affect the real interest rate and the nominal interest rate?

6. What are the costs of inflation? Which of these costs do you think are most important for the U.S. economy?

7. If inflation is less than expected, who benefits— debtors or creditors? Explain.

PROBLEMS AND APPLICATIONS

1. Suppose that this year's money supply is $500 billion, nominal GDP is $10 trillion, and real GDP is $5 trillion.
   a. What is the price level? What is the velocity of money?
   b. Suppose that velocity is constant and the economy's output of goods and services rises by 5 percent each year. What will happen to nominal GDP and the price level next year if the Fed keeps the money supply constant?
   c. What money supply should the Fed set next year if it wants to keep the price level stable?
   d. What money supply should the Fed set next year if it wants inflation of 10 percent?

139

2. Suppose that changes in bank regulations expand the availability of credit cards so that people need to hold less cash.
   a. How does this event affect the demand for money?
   b. If the Fed does not respond to this event, what will happen to the price level?
   c. If the Fed wants to keep the price level stable, what should it do?

3. It is sometimes suggested that the Federal Reserve should try to achieve zero inflation. If we assume that velocity is constant, does this zero-inflation goal require that the rate of money growth equal zero? If yes, explain why. If no, explain what the rate of money growth should equal.

4. Suppose that a country's inflation rate increases sharply. What happens to the inflation tax on the holders of money? Why is wealth that is held in savings accounts *not* subject to a change in the inflation tax? Can you think of any way holders of savings accounts are hurt by the increase in the inflation rate?

5. Let's consider the effects of inflation in an economy composed of only two people: Bob, a bean farmer, and Rita, a rice farmer. Bob and Rita both always consume equal amounts of rice and beans. In 2016, the price of beans was $1 and the price of rice was $3.
   a. Suppose that in 2017 the price of beans was $2 and the price of rice was $6. What was inflation? Was Bob better off, worse off, or unaffected by the changes in prices? What about Rita?
   b. Now suppose that in 2017 the price of beans was $2 and the price of rice was $4. What was inflation? Was Bob better off, worse off, or unaffected by the changes in prices? What about Rita?
   c. Finally, suppose that in 2017 the price of beans was $2 and the price of rice was $1.50. What was inflation? Was Bob better off, worse off, or unaffected by the changes in prices? What about Rita?

   d. What matters more to Bob and Rita—the overall inflation rate or the relative price of rice and beans?

6. If the tax rate is 40 percent, compute the before-tax real interest rate and the after-tax real interest rate in each of the following cases.
   a. The nominal interest rate is 10 percent, and the inflation rate is 5 percent.
   b. The nominal interest rate is 6 percent, and the inflation rate is 2 percent.
   c. The nominal interest rate is 4 percent, and the inflation rate is 1 percent.

7. Recall that money serves three functions in the economy. What are those functions? How does inflation affect the ability of money to serve each of these functions?

8. Suppose that people expect inflation to equal 3 percent, but in fact, prices rise by 5 percent. Describe how this unexpectedly high inflation rate would help or hurt the following:
   a. the government
   b. a homeowner with a fixed-rate mortgage
   c. a union worker in the second year of a labor contract
   d. a college that has invested some of its endowment in government bonds

9. Explain whether the following statements are true, false, or uncertain.
   a. "Inflation hurts borrowers and helps lenders, because borrowers must pay a higher rate of interest."
   b. "If prices change in a way that leaves the overall price level unchanged, then no one is made better or worse off."
   c. "Inflation does not reduce the purchasing power of most workers."

To find additional study resources, visit cengagebrain.com, and search for "Mankiw."

PART XII

Short-Run Economic Fluctuations

Aggregate Demand and Aggregate Supply

Economic activity fluctuates from year to year. In most years, the production of goods and services rises. Because of increases in the labor force, increases in the capital stock, and advances in technological knowledge, the economy can produce more and more over time. This growth allows everyone to enjoy a higher standard of living. On average, over the past half century, the production of the U.S. economy as measured by real GDP has grown by about 3 percent per year.

In some years, however, instead of expanding, the economy contracts. Firms find themselves unable to sell all the goods and services they have to offer, so

recession
a period of declining
real incomes and rising
unemployment

depression
a severe recession

they reduce production. Workers are laid off, unemployment becomes widespread, and factories are left idle. With the economy producing fewer goods and services, real GDP and other measures of income decline. Such a period of falling incomes and rising unemployment is called a **recession** if it is relatively mild and a **depression** if it is more severe.

An example of such a downturn occurred in 2008 and 2009. From the fourth quarter of 2007 to the second quarter of 2009, real GDP for the U.S. economy fell by 4.2 percent. The rate of unemployment rose from 4.4 percent in May 2007 to 10.0 percent in October 2009—the highest level in more than a quarter century. Not surprisingly, students graduating during this time found that desirable jobs were hard to come by.

What causes short-run fluctuations in economic activity? What, if anything, can public policy do to prevent periods of falling incomes and rising unemployment? When recessions and depressions occur, how can policymakers reduce their length and severity? These are the questions we take up now.

The variables that we study are largely those we have seen in previous chapters. They include GDP, unemployment, interest rates, and the price level. Also familiar are the policy instruments of government spending, taxes, and the money supply. What differs from our earlier analysis is the time horizon. So far, our goal has been to explain the behavior of these variables in the long run. Our goal now is to explain their short-run deviations from long-run trends. In other words, instead of focusing on the forces that explain economic growth from generation to generation, we are now interested in the forces that explain economic fluctuations from year to year.

There is some debate among economists about how best to analyze short-run fluctuations, but most economists use the *model of aggregate demand and aggregate supply*. Learning how to use this model for analyzing the short-run effects of various events and policies is the primary task ahead. This chapter introduces the model's two pieces: the aggregate-demand curve and the aggregate-supply curve. Before turning to the model, however, let's look at some of the key facts that describe the ups and downs of the economy.

33-1 Three Key Facts about Economic Fluctuations

Short-run fluctuations in economic activity have occurred in all countries throughout history. As a starting point for understanding these year-to-year fluctuations, let's discuss some of their most important properties.

33-1a Fact 1: Economic Fluctuations Are Irregular and Unpredictable

Fluctuations in the economy are often called *the business cycle*. As this term suggests, economic fluctuations correspond to changes in business conditions. When real GDP grows rapidly, business is good. During such periods of economic expansion, most firms find that customers are plentiful and that profits are growing. When real GDP falls during recessions, businesses have trouble. During such periods of economic contraction, most firms experience declining sales and dwindling profits.

The term *business cycle* is somewhat misleading because it suggests that economic fluctuations follow a regular, predictable pattern. In fact, economic fluctuations are not at all regular, and they are almost impossible to predict with much accuracy. Panel (a) of Figure 1 shows the real GDP of the

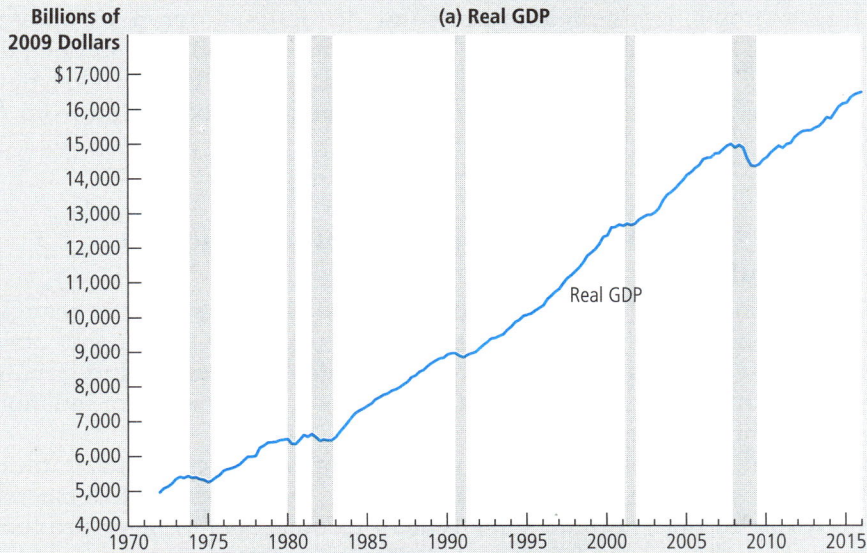

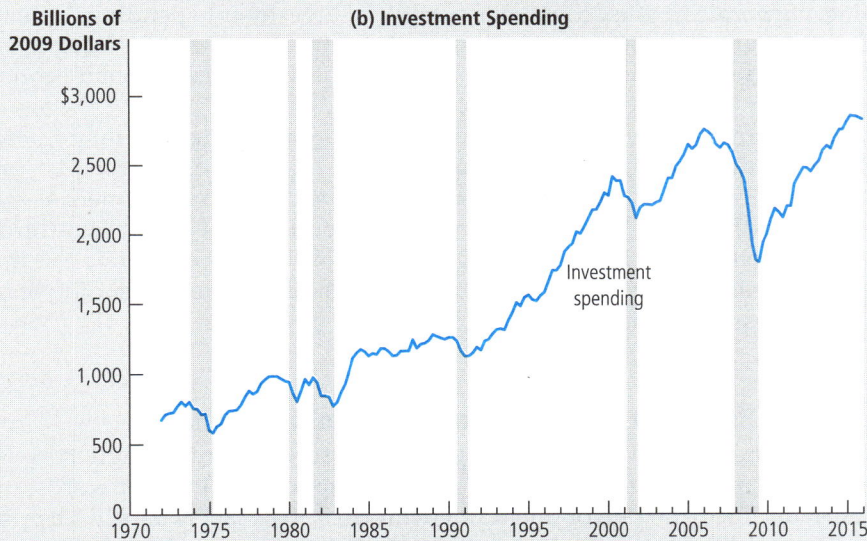

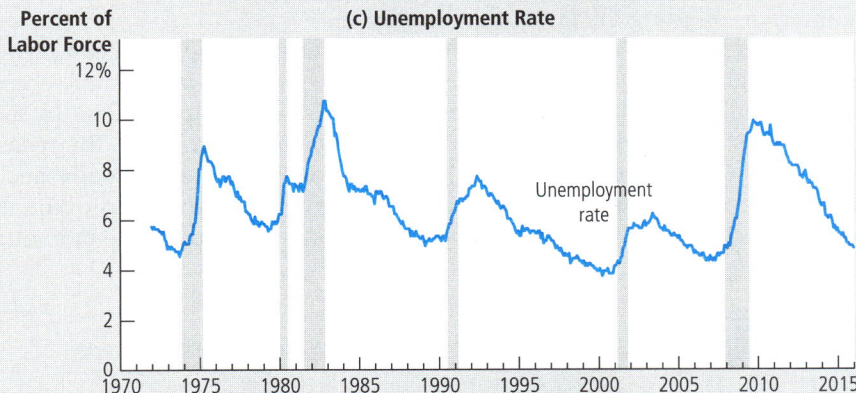

FIGURE 1

A Look at Short-Run Economic Fluctuations
This figure shows real GDP in panel (a), investment spending in panel (b), and unemployment in panel (c) for the U.S. economy. Recessions are shown as the shaded areas. Notice that real GDP and investment spending decline during recessions, while unemployment rises.

Source: U.S. Department of Commerce; U.S. Department of Labor.

U.S. economy since 1972. The shaded areas represent times of recession. As the figure shows, recessions do not come at regular intervals. Sometimes recessions are close together, such as the recessions of 1980 and 1982. Sometimes the economy goes many years without a recession. The longest period in U.S. history without a recession was the economic expansion from 1991 to 2001.

33-1b Fact 2: Most Macroeconomic Quantities Fluctuate Together

Real GDP is the variable most commonly used to monitor short-run changes in the economy because it is the most comprehensive measure of economic activity. Real GDP measures the value of all final goods and services produced within a given period of time. It also measures the total income (adjusted for inflation) of everyone in the economy.

It turns out, however, that for monitoring short-run fluctuations, it does not really matter which measure of economic activity one looks at. Most macroeconomic variables that measure some type of income, spending, or production fluctuate closely together. When real GDP falls in a recession, so do personal income, corporate profits, consumer spending, investment spending, industrial production, retail sales, home sales, auto sales, and so on. Because recessions are economy-wide phenomena, they show up in many sources of macroeconomic data.

Although many macroeconomic variables fluctuate together, they fluctuate by different amounts. In particular, as panel (b) of Figure 1 shows, investment spending varies greatly over the business cycle. Even though investment averages about one-sixth of GDP, declines in investment account for about two-thirds of the declines in GDP during recessions. In other words, when economic conditions deteriorate, much of the decline is attributable to reductions in spending on new factories, housing, and inventories.

33-1c Fact 3: As Output Falls, Unemployment Rises

Changes in the economy's output of goods and services are strongly correlated with changes in the economy's utilization of its labor force. In other words, when real GDP declines, the rate of unemployment rises. This fact is hardly surprising: When firms choose to produce a smaller quantity of goods and services, they lay off workers, expanding the pool of unemployed.

Panel (c) of Figure 1 shows the unemployment rate in the U.S. economy since 1972. Once again, the shaded areas in the figure indicate periods of recession. The figure shows clearly the impact of recessions on unemployment. In each of the recessions, the unemployment rate rises substantially. When the recession ends and real GDP starts to expand, the unemployment rate gradually declines. Because there are always some workers between jobs, the unemployment rate never approaches zero. Instead, it fluctuates around its natural rate of about 5 or 6 percent.

QuickQuiz *List and discuss three key facts about economic fluctuations.*

"You're fired. Pass it on."

© ROBERT MANKOFF/THE NEW YORKER COLLECTION/ WWW.CARTOONBANK.COM

33-2 Explaining Short-Run Economic Fluctuations

Describing what happens to economies as they fluctuate over time is easy. Explaining what causes these fluctuations is more difficult. Indeed, compared to the topics we have studied in previous chapters, the theory of economic fluctuations remains controversial. In this chapter, we begin to develop the model that most economists use to explain short-run fluctuations in economic activity.

33-2a The Assumptions of Classical Economics

In previous chapters, we developed theories to explain what determines most important macroeconomic variables in the long run. Chapter 25 explained the level and growth of productivity and real GDP. Chapters 26 and 27 explained how the financial system works and how the real interest rate adjusts to balance saving and investment. Chapter 28 explained why there is always some unemployment in the economy. Chapters 29 and 30 explained the monetary system and how changes in the money supply affect the price level, the inflation rate, and the nominal interest rate.

All of this previous analysis was based on two related ideas: the classical dichotomy and monetary neutrality. Recall that the classical dichotomy is the separation of variables into real variables (those that measure quantities or relative prices) and nominal variables (those measured in terms of money). According to classical macroeconomic theory, changes in the money supply affect nominal variables but not real variables. As a result of this monetary neutrality, Chapters 25 through 28 were able to examine the determinants of real variables (real GDP, the real interest rate, and unemployment) without introducing nominal variables (the money supply and the price level).

In a sense, money does not matter in a classical world. If the quantity of money in the economy were to double, everything would cost twice as much, and everyone's income would be twice as high. But so what? The change would be *nominal* (by the standard meaning of "nearly insignificant"). The things that people *really* care about—whether they have a job, how many goods and services they can afford, and so on—would be exactly the same.

This classical view is sometimes described by the saying, "Money is a veil." That is, nominal variables may be the first things we see when we observe an economy because economic variables are often expressed in units of money. But what's important are the real variables and the economic forces that determine them. According to classical theory, to understand these real variables, we need to look behind the veil.

33-2b The Reality of Short-Run Fluctuations

Do these assumptions of classical macroeconomic theory apply to the world in which we live? The answer to this question is of central importance to understanding how the economy works. *Most economists believe that classical theory describes the world in the long run but not in the short run.*

Consider again the impact of money on the economy. Most economists believe that, beyond a period of several years, changes in the money supply affect prices and other nominal variables but do not affect real GDP, unemployment, and other real variables—just as classical theory says. When studying year-to-year changes in the economy, however, the assumption of monetary neutrality is no longer appropriate. In the short run, real and nominal variables are highly intertwined, and changes in the money supply can temporarily push real GDP away from its long-run trend.

Even the classical economists themselves, such as David Hume, realized that classical economic theory did not hold in the short run. From his vantage point in 18th-century England, Hume observed that when the money supply expanded after gold discoveries, it took some time for prices to rise, and in the meantime, the economy enjoyed higher employment and production.

To understand how the economy works in the short run, we need a new model. This new model can be built using many of the tools we developed in previous chapters, but it must abandon the classical dichotomy and the neutrality of money. We can no longer separate our analysis of real variables such as output and employment from our analysis of nominal variables such as money and the price level. Our new model focuses on how real and nominal variables interact.

model of aggregate demand and aggregate supply
the model that most economists use to explain short-run fluctuations in economic activity around its long-run trend

33-2c The Model of Aggregate Demand and Aggregate Supply

Our model of short-run economic fluctuations focuses on the behavior of two variables. The first variable is the economy's output of goods and services, as measured by real GDP. The second is the average level of prices, as measured by the CPI or the GDP deflator. Notice that output is a real variable, whereas the price level is a nominal variable. By focusing on the relationship between these two variables, we are departing from the classical assumption that real and nominal variables can be studied separately.

aggregate-demand curve
a curve that shows the quantity of goods and services that households, firms, the government, and customers abroad want to buy at each price level

We analyze fluctuations in the economy as a whole with the **model of aggregate demand and aggregate supply**, which is illustrated in Figure 2. On the vertical axis is the overall price level in the economy. On the horizontal axis is the overall quantity of goods and services produced in the economy. The **aggregate-demand curve** shows the quantity of goods and services that households, firms,

FIGURE 2

Aggregate Demand and Aggregate Supply
Economists use the model of aggregate demand and aggregate supply to analyze economic fluctuations. On the vertical axis is the overall level of prices. On the horizontal axis is the economy's total output of goods and services. Output and the price level adjust to the point at which the aggregate-supply and aggregate-demand curves intersect.

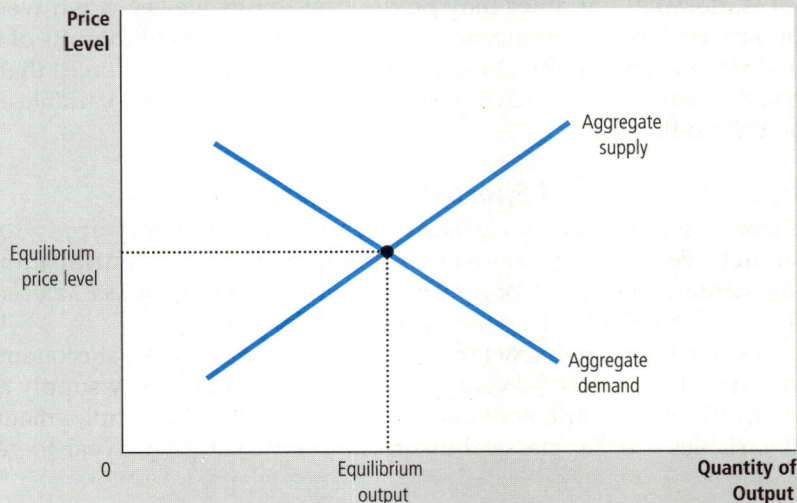

the government, and customers abroad want to buy at each price level. The **aggregate-supply curve** shows the quantity of goods and services that firms produce and sell at each price level. According to this model, the price level and the quantity of output adjust to bring aggregate demand and aggregate supply into balance.

It is tempting to view the model of aggregate demand and aggregate supply as nothing more than a large version of the model of market demand and market supply introduced in Chapter 4. But in fact, this model is quite different. When we consider demand and supply in a specific market—ice cream, for instance—the behavior of buyers and sellers depends on the ability of resources to move from one market to another. When the price of ice cream rises, the quantity demanded falls because buyers will use their incomes to buy products other than ice cream. Similarly, a higher price of ice cream raises the quantity supplied because firms that produce ice cream can increase production by hiring workers away from other parts of the economy. This *microeconomic* substitution from one market to another is impossible for the economy as a whole. After all, the quantity that our model is trying to explain—real GDP—measures the *total* quantity of goods and services produced by *all* firms in *all* markets. To understand why the aggregate-demand curve slopes downward and why the aggregate-supply curve slopes upward, we need a *macroeconomic* theory that explains the total quantity of goods and services demanded and the total quantity of goods and services supplied. Developing such a theory is our next task.

Quick Quiz *How does the economy's behavior in the short run differ from its behavior in the long run? • Draw the model of aggregate demand and aggregate supply. What variables are on the two axes?*

33-3 The Aggregate-Demand Curve

The aggregate-demand curve tells us the quantity of all goods and services demanded in the economy at any given price level. As Figure 3 illustrates, the aggregate-demand curve slopes downward. This means that, other things being equal, a decrease in the economy's overall level of prices (from, say, P_1 to P_2) raises the quantity of goods and services demanded (from Y_1 to Y_2). Conversely, an increase in the price level reduces the quantity of goods and services demanded.

33-3a Why the Aggregate-Demand Curve Slopes Downward
Why does a change in the price level move the quantity of goods and services demanded in the opposite direction? To answer this question, it is useful to recall that an economy's GDP (which we denote as Y) is the sum of its consumption (C), investment (I), government purchases (G), and net exports (NX):

$$Y = C + I + G + NX.$$

Each of these four components contributes to the aggregate demand for goods and services. For now, we assume that government spending is fixed by policy. The other three components of spending—consumption, investment, and net exports—depend on economic conditions and, in particular, on the price level. Therefore, to understand the downward slope of the aggregate-demand curve, we must examine how the price level affects the quantity of goods and services demanded for consumption, investment, and net exports.

aggregate-supply curve
a curve that shows the quantity of goods and services that firms choose to produce and sell at each price level

FIGURE 3

The Aggregate-Demand Curve
A fall in the price level from P_1 to P_2 increases the quantity of goods and services demanded from Y_1 to Y_2. There are three reasons for this negative relationship. As the price level falls, real wealth rises, interest rates fall, and the exchange rate depreciates. These effects stimulate spending on consumption, investment, and net exports. Increased spending on any or all of these components of output means a larger quantity of goods and services demanded.

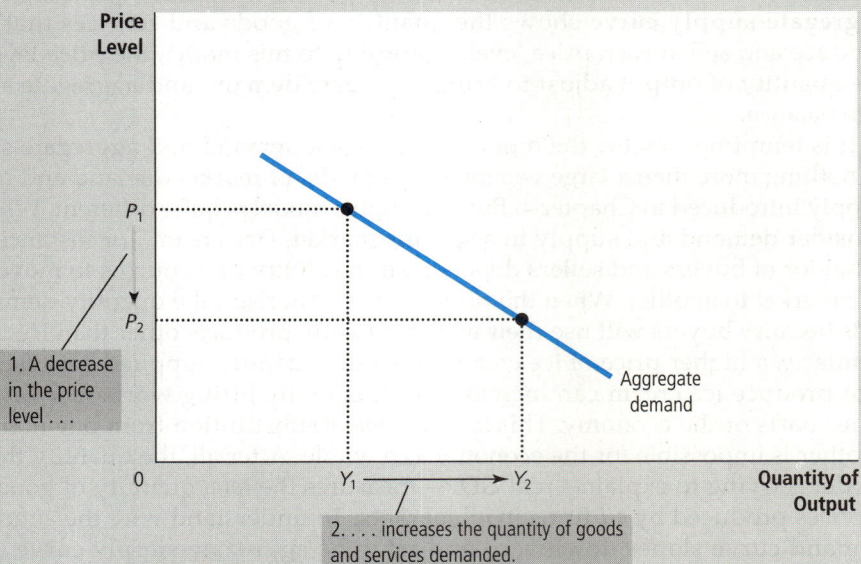

1. A decrease in the price level . . .

2. . . . increases the quantity of goods and services demanded.

The Price Level and Consumption: The Wealth Effect   Consider the money that you hold in your wallet and your bank account. The nominal value of this money is fixed: One dollar is always worth one dollar. Yet the *real* value of a dollar is not fixed. If a candy bar costs one dollar, then a dollar is worth one candy bar. If the price of a candy bar falls to 50 cents, then one dollar is worth two candy bars. Thus, when the price level falls, the dollars you are holding rise in value, which increases your real wealth and your ability to buy goods and services.

This logic gives us the first reason the aggregate-demand curve slopes downward. *A decrease in the price level raises the real value of money and makes consumers wealthier, which in turn encourages them to spend more. The increase in consumer spending means a larger quantity of goods and services demanded. Conversely, an increase in the price level reduces the real value of money and makes consumers poorer, which in turn reduces consumer spending and the quantity of goods and services demanded.*

The Price Level and Investment: The Interest-Rate Effect   The price level is one determinant of the quantity of money demanded. When the price level is lower, households do not need to hold as much money to buy the goods and services they want. Therefore, when the price level falls, households try to reduce their holdings of money by lending some of it out. For instance, a household might use its excess money to buy interest-bearing bonds. Or it might deposit its excess money in an interest-bearing savings account, and the bank would use these funds to make more loans. In either case, as households try to convert some of their money into interest-bearing assets, they drive down interest rates. (The next chapter analyzes this process in more detail.)

Interest rates, in turn, affect spending on goods and services. Because a lower interest rate makes borrowing less expensive, it encourages firms to borrow more to invest in new plants and equipment, and it encourages households to borrow more to invest in new housing. (A lower interest rate might also stimulate consumer spending, especially spending on large durable purchases such as cars, which are often bought on credit.) Thus, a lower interest rate increases the quantity of goods and services demanded.

This logic gives us the second reason the aggregate-demand curve slopes downward. *A lower price level reduces the interest rate, encourages greater spending on investment goods, and thereby increases the quantity of goods and services demanded. Conversely, a higher price level raises the interest rate, discourages investment spending, and decreases the quantity of goods and services demanded.*

The Price Level and Net Exports: The Exchange-Rate Effect As we have just discussed, a lower price level in the United States lowers the U.S. interest rate. In response to the lower interest rate, some U.S. investors will seek higher returns by investing abroad. For instance, as the interest rate on U.S. government bonds falls, a mutual fund might sell U.S. government bonds to buy German government bonds. As the mutual fund tries to convert its dollars into euros to buy the German bonds, it increases the supply of dollars in the market for foreign-currency exchange.

The increased supply of dollars to be turned into euros causes the dollar to depreciate relative to the euro. This leads to a change in the real exchange rate—the relative price of domestic and foreign goods. Because each dollar buys fewer units of foreign currencies, foreign goods become more expensive relative to domestic goods.

The change in relative prices affects spending, both at home and abroad. Because foreign goods are now more expensive, Americans buy less from other countries, causing U.S. imports of goods and services to decrease. At the same time, because U.S. goods are now cheaper, foreigners buy more from the United States, so U.S. exports increase. Net exports equal exports minus imports, so both of these changes cause U.S. net exports to increase. Thus, the fall in the real exchange value of the dollar leads to an increase in the quantity of goods and services demanded.

This logic yields the third reason the aggregate-demand curve slopes downward. *When a fall in the U.S. price level causes U.S. interest rates to fall, the real value of the dollar declines in foreign exchange markets. This depreciation stimulates U.S. net exports and thereby increases the quantity of goods and services demanded. Conversely, when the U.S. price level rises and causes U.S. interest rates to rise, the real value of the dollar increases, and this appreciation reduces U.S. net exports and the quantity of goods and services demanded.*

Summing Up There are three distinct but related reasons a fall in the price level increases the quantity of goods and services demanded:

1. Consumers are wealthier, which stimulates the demand for consumption goods.
2. Interest rates fall, which stimulates the demand for investment goods.
3. The currency depreciates, which stimulates the demand for net exports.

The same three effects work in reverse: When the price level rises, decreased wealth depresses consumer spending, higher interest rates depress investment spending, and a currency appreciation depresses net exports.

Here is a thought experiment to hone your intuition about these effects. Imagine that one day you wake up and notice that, for some mysterious reason, the prices of all goods and services have fallen by half, so the dollars you are holding are worth twice as much. In real terms, you now have twice as much money as you had when you went to bed the night before. What would you do with the extra money? You could spend it at your favorite restaurant, increasing consumer spending. You could lend it out (by buying a bond or depositing it in your bank), reducing interest rates and increasing investment spending. Or you could invest it overseas (by buying shares in an international mutual fund), reducing the real exchange value of the dollar and increasing net exports. Whichever of these three responses you choose, the fall in the price level leads to an increase in the quantity of goods and services demanded. This is what the downward slope of the aggregate-demand curve represents.

It is important to keep in mind that the aggregate-demand curve (like all demand curves) is drawn holding "other things equal." In particular, our three explanations of the downward-sloping aggregate-demand curve assume that the money supply is fixed. That is, we have been considering how a change in the price level affects the demand for goods and services, holding the amount of money in the economy constant. As we will see, a change in the quantity of money shifts the aggregate-demand curve. At this point, just keep in mind that the aggregate-demand curve is drawn for a given quantity of the money supply.

33-3b Why the Aggregate-Demand Curve Might Shift

The downward slope of the aggregate-demand curve shows that a fall in the price level raises the overall quantity of goods and services demanded. Many other factors, however, affect the quantity of goods and services demanded at a given price level. When one of these other factors changes, the quantity of goods and services demanded at every price level changes and the aggregate-demand curve shifts.

Let's consider some examples of events that shift aggregate demand. We can categorize them according to the component of spending that is most directly affected.

Shifts Arising from Changes in Consumption   Suppose Americans suddenly become more concerned about saving for retirement and, as a result, reduce their current consumption. Because the quantity of goods and services demanded at any price level is lower, the aggregate-demand curve shifts to the left. Conversely, imagine that a stock market boom makes people wealthier and less concerned about saving. The resulting increase in consumer spending means a greater quantity of goods and services demanded at any given price level, so the aggregate-demand curve shifts to the right.

Thus, any event that changes how much people want to consume at a given price level shifts the aggregate-demand curve. One policy variable that has this effect is the level of taxation. When the government cuts taxes, it encourages people to spend more, so the aggregate-demand curve shifts to the right. When the government raises taxes, people cut back on their spending and the aggregate-demand curve shifts to the left.

Shifts Arising from Changes in Investment   Any event that changes how much firms want to invest at a given price level also shifts the aggregate-demand curve. For instance, imagine that the computer industry introduces a faster line of computers and many firms decide to invest in new computer systems. Because the quantity of goods and services demanded at any price level is higher, the aggregate-demand curve shifts to the right. Conversely, if firms become pessimistic about future business conditions, they may cut back on investment spending, shifting the aggregate-demand curve to the left.

Tax policy can also influence aggregate demand through investment. For example, an investment tax credit (a tax rebate tied to a firm's investment spending) increases the quantity of investment goods that firms demand at any given interest rate and therefore shifts the aggregate-demand curve to the right. The repeal of an investment tax credit reduces investment and shifts the aggregate-demand curve to the left.

Another policy variable that can influence investment and aggregate demand is the money supply. As we discuss more fully in the next chapter, an increase in the money supply lowers the interest rate in the short run. This decrease in the interest rate makes borrowing less costly, which stimulates investment spending and thereby shifts the aggregate-demand curve to the right. Conversely, a decrease in the money supply raises the interest rate, discourages investment spending, and thereby shifts the aggregate-demand curve to the left. Many economists believe that throughout U.S. history, changes in monetary policy have been an important source of shifts in aggregate demand.

Shifts Arising from Changes in Government Purchases   The most direct way that policymakers shift the aggregate-demand curve is through government purchases. For example, suppose Congress decides to reduce purchases of new weapons systems. Because the quantity of goods and services demanded at any price level is lower, the aggregate-demand curve shifts to the left. Conversely, if state governments start building more highways, the result is a greater quantity of goods and services demanded at any price level, so the aggregate-demand curve shifts to the right.

Shifts Arising from Changes in Net Exports   Any event that changes net exports for a given price level also shifts aggregate demand. For instance, when Europe experiences a recession, it buys fewer goods from the United States. This reduces U.S. net exports at every price level and shifts the aggregate-demand curve for the U.S. economy to the left. When Europe recovers from its recession, it starts buying U.S. goods again and the aggregate-demand curve shifts to the right.

Net exports can also change because international speculators cause movements in the exchange rate. Suppose, for instance, that these speculators lose confidence in foreign economies and want to move some of their wealth into the U.S. economy. In doing so, they bid up the value of the U.S. dollar in the foreign exchange market. This appreciation of the dollar makes U.S. goods more expensive compared to foreign goods, which depresses net exports and shifts the aggregate-demand curve to the left. Conversely, speculation that causes a depreciation of the dollar stimulates net exports and shifts the aggregate-demand curve to the right.

Summing Up   In the next chapter, we analyze the aggregate-demand curve in more detail. There we examine more precisely how the tools of monetary and fiscal policy can shift aggregate demand and whether policymakers should use these tools for that purpose. At this point, however, you should have some idea about why the aggregate-demand curve slopes downward and what kinds of events and policies can shift this curve. Table 1 summarizes what we have learned so far.

TABLE 1

The Aggregate-Demand Curve: Summary

Why Does the Aggregate-Demand Curve Slope Downward?

1. *The Wealth Effect:* A lower price level increases real wealth, which stimulates spending on consumption.
2. *The Interest-Rate Effect:* A lower price level reduces the interest rate, which stimulates spending on investment.
3. *The Exchange-Rate Effect:* A lower price level causes the real exchange rate to depreciate, which stimulates spending on net exports.

Why Might the Aggregate-Demand Curve Shift?

1. *Shifts Arising from Changes in Consumption:* An event that causes consumers to spend more at a given price level (a tax cut, a stock market boom) shifts the aggregate-demand curve to the right. An event that causes consumers to spend less at a given price level (a tax hike, a stock market decline) shifts the aggregate-demand curve to the left.
2. *Shifts Arising from Changes in Investment:* An event that causes firms to invest more at a given price level (optimism about the future, a fall in interest rates due to an increase in the money supply) shifts the aggregate-demand curve to the right. An event that causes firms to invest less at a given price level (pessimism about the future, a rise in interest rates due to a decrease in the money supply) shifts the aggregate-demand curve to the left.
3. *Shifts Arising from Changes in Government Purchases:* An increase in government purchases of goods and services (greater spending on defense or highway construction) shifts the aggregate-demand curve to the right. A decrease in government purchases on goods and services (a cutback in defense or highway spending) shifts the aggregate-demand curve to the left.
4. *Shifts Arising from Changes in Net Exports:* An event that raises spending on net exports at a given price level (a boom overseas, speculation that causes an exchange-rate depreciation) shifts the aggregate-demand curve to the right. An event that reduces spending on net exports at a given price level (a recession overseas, speculation that causes an exchange-rate appreciation) shifts the aggregate-demand curve to the left.

Quick Quiz *Explain the three reasons the aggregate-demand curve slopes downward.*
• *Give an example of an event that would shift the aggregate-demand curve. In which direction would this event shift the curve?*

33-4 The Aggregate-Supply Curve

The aggregate-supply curve tells us the total quantity of goods and services that firms produce and sell at any given price level. Unlike the aggregate-demand curve, which always slopes downward, the aggregate-supply curve shows a relationship that depends crucially on the time horizon examined. *In the long run, the aggregate-supply curve is vertical, whereas in the short run, the aggregate-supply curve slopes upward.* To understand short-run economic fluctuations, and how the short-run behavior of the economy deviates from its long-run behavior, we need to examine both the long-run aggregate-supply curve and the short-run aggregate-supply curve.

33-4a Why the Aggregate-Supply Curve Is Vertical in the Long Run

What determines the quantity of goods and services supplied in the long run? We implicitly answered this question earlier in the book when we analyzed the process of economic growth. *In the long run, an economy's production of goods and services (its real GDP) depends on its supplies of labor, capital, and natural resources and on the available technology used to turn these factors of production into goods and services.*

When we analyzed these forces that govern long-run growth, we did not need to make any reference to the overall level of prices. We examined the price level in a separate chapter, where we saw that it was determined by the quantity of money. We learned that if two economies were identical except that one had twice as much money in circulation, the price level would be twice as high in the economy with more money. But since the amount of money does not affect technology or the supplies of labor, capital, and natural resources, the output of goods and services in the two economies would be the same.

Because the price level does not affect the long-run determinants of real GDP, the long-run aggregate-supply curve is vertical, as in Figure 4. In other words, in the long run, the economy's labor, capital, natural resources, and technology determine the total quantity of goods and services supplied, and this quantity supplied is the same regardless of what the price level happens to be.

The vertical long-run aggregate-supply curve is a graphical representation of the classical dichotomy and monetary neutrality. As we have already discussed, classical macroeconomic theory is based on the assumption that real variables do not depend on nominal variables. The long-run aggregate-supply curve is consistent with this idea because it implies that the quantity of output (a real variable) does not depend on the level of prices (a nominal variable). As noted earlier, most economists believe this principle works well when studying the economy over a period of many years but not when studying year-to-year changes. Thus, *the aggregate-supply curve is vertical only in the long run.*

33-4b Why the Long-Run Aggregate-Supply Curve Might Shift

Because classical macroeconomic theory predicts the quantity of goods and services produced by an economy in the long run, it also explains the position of the long-run aggregate-supply curve. The long-run level of production is

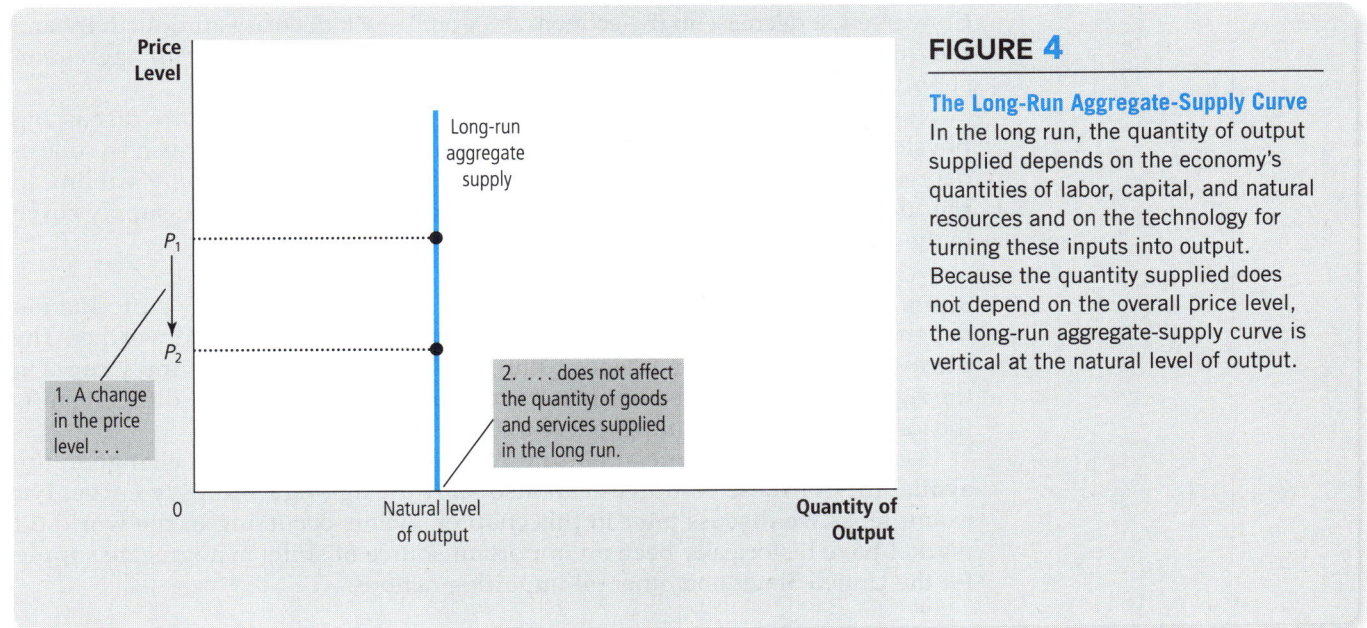

FIGURE 4

The Long-Run Aggregate-Supply Curve
In the long run, the quantity of output supplied depends on the economy's quantities of labor, capital, and natural resources and on the technology for turning these inputs into output. Because the quantity supplied does not depend on the overall price level, the long-run aggregate-supply curve is vertical at the natural level of output.

natural level of output
the production of goods and services that an economy achieves in the long run when unemployment is at its normal rate

sometimes called *potential output* or *full-employment output*. To be more precise, we call it the **natural level of output** because it shows what the economy produces when unemployment is at its natural, or normal, rate. The natural level of output is the rate of production toward which the economy gravitates in the long run.

Any change in the economy that alters the natural level of output shifts the long-run aggregate-supply curve. Because output in the classical model depends on labor, capital, natural resources, and technological knowledge, we can categorize shifts in the long-run aggregate-supply curve as arising from these four sources.

Shifts Arising from Changes in Labor   Imagine that an economy experiences an increase in immigration. Because there would be a greater number of workers, the quantity of goods and services supplied would increase. As a result, the long-run aggregate-supply curve would shift to the right. Conversely, if many workers left the economy to go abroad, the long-run aggregate-supply curve would shift to the left.

The position of the long-run aggregate-supply curve also depends on the natural rate of unemployment, so any change in the natural rate of unemployment shifts the long-run aggregate-supply curve. For example, if Congress were to raise the minimum wage substantially, the natural rate of unemployment would rise and the economy would produce a smaller quantity of goods and services. As a result, the long-run aggregate-supply curve would shift to the left. Conversely, if a reform of the unemployment insurance system were to encourage unemployed workers to search harder for new jobs, the natural rate of unemployment would fall and the long-run aggregate-supply curve would shift to the right.

Shifts Arising from Changes in Capital   An increase in the economy's capital stock increases productivity and, thereby, the quantity of goods and services supplied. As a result, the long-run aggregate-supply curve shifts to the right. Conversely, a decrease in the economy's capital stock decreases productivity and the quantity of goods and services supplied, shifting the long-run aggregate-supply curve to the left.

Notice that the same logic applies regardless of whether we are discussing physical capital such as machines and factories or human capital such as college degrees. An increase in either type of capital will raise the economy's ability to produce goods and services and, thus, shift the long-run aggregate-supply curve to the right.

Shifts Arising from Changes in Natural Resources   An economy's production depends on its natural resources, including its land, minerals, and weather. The discovery of a new mineral deposit shifts the long-run aggregate-supply curve to the right. A change in weather patterns that makes farming more difficult shifts the long-run aggregate-supply curve to the left.

In many countries, crucial natural resources are imported. A change in the availability of these resources can also shift the aggregate-supply curve. For example, as we discuss later in this chapter, events occurring in the world oil market have historically been an important source of shifts in aggregate supply for the United States and other oil-importing nations.

Shifts Arising from Changes in Technological Knowledge   Perhaps the most important reason that the economy today produces more than it did a generation ago is that our technological knowledge has advanced. The invention of the computer, for instance, has allowed us to produce more goods and services from any given amounts of labor, capital, and natural resources. As computer use has spread throughout the economy, it has shifted the long-run aggregate-supply curve to the right.

Although not literally technological, many other events act like changes in technology. For instance, opening up international trade has effects similar to inventing new production processes because it allows a country to specialize in higher-productivity industries; therefore, it also shifts the long-run aggregate-supply curve to the right. Conversely, if the government passes new regulations preventing firms from using some production methods, perhaps to address worker safety or environmental concerns, the result is a leftward shift in the long-run aggregate-supply curve.

Summing Up   Because the long-run aggregate-supply curve reflects the classical model of the economy we developed in previous chapters, it provides a new way to describe our earlier analysis. Any policy or event that raised real GDP in previous chapters can now be described as increasing the quantity of goods and services supplied and shifting the long-run aggregate-supply curve to the right. Any policy or event that lowered real GDP in previous chapters can now be described as decreasing the quantity of goods and services supplied and shifting the long-run aggregate-supply curve to the left.

33-4c Using Aggregate Demand and Aggregate Supply to Depict Long-Run Growth and Inflation

Having introduced the economy's aggregate-demand curve and the long-run aggregate-supply curve, we now have a new way to describe the economy's long-run trends. Figure 5 illustrates the changes that occur in an economy from decade to decade. Notice that both curves are shifting. Although many forces influence the economy in the long run and can in theory cause such shifts, the two most important forces in practice are technology and monetary policy. Technological progress enhances an economy's ability to produce goods and services, and the resulting increases in output are reflected in continual shifts of the long-run aggregate-supply curve to the right. At the same time, because the Fed increases the money supply over time, the aggregate-demand curve also shifts to the right. As the figure illustrates, the result is continuing growth in output (as shown by increasing Y) and continuing inflation (as shown by increasing P). This is just another way of representing the classical analysis of growth and inflation we conducted in earlier chapters.

The purpose of developing the model of aggregate demand and aggregate supply, however, is not to dress our previous long-run conclusions in new clothing. Instead, it is to provide a framework for short-run analysis, as we will see in a moment. As we develop the short-run model, we keep the analysis simple by omitting the continuing growth and inflation shown by the shifts in Figure 5. But always remember that long-run trends are the background on which short-run fluctuations are superimposed. *The short-run fluctuations in output and the price level that we will be studying should be viewed as deviations from the long-run trends of output growth and inflation.*

FIGURE 5

Long-Run Growth and Inflation in the Model of Aggregate Demand and Aggregate Supply

As the economy becomes better able to produce goods and services over time, primarily because of technological progress, the long-run aggregate-supply curve shifts to the right. At the same time, as the Fed increases the money supply, the aggregate-demand curve also shifts to the right. In this figure, output grows from Y_{1990} to Y_{2000} and then to Y_{2010} and the price level rises from P_{1990} to P_{2000} and then to P_{2010}. Thus, the model of aggregate demand and aggregate supply offers a new way to describe the classical analysis of growth and inflation.

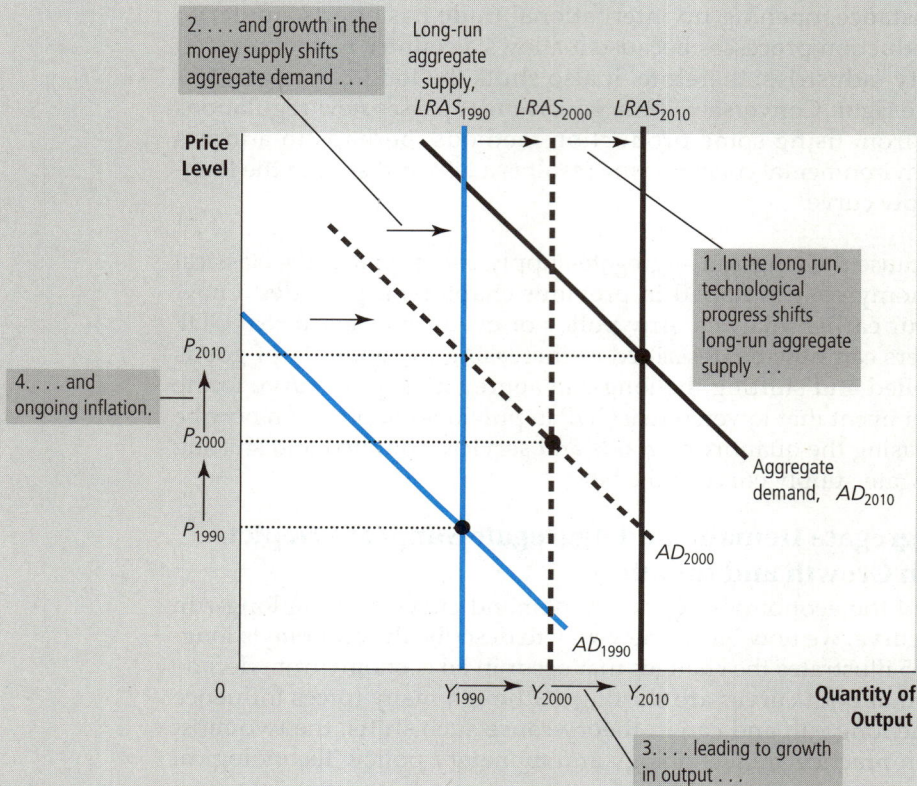

2. . . . and growth in the money supply shifts aggregate demand . . .

Long-run aggregate supply, $LRAS_{1990}$ $LRAS_{2000}$ $LRAS_{2010}$

Price Level

1. In the long run, technological progress shifts long-run aggregate supply . . .

4. . . . and ongoing inflation.

P_{2010}

P_{2000}

P_{1990}

Aggregate demand, AD_{2010}

AD_{2000}

AD_{1990}

0   Y_{1990} Y_{2000} Y_{2010} Quantity of Output

3. . . . leading to growth in output . . .

33-4d   Why the Aggregate-Supply Curve Slopes Upward in the Short Run

The key difference between the economy in the short run and in the long run is the behavior of aggregate supply. The long-run aggregate-supply curve is vertical because, in the long run, the overall level of prices does not affect the economy's ability to produce goods and services. By contrast, in the short run, the price level *does* affect the economy's output. That is, over a period of a year or two, an increase in the overall level of prices in the economy tends to raise the quantity of goods and services supplied, and a decrease in the level of prices tends to reduce the quantity of goods and services supplied. As a result, the short-run aggregate-supply curve slopes upward, as shown in Figure 6.

Why do changes in the price level affect output in the short run? Macro-economists have proposed three theories for the upward slope of the short-run

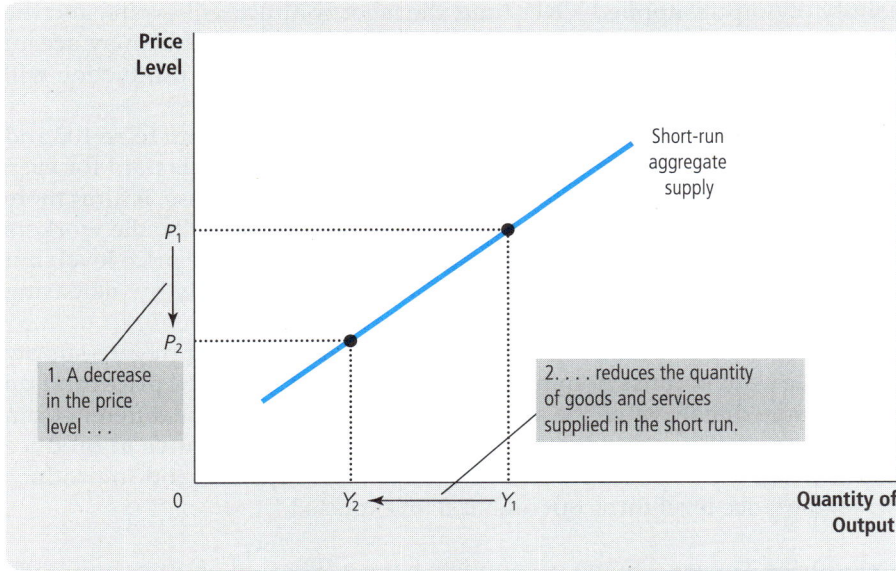

FIGURE 6

The Short-Run Aggregate-Supply Curve
In the short run, a fall in the price level from P_1 to P_2 reduces the quantity of output supplied from Y_1 to Y_2. This positive relationship could be due to sticky wages, sticky prices, or misperceptions. Over time, wages, prices, and perceptions adjust, so this positive relationship is only temporary.

aggregate-supply curve. In each theory, a specific market imperfection causes the supply side of the economy to behave differently in the short run than it does in the long run. The following theories differ in their details, but they share a common theme: *The quantity of output supplied deviates from its long-run, or natural, level when the actual price level in the economy deviates from the price level that people expected to prevail.* When the price level rises above the level that people expected, output rises above its natural level, and when the price level falls below the expected level, output falls below its natural level.

The Sticky-Wage Theory The first explanation of the upward slope of the short-run aggregate-supply curve is the sticky-wage theory. This theory is the simplest of the three approaches to aggregate supply, and some economists believe it highlights the most important reason why the economy in the short run differs from the economy in the long run. Therefore, it is the theory of short-run aggregate supply that we emphasize in this book.

According to this theory, the short-run aggregate-supply curve slopes upward because nominal wages are slow to adjust to changing economic conditions. In other words, wages are "sticky" in the short run. To some extent, the slow adjustment of nominal wages is attributable to long-term contracts between workers and firms that fix nominal wages, sometimes for as long as 3 years. In addition, this prolonged adjustment may be attributable to slowly changing social norms and notions of fairness that influence wage setting.

An example can help explain how sticky nominal wages can result in a short-run aggregate-supply curve that slopes upward. Imagine that a year ago a firm expected the price level today to be 100, and based on this expectation, it signed a contract with its workers agreeing to pay them, say, $20 an hour. In fact, the price level turns out to be only 95. Because prices have fallen below expectations, the firm gets 5 percent less than expected for each unit of its product that it sells. The cost of labor used to make the output, however, is stuck at $20 per hour. Production is now less profitable, so the firm hires fewer workers and reduces the quantity of output supplied. Over time, the labor contract will expire, and the firm can renegotiate with its workers for a lower wage (which they may accept because prices are lower), but in the meantime, employment and production will remain below their long-run levels.

The same logic works in reverse. Suppose the price level turns out to be 105 and the wage remains stuck at $20. The firm sees that the amount it is paid for each unit sold is up by 5 percent, while its labor costs are not. In response, it hires more workers and increases the quantity of output supplied. Eventually, the workers will demand higher nominal wages to compensate for the higher price level, but for a while, the firm can take advantage of the profit opportunity by increasing employment and production above their long-run levels.

In short, according to the sticky-wage theory, the short-run aggregate-supply curve slopes upward because nominal wages are based on expected prices and do not respond immediately when the actual price level turns out to be different from what was expected. This stickiness of wages gives firms an incentive to produce less output when the price level turns out lower than expected and to produce more when the price level turns out higher than expected.

The Sticky-Price Theory Some economists have advocated another approach to explaining the upward slope of the short-run aggregate-supply curve, called the sticky-price theory. As we just discussed, the sticky-wage theory emphasizes that nominal wages adjust slowly over time. The sticky-price theory emphasizes that the prices of some goods and services also adjust sluggishly in response to changing economic conditions. This slow adjustment of prices occurs in part because there are costs to adjusting prices, called *menu costs*. These menu costs include the cost of printing and distributing catalogs and the time required to change price tags. As a result of these costs, prices as well as wages may be sticky in the short run.

To see how sticky prices explain the aggregate-supply curve's upward slope, suppose that each firm in the economy announces its prices in advance based on the economic conditions it expects to prevail over the coming year. Suppose further that after prices are announced, the economy experiences an unexpected contraction in the money supply, which (as we have learned) will reduce the overall price level in the long run. What happens in the short run? Although some firms reduce their prices quickly in response to the unexpected change in economic conditions, many other firms want to avoid additional menu costs. As a result, they temporarily lag behind in cutting their prices. Because these lagging firms have prices that are too high, their sales decline. Declining sales, in turn, cause these firms to cut back on production and employment. In other words, because not all prices adjust immediately to changing conditions, an unexpected fall in the price level leaves some firms with higher-than-desired prices, and these higher-than-desired prices depress sales and induce firms to reduce the quantity of goods and services they produce.

Similar reasoning applies when the money supply and price level turn out to be above what firms expected when they originally set their prices. While some firms raise their prices quickly in response to the new economic environment, other firms lag behind, keeping their prices at the lower-than-desired levels. These low prices attract customers, which induces these firms to increase employment and production. Thus, during the time these lagging firms are operating with outdated prices, there is a positive association between the overall price level and the quantity of output. This positive association is represented by the upward slope of the short-run aggregate-supply curve.

The Misperceptions Theory   A third approach to explaining the upward slope of the short-run aggregate-supply curve is the misperceptions theory. According to this theory, changes in the overall price level can temporarily mislead suppliers about what is happening in the individual markets in which they sell their output. As a result of these short-run misperceptions, suppliers respond to changes in the level of prices, and this response leads to an upward-sloping aggregate-supply curve.

To see how this might work, suppose the overall price level falls below the level that suppliers expected. When suppliers see the prices of their products fall, they may mistakenly believe that their *relative* prices have fallen; that is, they may believe that their prices have fallen compared to other prices in the economy. For example, wheat farmers may notice a fall in the price of wheat before they notice a fall in the prices of the many items they buy as consumers. They may infer from this observation that the reward for producing wheat is temporarily low, and they may respond by reducing the quantity of wheat they supply. Similarly, workers may notice a fall in their nominal wages before they notice that the prices of the goods they buy are also falling. They may infer that the reward for working is temporarily low and respond by reducing the quantity of labor they supply. In both cases, a lower price level causes misperceptions about relative prices, and these misperceptions induce suppliers to respond to the lower price level by decreasing the quantity of goods and services supplied.

Similar misperceptions arise when the price level is above what was expected. Suppliers of goods and services may notice the price of their output rising and infer, mistakenly, that their relative prices are rising. They would conclude that it is a good time to produce. Until their misperceptions are corrected, they respond to the higher price level by increasing the quantity of goods and services supplied. This behavior results in a short-run aggregate-supply curve that slopes upward.

Summing Up   There are three alternative explanations for the upward slope of the short-run aggregate-supply curve: (1) sticky wages, (2) sticky prices, and (3) misperceptions about relative prices. Economists debate which of these theories is correct, and it is possible that each contains an element of truth. For our purposes in this book, the similarities of the theories are more important than the differences. All three theories suggest that output deviates in the short run from its natural level when the actual price level deviates from the price level that people had expected to prevail. We can express this mathematically as follows:

$$\begin{matrix} \text{Quantity} \\ \text{of output} \\ \text{supplied} \end{matrix} = \begin{matrix} \text{Natural} \\ \text{level of} \\ \text{output} \end{matrix} + a \left(\begin{matrix} \text{Actual} \\ \text{price} \\ \text{level} \end{matrix} - \begin{matrix} \text{Expected} \\ \text{price} \\ \text{level} \end{matrix} \right)$$

where a is a number that determines how much output responds to unexpected changes in the price level.

Notice that each of the three theories of short-run aggregate supply emphasizes a problem that is likely to be temporary. Whether the upward slope of the aggregate-supply curve is attributable to sticky wages, sticky prices, or misperceptions, these conditions will not persist forever. Over time, nominal wages will become unstuck, prices will become unstuck, and misperceptions about relative prices will be corrected. In the long run, it is reasonable to assume that wages and prices are flexible rather than sticky and that people are not confused about relative prices. Thus, while we have several good theories to explain why the short-run aggregate-supply curve slopes upward, they are all consistent with a long-run aggregate-supply curve that is vertical.

33-4e Why the Short-Run Aggregate-Supply Curve Might Shift

The short-run aggregate-supply curve tells us the quantity of goods and services supplied in the short run for any given level of prices. This curve is similar to the long-run aggregate-supply curve, but it is upward-sloping rather than vertical because of sticky wages, sticky prices, and misperceptions. Thus, when thinking about what shifts the short-run aggregate-supply curve, we have to consider all those variables that shift the long-run aggregate-supply curve. In addition, we have to consider a new variable—the expected price level—that influences the wages that are stuck, the prices that are stuck, and the perceptions about relative prices that may be flawed.

Let's start with what we know about the long-run aggregate-supply curve. As we discussed earlier, shifts in the long-run aggregate-supply curve normally arise from changes in labor, capital, natural resources, or technological knowledge. These same variables shift the short-run aggregate-supply curve. For example, when an increase in the economy's capital stock increases productivity, the economy is able to produce more output, so both the long-run and short-run aggregate-supply curves shift to the right. When an increase in the minimum wage raises the natural rate of unemployment, the economy has fewer employed workers and thus produces less output, so both the long-run and short-run aggregate-supply curves shift to the left.

The important new variable that affects the position of the short-run aggregate-supply curve is the price level that people expected to prevail. As we have discussed, the quantity of goods and services supplied depends, in the short run, on sticky wages, sticky prices, and misperceptions. Yet wages, prices, and perceptions are set based on the expected price level. So when people change their expectations of the price level, the short-run aggregate-supply curve shifts.

To make this idea more concrete, let's consider a specific theory of aggregate supply—the sticky-wage theory. According to this theory, when workers and firms expect the price level to be high, they are likely to reach a bargain with a higher level of nominal wages. Higher wages raise firms' costs, and for any given actual price level, higher costs reduce the quantity of goods and services supplied. Thus, when the expected price level rises, wages are higher, costs increase, and firms produce a smaller quantity of goods and services at any given actual price level. Thus, the short-run aggregate-supply curve shifts to the left. Conversely, when the expected price level falls, wages are lower, costs decline, firms increase output at any given price level, and the short-run aggregate-supply curve shifts to the right.

A similar logic applies in each theory of aggregate supply. The general lesson is the following: *An increase in the expected price level reduces the quantity of goods and services supplied and shifts the short-run aggregate-supply curve to the left. A decrease in the expected price level raises the quantity of goods and services supplied and shifts the short-run aggregate-supply curve to the right.* As we will see in the next section, the influence of expectations on the position of the short-run aggregate-supply curve plays a key role in explaining how the economy makes the transition from the short run to the long run. In the short run, expectations are fixed and the economy finds itself at the intersection of the aggregate-demand curve and the short-run aggregate-supply curve. In the long run, if people observe that the price level is different from what they expected, their expectations adjust and the short-run aggregate-supply curve shifts. This shift ensures that the economy eventually finds itself at the intersection of the aggregate-demand curve and the long-run aggregate-supply curve.

You should now have some understanding about why the short-run aggregate-supply curve slopes upward and what events and policies can cause this curve to shift. Table 2 summarizes our discussion.

TABLE 2

The Short-Run Aggregate-Supply Curve: Summary

Why Does the Short-Run Aggregate-Supply Curve Slope Upward?
1. *The Sticky-Wage Theory:* An unexpectedly low price level raises the real wage, which causes firms to hire fewer workers and produce a smaller quantity of goods and services.
2. *The Sticky-Price Theory:* An unexpectedly low price level leaves some firms with higher-than-desired prices, which depresses their sales and leads them to cut back production.
3. *The Misperceptions Theory:* An unexpectedly low price level leads some suppliers to think their relative prices have fallen, which induces a fall in production.

Why Might the Short-Run Aggregate-Supply Curve Shift?
1. *Shifts Arising from Changes in Labor:* An increase in the quantity of labor available (perhaps due to a fall in the natural rate of unemployment) shifts the aggregate-supply curve to the right. A decrease in the quantity of labor available (perhaps due to a rise in the natural rate of unemployment) shifts the aggregate-supply curve to the left.
2. *Shifts Arising from Changes in Capital:* An increase in physical or human capital shifts the aggregate-supply curve to the right. A decrease in physical or human capital shifts the aggregate-supply curve to the left.
3. *Shifts Arising from Changes in Natural Resources:* An increase in the availability of natural resources shifts the aggregate-supply curve to the right. A decrease in the availability of natural resources shifts the aggregate-supply curve to the left.
4. *Shifts Arising from Changes in Technology:* An advance in technological knowledge shifts the aggregate-supply curve to the right. A decrease in the available technology (perhaps due to government regulation) shifts the aggregate-supply curve to the left.
5. *Shifts Arising from Changes in the Expected Price Level:* A decrease in the expected price level shifts the short-run aggregate-supply curve to the right. An increase in the expected price level shifts the short-run aggregate-supply curve to the left.

QuickQuiz *Explain why the long-run aggregate-supply curve is vertical. • Explain three theories for why the short-run aggregate-supply curve slopes upward. • What variables shift both the long-run and short-run aggregate-supply curves? • What variable shifts the short-run aggregate-supply curve but not the long-run aggregate-supply curve?*

33-5 Two Causes of Economic Fluctuations

Now that we have introduced the model of aggregate demand and aggregate supply, we have the basic tools we need to analyze fluctuations in economic activity. In particular, we can use what we have learned about aggregate demand and aggregate supply to examine the two basic causes of short-run fluctuations : shifts in aggregate demand and shifts in aggregate supply.

To keep things simple, we assume the economy begins in long-run equilibrium, as shown in Figure 7. Output and the price level are determined in the long run by the intersection of the aggregate-demand curve and the long-run aggregate-supply curve, shown as point A in the figure. At this point, output is at its natural level. Because the economy is always in a short-run equilibrium, the short-run aggregate-supply curve passes through this point as well, indicating that the expected price level has adjusted to this long-run equilibrium. That is, when an economy is in its long-run equilibrium, the expected price level must equal the actual price level so that the intersection of aggregate demand with short-run

FIGURE 7

The Long-Run Equilibrium
The long-run equilibrium of the economy is found where the aggregate-demand curve crosses the long-run aggregate-supply curve (point A). When the economy reaches this long-run equilibrium, the expected price level will have adjusted to equal the actual price level. As a result, the short-run aggregate-supply curve crosses this point as well.

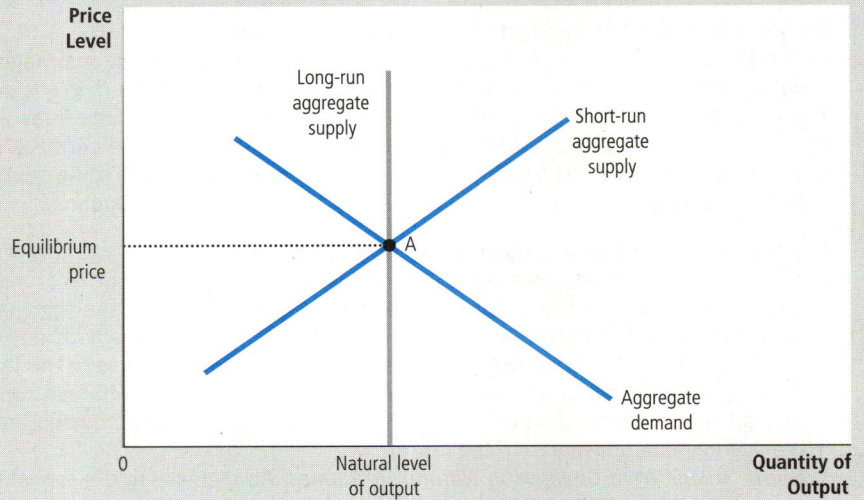

aggregate supply is the same as the intersection of aggregate demand with long-run aggregate supply.

33-5a The Effects of a Shift in Aggregate Demand

Suppose that a wave of pessimism suddenly overtakes the economy. The cause might be a scandal in the White House, a crash in the stock market, or the outbreak of war overseas. Because of this event, many people lose confidence in the future and alter their plans. Households cut back on their spending and delay major purchases, and firms put off buying new equipment.

What is the macroeconomic impact of such a wave of pessimism? In answering this question, we can follow the three steps we used in Chapter 4 when analyzing supply and demand in specific markets. First, we determine whether the event affects aggregate demand or aggregate supply. Second, we determine the direction that the curve shifts. Third, we use the diagram of aggregate demand and aggregate supply to compare the initial and the new equilibrium. The new wrinkle is that we need to add a fourth step: We have to keep track of a new short-run equilibrium, a new long-run equilibrium, and the transition between them. Table 3 summarizes the four steps to analyzing economic fluctuations.

TABLE 3

Four Steps for Analyzing Macroeconomic Fluctuations

1. Decide whether the event shifts the aggregate-demand curve or the aggregate-supply curve (or perhaps both).
2. Decide the direction in which the curve shifts.
3. Use the diagram of aggregate demand and aggregate supply to determine the impact on output and the price level in the short run.
4. Use the diagram of aggregate demand and aggregate supply to analyze how the economy moves from its new short-run equilibrium to its new long-run equilibrium.

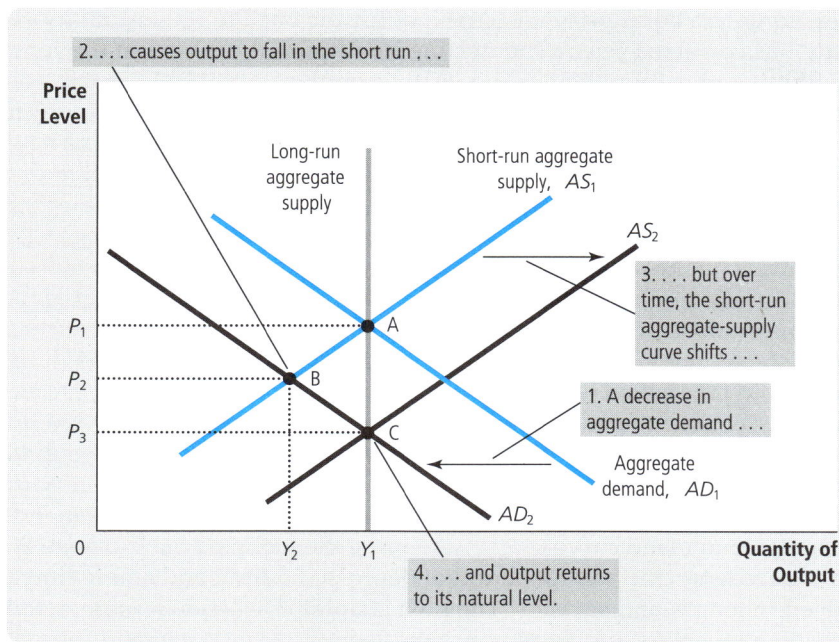

2. . . . causes output to fall in the short run . . .

Long-run aggregate supply

Short-run aggregate supply, AS_1

AS_2

3. . . . but over time, the short-run aggregate-supply curve shifts . . .

1. A decrease in aggregate demand . . .

Aggregate demand, AD_1

AD_2

4. . . . and output returns to its natural level.

FIGURE 8

A Contraction in Aggregate Demand
A fall in aggregate demand is represented with a leftward shift in the aggregate-demand curve from AD_1 to AD_2. In the short run, the economy moves from point A to point B. Output falls from Y_1 to Y_2, and the price level falls from P_1 to P_2. Over time, as the expected price level adjusts, the short-run aggregate-supply curve shifts to the right from AS_1 to AS_2, and the economy reaches point C, where the new aggregate-demand curve crosses the long-run aggregate-supply curve. In the long run, the price level falls to P_3, and output returns to its natural level, Y_1.

The first two steps are straightforward. First, because the wave of pessimism affects spending plans, it affects the aggregate-demand curve. Second, because households and firms now want to buy a smaller quantity of goods and services for any given price level, the event reduces aggregate demand. As Figure 8 shows, the aggregate-demand curve shifts to the left from AD_1 to AD_2.

With this figure, we can perform step three: By comparing the initial and the new equilibrium, we can see the effects of the fall in aggregate demand. In the short run, the economy moves along the initial short-run aggregate-supply curve, AS_1, going from point A to point B. As the economy moves between these two points, output falls from Y_1 to Y_2 and the price level falls from P_1 to P_2. The falling level of output indicates that the economy is in a recession. Although not shown in the figure, firms respond to lower sales and production by reducing employment. Thus, the pessimism that caused the shift in aggregate demand is, to some extent, self-fulfilling: Pessimism about the future leads to falling incomes and rising unemployment.

Now comes step four—the transition from the short-run equilibrium to the new long-run equilibrium. Because of the reduction in aggregate demand, the price level initially falls from P_1 to P_2. The price level is thus below the level that people were expecting (P_1) before the sudden fall in aggregate demand. People can be surprised in the short run, but they will not remain surprised. Over time, their expectations catch up with this new reality, and the expected price level falls as well. The fall in the expected price level alters wages, prices, and perceptions, which in turn influences the position of the short-run aggregate-supply curve. For example, according to the sticky-wage theory, once workers and firms come to expect a lower level of prices, they start to strike bargains for lower nominal wages; the reduction in labor costs encourages firms to hire more workers and expand production at any given level of prices. Thus, the fall in the expected price level shifts the short-run aggregate-supply curve to the right from AS_1 to AS_2 in Figure 8. This shift allows the economy to approach point C, where the new aggregate-demand curve (AD_2) crosses the long-run aggregate-supply curve.

In the new long-run equilibrium, point C, output is back to its natural level. The economy has corrected itself: The decline in output is reversed in the long run, even without action by policymakers. Although the wave of pessimism has reduced aggregate demand, the price level has fallen sufficiently (to P_3) to offset the shift in the aggregate-demand curve, and people have come to expect this new lower price level as well. Thus, in the long run, the shift in aggregate demand is reflected fully in the price level and not at all in the level of output. In other words, the long-run effect of a shift in aggregate demand is a nominal change (the price level is lower) but not a real change (output is the same).

What should policymakers do when faced with a sudden fall in aggregate demand? In this analysis, we assumed they did nothing. Another possibility is that, as soon as the economy heads into recession (moving from point A to point B), policymakers could take action to increase aggregate demand. As we noted earlier, an increase in government spending or an increase in the money supply would increase the quantity of goods and services demanded at any price and, therefore, would shift the aggregate-demand curve to the right. If policymakers act with sufficient speed and precision, they can offset the initial shift in aggregate demand, return the aggregate-demand curve to AD_1, and bring the economy back to point A. If the policy is successful, the painful period of depressed output and employment can be reduced in length and severity. The next chapter discusses in more detail the ways in which monetary and fiscal policy influence aggregate demand, as well as some of the practical difficulties in using these policy instruments.

To sum up, this story about shifts in aggregate demand has three important lessons:

- In the short run, shifts in aggregate demand cause fluctuations in the economy's output of goods and services.
- In the long run, shifts in aggregate demand affect the overall price level but do not affect output.
- Because policymakers influence aggregate demand, they can potentially mitigate the severity of economic fluctuations.

FYI

Monetary Neutrality Revisited

According to classical economic theory, money is neutral. That is, changes in the quantity of money affect nominal variables such as the price level but not real variables such as output. Earlier in this chapter, we noted that most economists accept this conclusion as a description of how the economy works in the long run but not in the short run. With the model of aggregate demand and aggregate supply, we can illustrate this conclusion and explain it more fully.

Suppose that the Federal Reserve reduces the quantity of money in the economy. What effect does this change have? As we discussed, the money supply is one determinant of aggregate demand. The reduction in the money supply shifts the aggregate-demand curve to the left.

The analysis looks just like Figure 8. Even though the cause of the shift in aggregate demand is different, we would observe the same effects on output and the price level. In the short run, both output and the price level fall. The economy experiences a recession. But over time, the expected price level falls as well. Firms and workers respond to their new expectations by, for instance, agreeing to lower nominal wages. As they do so, the short-run aggregate-supply curve shifts to the right. Eventually, the economy finds itself back on the long-run aggregate-supply curve.

Figure 8 shows when money matters for real variables and when it does not. In the long run, money is neutral, as represented by the movement of the economy from point A to point C. But in the short run, a change in the money supply has real effects, as represented by the movement of the economy from point A to point B. An old saying summarizes the analysis: "Money is a veil, but when the veil flutters, real output sputters." ∎

CASE STUDY

TWO BIG SHIFTS IN AGGREGATE DEMAND: THE GREAT DEPRESSION AND WORLD WAR II

At the beginning of this chapter, we established three key facts about economic fluctuations by looking at data since 1972. Let's now take a longer look at U.S. economic history. Figure 9 shows data since 1900 on the percentage change in real GDP over the previous 3 years. In an average 3-year period, real GDP grows about 10 percent—a bit more than 3 percent per year. The business cycle, however, causes fluctuations around this average. Two episodes jump out as being particularly significant: the large drop in real GDP in the early 1930s and the large increase in real GDP in the early 1940s. Both of these events are attributable to shifts in aggregate demand.

The economic calamity of the early 1930s is called the *Great Depression*, and it is by far the largest economic downturn in U.S. history. Real GDP fell by 27 percent from 1929 to 1933, and unemployment rose from 3 percent to 25 percent. At the same time, the price level fell by 22 percent over these 4 years. Many other countries experienced similar declines in output and prices during this period.

Economic historians continue to debate the causes of the Great Depression, but most explanations center on a large decline in aggregate demand. What caused aggregate demand to contract? Here is where the disagreement arises.

Many economists place primary blame on the decline in the money supply: From 1929 to 1933, the money supply fell by 28 percent. As you may recall from our discussion of the monetary system, this decline in the money supply was due to problems in the banking system. As households withdrew their money from financially shaky banks and bankers became more cautious and started holding greater reserves, the process of money creation under fractional-reserve banking went into reverse. The Fed, meanwhile, failed to offset this fall in the money multiplier with expansionary open-market operations. As a result, the money supply declined. Many economists blame the Fed's failure to act for the Great Depression's severity.

Over the course of U.S. economic history, two fluctuations stand out as especially large. During the early 1930s, the economy went through the Great Depression, when the production of goods and services plummeted. During the early 1940s, the United States entered World War II and the economy experienced rapidly rising production. Both of these events are usually explained by large shifts in aggregate demand.

Source: Louis D. Johnston and Samuel H. Williamson, "What Was GDP Then?" http://www.measuringworth.com/usgdp/; Department of Commerce (Bureau of Economic Analysis).

FIGURE 9

U.S. Real GDP Growth since 1900

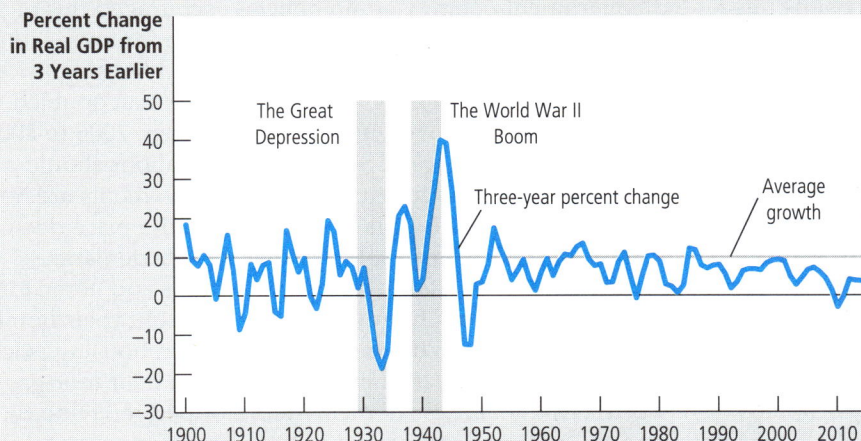

The outcome of a massive decrease in aggregate demand

Other economists have suggested alternative reasons for the collapse in aggregate demand. For example, stock prices fell about 90 percent during this period, depressing household wealth and thereby consumer spending. In addition, the banking problems may have prevented some firms from obtaining the financing they wanted for new projects and business expansions, reducing investment spending. It is possible that all these forces may have acted together to contract aggregate demand during the Great Depression.

The second significant episode in Figure 9—the economic boom of the early 1940s—is easier to explain. The cause of this event was World War II. As the United States entered the war overseas, the federal government had to devote more resources to the military. Government purchases of goods and services increased almost fivefold from 1939 to 1944. This huge expansion in aggregate demand almost doubled the economy's production of goods and services and led to a 20 percent increase in the price level (although widespread government price controls limited the rise in prices). Unemployment fell from 17 percent in 1939 to about 1 percent in 1944—the lowest level in U.S. history. ●

CASE STUDY

THE GREAT RECESSION OF 2008–2009
In 2008 and 2009, the U.S. economy experienced a financial crisis and a severe downturn in economic activity. In many ways, it was the worst macroeconomic event in more than half a century.

The story of this downturn begins a few years earlier with a substantial boom in the housing market. The boom was, in part, fueled by low interest rates. In the aftermath of the recession of 2001, the Federal Reserve lowered interest rates to historically low levels. Low interest rates helped the economy recover, but by making it less expensive to get a mortgage and buy a home, they also contributed to a rise in housing prices.

In addition to low interest rates, various developments in the mortgage market made it easier for *subprime borrowers*—those borrowers with a higher risk of default based on their income and credit history—to get loans to buy homes. One development was *securitization*, the process by which a financial institution (specifically, a mortgage originator) makes loans and then (with the help of an investment bank) bundles them together into financial instruments called *mortgage-backed securities*. These mortgage-backed securities were then sold to other institutions (such as banks and insurance companies), which may not have fully appreciated the risks in these securities. Some economists blame inadequate regulation for these high-risk loans. Others blame misguided government policy: Certain policies encouraged this high-risk lending to make the goal of homeownership more attainable for low-income families. Together, these many forces drove up housing demand and housing prices. From 1995 to 2006, average housing prices in the United States more than doubled.

The high price of housing, however, proved unsustainable. From 2006 to 2009, housing prices nationwide fell about 30 percent. Such price fluctuations should not necessarily be a problem in a market economy. After all, price movements are how markets equilibrate supply and demand. In this case, however, the price decline had two related repercussions that caused a sizable fall in aggregate demand.

The first repercussion was a substantial rise in mortgage defaults and home foreclosures. During the housing boom, many homeowners had bought their homes with mostly borrowed money and minimal down payments. When housing prices declined, these homeowners were *underwater* (they owed more on their mortgages than their homes were worth). Many of these homeowners stopped repaying their loans. The banks servicing the mortgages responded to these defaults by taking the houses away in foreclosure procedures and then selling them off. The banks' goal was to recoup whatever they could from the bad loans. As you might have expected from your study of supply and demand, the increase in the number of homes for sale exacerbated the downward spiral of house prices. As house prices fell, spending on the construction of housing also collapsed.

A second repercussion was that the various financial institutions that owned mortgage-backed securities suffered huge losses. In essence, by borrowing large sums to buy high-risk mortgages, these companies had bet that house prices would keep rising; when this bet turned bad, they found themselves at or near the point of bankruptcy. Because of these large losses, many financial institutions did not have funds to loan out and the ability of the financial system to channel resources to those who could best use them was impaired. Even creditworthy customers found themselves unable to borrow to finance investment spending.

As a result of all these events, the economy experienced a large contractionary shift in aggregate demand. Real GDP and employment both fell sharply. The introduction to this chapter has already cited the figures, but they are worth repeating: Real GDP declined by 4.2 percent between the fourth quarter of 2007 and the second quarter of 2009, and the rate of unemployment rose from 4.4 percent in May 2007 to 10.0 percent in October 2009. This experience served as a vivid reminder that deep economic downturns and personal hardship they cause are not a relic of history but a constant risk in the modern economy.

As the crisis unfolded, the U.S. government responded in a variety of ways. Three policy actions—all aimed in part at returning aggregate demand to its previous level—are most noteworthy.

First, the Fed cut its target for the federal funds rate from 5.25 percent in September 2007 to about zero in December 2008. The Federal Reserve also started buying mortgage-backed securities and other private loans in open-market operations. By purchasing these instruments from the banking system, the Fed provided banks with additional funds in the hope that the banks would makes loans more readily available.

Second, in an even more unusual move in October 2008, Congress appropriated $700 billion for the Treasury to use to rescue the financial system. Much of this money was used for equity injections into banks. That is, the Treasury put funds into the banking system, which the banks could use to make loans and otherwise continue their normal operations; in exchange for these funds, the U.S. government became a part owner of these banks, at least temporarily. The goal of this policy was to stem the crisis on Wall Street and make it easier for businesses and individuals to obtain loans.

Finally, when Barack Obama became president in January 2009, his first major initiative was a large increase in government spending. After a relatively brief congressional debate over the form of the legislation, the new president signed a $787 billion stimulus bill on February 17, 2009. This policy move is discussed more fully in the next chapter when we consider the impact of fiscal policy on aggregate demand.

The recovery from this recession officially began in June 2009. But it was, by historical standards, only a meager recovery. From the second quarter of 2009 to the fourth quarter of 2015, real GDP growth averaged only 2.1 percent per year, well below the average rate of growth over the past half century of about 3 percent. Although unemployment fell to 5.0 percent by the end of 2015, much of the decline was attributable to individuals leaving the labor force rather than finding jobs. In December 2015, the employment-to-population ratio was only 1.3 percentage points higher than at its trough during the Great Recession and was more than 3 percentage points lower than before the downturn began.

Which, if any, of the many policy moves were most important for ending the recession? And what other policies might have promoted a more robust recovery? These are surely questions that macroeconomic historians will debate in the years to come. ●

What Have We Learned?

Since the financial crisis and Great Recession of 2008–2009, economists have asked themselves how this episode should change the field of macroeconomics.

Olivier Blanchard's Five Lessons for Economists from the Financial Crisis

By David Wessel

What did the worst financial crisis and deepest recession in 75 years teach academic economists and policymakers on whose watch it happened? At a recent London School of Economics forum, convened to honor Bank of England Governor Mervyn King, Olivier Blanchard offered some answers.

Mr. Blanchard, 64 years old, is well positioned to offer such reconsideration. An internationally prominent macroeconomist, he spent 25 years on the MIT faculty before becoming chief economist at the International Monetary Fund in September 2008, just before the collapse of Lehman Brothers.

Here are Mr. Blanchard's five lessons in his own words, lightly edited by The Wall Street Journal's David Wessel:

#1: Humility is in order.

The Great Moderation [the economically tranquil period from 1987 to 2007] convinced too many of us that the large-economy crisis—a financial crisis, a banking crisis— was a thing of the past. It wasn't going to happen again, except maybe in emerging markets. History was marching on.

My generation, which was born after World War II, lived with the notion that the world was getting to be a better and better place. We knew how to do things better, not only in economics but in other fields as well. What we have learned is that's not true. History repeats itself. We should have known.

#2: The financial system matters— a lot.

It's not the first time that we're confronted with what [former U.S. Defense Secretary Donald] Rumsfeld called "unknown unknowns," things that happened that we hadn't thought about. There is another example in macroeconomics:

The oil shocks of the 1970s during which we were students and we hadn't thought about it. It took a few years, more than a few years, for economists to understand what was going on. After a few years, we concluded that we could think of the oil shock as yet another macroeconomic shock. We did not need to understand the plumbing. We didn't need to understand the details of the oil market. When there's an increase in the price of energy or materials, we can just integrate it into our macro models—the implications of energy prices on inflation and so on.

This is different. What we have learned about the financial system is that the problem is in the plumbing and that we have to understand the plumbing. Before I came to the Fund, I thought of the financial system as a set of arbitrage equations. Basically the Federal Reserve would choose one interest rate, and then the expectations hypothesis would give all the rates everywhere else with premia which might vary, but not very much.

It was really easy. I thought of people on Wall Street as basically doing this for me so I didn't have to think about it.

What we have learned is that that's not the case. In the financial system, a myriad of distortions or small shocks build on each other. When there are enough small shocks, enough distortions, things can go very bad. This has fundamental implications for macroeconomics. We do macro on the assumption that we can look at aggregates in some way and then just have them interact in simple models. I still think that's the way to go, but this shows the limits of that approach. When it comes to the financial system, it's very clear that the details of the plumbing matter.

#3 Interconnectedness matters.

This crisis started in the U.S. and across the ocean in a matter of days and weeks. Each crisis, even in small islands, potentially has effects on the rest of the world. The complexity of the cross border claims by creditors and by debtors clearly is something that many of us had not fully realized: the cross border movements triggered by the risk-on/risk-off movements, which countries are safe havens, and when and why? Understanding this has become absolutely essential. What happens in one part of the world cannot be ignored by the rest of the world. The fact that we all spend so

33-5b   The Effects of a Shift in Aggregate Supply

Imagine once again an economy in its long-run equilibrium. Now suppose that suddenly some firms experience an increase in their costs of production. For example, bad weather in farm states might destroy some crops, driving up the

much time thinking about Cyprus in the last few days is an example of that.

It's also true on the trade side. We used to think if one country was doing badly, then exports to that country would do badly and therefore the exporting countries would do badly. In our models, the effect was relatively small. One absolutely striking fact of the crisis is the collapse of trade in 2009. Output went down. Trade collapsed. Countries which felt they were not terribly exposed through trade turned out to be enormously exposed.

#4 We don't know if macro-prudential tools work.

It's very clear that the traditional monetary and fiscal tools are just not good enough to deal with the very specific problems in the financial system. This has led to the development of macro-prudential tools, which may or may not become the third leg of macroeconomic policies.

[Macro-prudential tools allow a central bank to restrain lending in specific sectors without raising interest rates for the whole economy, such as increasing the minimum down payment required to get a mortgage, which reduces the loan-to-value ratio.] In principle, they can address specific issues in the financial sector. If there is a problem somewhere you can target the tool at the problem and not use the policy interest rate, which basically is kind of an atomic bomb without any precision.

The big question here is: How reliable are these tools? How much can they be used? The answer—from some experiments before the crisis with loan-to-value ratios and during the crisis with variations in cyclical bank capital ratios or loan-to-value ratios or capital controls, such as in Brazil—is this: They work but they don't work great. People

and institutions find ways around them. In the process of reducing the problem somewhere you tend to create distortions elsewhere.

#5 Central bank independence wasn't designed for what central banks are now asked to do.

There is two-way interaction between monetary policy and macro-prudential tools. When [Fed chair] Ben Bernanke does expansionary monetary policy, quantitative easing, and interest rates on many assets

Olivier Blanchard

are close to zero, there's a tendency by many players to take risks to increase their rate of return. Some of this risk actually we want them to take. Some we don't want them to take. That is the interaction of monetary policy on the financial system.

You also have it the other way around. If you use macro-prudential tools to, say, slow down the building in the housing sector you have an effect on aggregate demand, which is going to decrease output.

The question is: How do you organize the use of these tools? It makes sense to have them under the same roof. In practice this means the central bank. But that poses questions not only about coordination between the two functions, but also about central bank independence.

One of the major achievements of the last 20 years is that most central banks have become independent of elected governments. Independence was given because the mandate and the tools were very clear. The mandate was primarily inflation, which can be observed over time. The tool was some short-term interest rate that could be used by the central bank to try to achieve the inflation target. In this case, you can give some independence to the institution in charge of this because the objective is perfectly well defined, and everybody can basically observe how well the central bank does..

If you think now of central banks as having a much larger set of responsibilities and a much larger set of tools, then the issue of central bank independence becomes much more difficult. Do you actually want to give the central bank the independence to choose loan-to-value ratios without any supervision from the political process? Isn't this going to lead to a democratic deficit in a way in which the central bank becomes too powerful? I'm sure there are ways out. Perhaps there could be independence with respect to some dimensions of monetary policy—the traditional ones—and some supervision for the rest or some interaction with a political process. ■

cost of producing food products. Or a war in the Middle East might interrupt the shipping of crude oil, driving up the cost of producing oil products.

To analyze the macroeconomic impact of such an increase in production costs, we follow the same four steps as always. First, which curve is affected? Because production costs affect the firms that supply goods and services, changes in

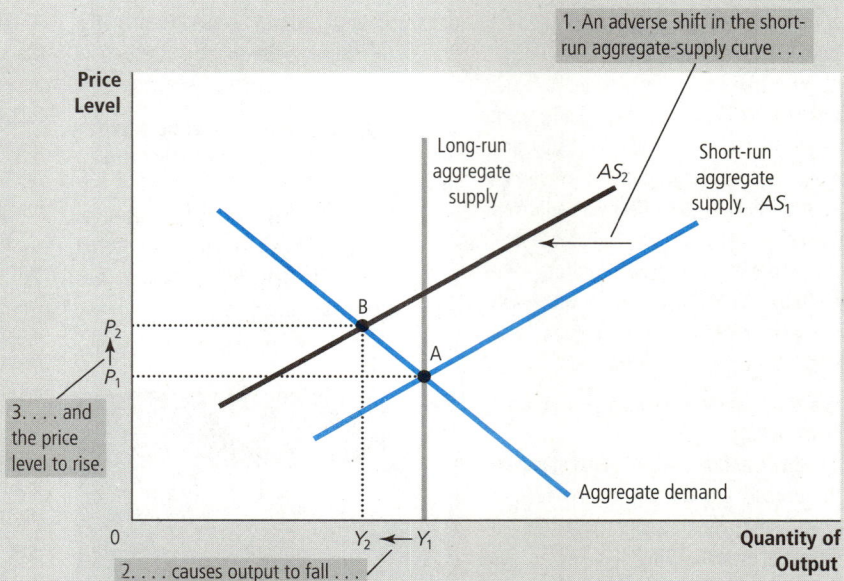

FIGURE 10

An Adverse Shift in Aggregate Supply
When some event increases firms' costs, the short-run aggregate-supply curve shifts to the left from AS_1 to AS_2. The economy moves from point A to point B. The result is stagflation: Output falls from Y_1 to Y_2, and the price level rises from P_1 to P_2.

production costs alter the position of the aggregate-supply curve. Second, in which direction does the curve shift? Because higher production costs make selling goods and services less profitable, firms now supply a smaller quantity of output for any given price level. Thus, as Figure 10 shows, the short-run aggregate-supply curve shifts to the left, from AS_1 to AS_2. (Depending on the event, the long-run aggregate-supply curve might also shift. To keep things simple, however, we will assume that it does not.)

The figure allows us to perform step three of comparing the initial and the new equilibrium. In the short run, the economy goes from point A to point B, moving along the existing aggregate-demand curve. The output of the economy falls from Y_1 to Y_2, and the price level rises from P_1 to P_2. Because the economy is experiencing both *stagnation* (falling output) and *inflation* (rising prices), such an event is sometimes called **stagflation**.

stagflation
a period of falling output and rising prices

Now consider step four—the transition from the short-run equilibrium to the long-run equilibrium. According to the sticky-wage theory, the key issue is how stagflation affects nominal wages. Firms and workers may at first respond to the higher level of prices by raising their expectations of the price level and setting higher nominal wages. In this case, firms' costs will rise yet again, and the short-run aggregate-supply curve will shift farther to the left, making the problem of stagflation even worse. This phenomenon of higher prices leading to higher wages, in turn leading to even higher prices, is sometimes called a *wage-price spiral*.

At some point, this spiral of ever-rising wages and prices will slow. The low level of output and employment will put downward pressure on workers' wages because workers have less bargaining power when unemployment is high. As nominal wages fall, producing goods and services becomes more profitable and the short-run aggregate-supply curve shifts to the right. As it shifts back toward AS_1, the price level falls and the quantity of output approaches its natural level. In

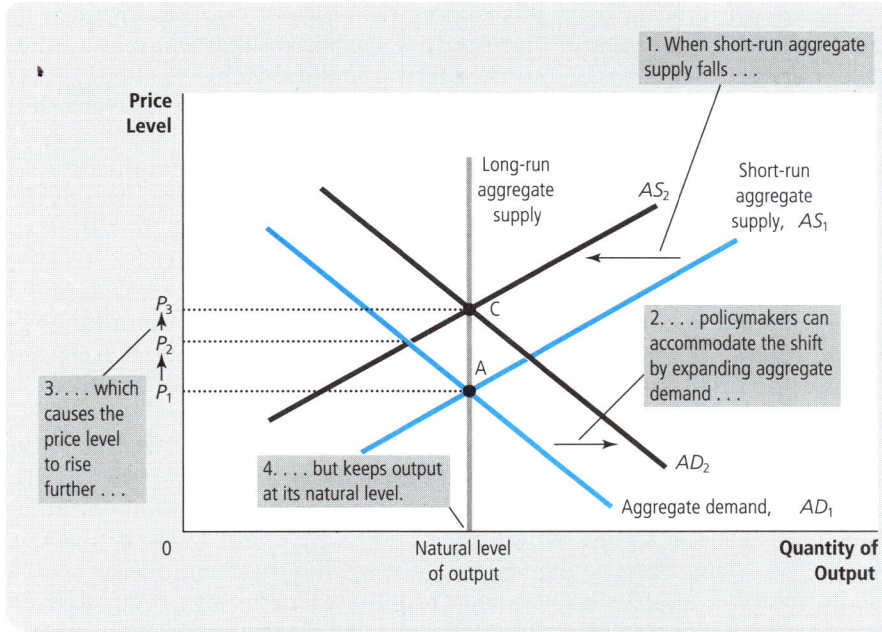

FIGURE 11

Accommodating an Adverse Shift in Aggregate Supply
Faced with an adverse shift in aggregate supply from AS_1 to AS_2, policymakers who can influence aggregate demand might try to shift the aggregate-demand curve to the right from AD_1 to AD_2. The economy would move from point A to point C. This policy would prevent the supply shift from reducing output in the short run, but the price level would permanently rise from P_1 to P_3.

the long run, the economy returns to point A, where the aggregate-demand curve crosses the long-run aggregate-supply curve.

This transition back to the initial equilibrium assumes, however, that aggregate demand is held constant throughout the process. In the real world, that may not be the case. Policymakers who control monetary and fiscal policy might attempt to offset some of the effects of the shift in the short-run aggregate-supply curve by shifting the aggregate-demand curve. This possibility is shown in Figure 11. In this case, changes in policy shift the aggregate-demand curve to the right, from AD_1 to AD_2—exactly enough to prevent the shift in aggregate supply from affecting output. The economy moves directly from point A to point C. Output remains at its natural level, and the price level rises from P_1 to P_3. In this case, policymakers are said to *accommodate* the shift in aggregate supply. An accommodative policy accepts a permanently higher level of prices to maintain a higher level of output and employment.

To sum up, this story about shifts in aggregate supply has two important lessons:

- Shifts in aggregate supply can cause stagflation—a combination of recession (falling output) and inflation (rising prices).
- Policymakers who can influence aggregate demand can potentially mitigate the adverse impact on output but only at the cost of exacerbating the problem of inflation.

CASE STUDY

OIL AND THE ECONOMY
Some of the largest economic fluctuations in the U.S. economy since 1970 have originated in the oil fields of the Middle East. Crude oil is a key input into the production of many goods and services, and much of the world's oil comes from Saudi Arabia, Kuwait, and other Middle Eastern countries. When some event (usually political in origin) reduces the

supply of crude oil flowing from this region, the price of oil rises around the world. Firms in the United States that produce gasoline, tires, and many other products experience rising costs, and they find it less profitable to supply their output of goods and services at any given price level. The result is a leftward shift in the aggregate-supply curve, which in turn leads to stagflation.

The first episode of this sort occurred in the mid-1970s. The countries with large oil reserves got together as members of OPEC, the Organization of the Petroleum Exporting Countries. OPEC is a *cartel*—a group of sellers that attempts to thwart competition and reduce production to raise prices. And indeed, oil prices rose substantially. From 1973 to 1975, oil approximately doubled in price. Oil-importing countries around the world experienced simultaneous inflation and recession. The U.S. inflation rate as measured by the CPI exceeded 10 percent for the first time in decades. Unemployment rose from 4.9 percent in 1973 to 8.5 percent in 1975.

Almost the same thing happened a few years later. In the late 1970s, the OPEC countries again restricted the supply of oil to raise the price. From 1978 to 1981, the price of oil more than doubled. Once again, the result was stagflation. Inflation, which had subsided somewhat after the first OPEC event, again rose above 10 percent per year. But because the Fed was not willing to accommodate such a large rise in inflation, a recession was soon to follow. Unemployment rose from about 6 percent in 1978 and 1979 to about 10 percent a few years later.

The world market for oil can also be a source of favorable shifts in aggregate supply. In 1986, squabbling broke out among members of OPEC. Member countries reneged on their agreements to restrict oil production. In the world market for crude oil, prices fell by about half. This fall in oil prices reduced costs to U.S. firms, which now found it more profitable to supply goods and services at any given price level. As a result, the aggregate-supply

The Origins of the Model of Aggregate Demand and Aggregate Supply

Now that we have a preliminary understanding of the model of aggregate demand and aggregate supply, it is worthwhile to step back from it and consider its history. How did this model of short-run fluctuations develop? The answer is that this model, to a large extent, is a by-product of the Great Depression of the 1930s. Economists and policymakers at the time were puzzled about what had caused this calamity and were uncertain about how to deal with it.

In 1936, economist John Maynard Keynes published a book titled *The General Theory of Employment, Interest, and Money*, which attempted to explain short-run economic fluctuations in general and the Great Depression in particular. Keynes's primary message was that recessions and depressions can occur because of inadequate aggregate demand for goods and services.

John Maynard Keynes

Keynes had long been a critic of classical economic theory—the theory we examined earlier in the book—because it could explain only the long-run effects of policies. A few years before offering *The General Theory*, Keynes had written the following about classical economics:

The long run is a misleading guide to current affairs. In the long run we are all dead. Economists set themselves too easy, too useless a task if in tempestuous seasons they can only tell us when the storm is long past, the ocean will be flat.

Keynes's message was aimed at policymakers as well as economists. As the world's economies suffered with high unemployment, Keynes advocated policies to increase aggregate demand, including government spending on public works.

In the next chapter, we examine in detail how policymakers can use the tools of monetary and fiscal policy to influence aggregate demand. The analysis in the next chapter, as well as in this one, owes much to the legacy of John Maynard Keynes. ■

curve shifted to the right. The U.S. economy experienced the opposite of stagflation: Output grew rapidly, unemployment fell, and the inflation rate reached its lowest level in many years.

In recent years, the world market for oil has not been as important a source of economic fluctuations for the U.S. economy. Part of the reason is that conservation efforts, changes in technology, and the availability of alternative energy sources have reduced the economy's dependence on oil. The amount of oil used to produce a unit of real GDP has declined by more than 50 percent since the OPEC shocks of the 1970s. As a result, the economic impact of any change in oil prices on the U.S. economy is much smaller today than it was in the past. (Of course, some nations rely on oil exports as a major source of their income, and this makes oil prices crucial for them, but that is another story.) ●

Changes in Middle East oil production are one source of U.S. economic fluctuations.

QuickQuiz *Suppose that the election of a popular presidential candidate suddenly increases people's confidence in the future. Use the model of aggregate demand and aggregate supply to analyze the effect on the economy.*

33-6 Conclusion

This chapter has achieved two goals. First, we have discussed some of the important facts about short-run fluctuations in economic activity. Second, we have introduced a basic model to explain those fluctuations, called the model of aggregate demand and aggregate supply. We continue our study of this model in the next chapter to understand more fully what causes fluctuations in the economy and how policymakers might respond to these fluctuations.

CHAPTER QuickQuiz

1. When the economy goes into a recession, real GDP _____ and unemployment _____.
   a. rises, rises
   b. rises, falls
   c. falls, rises
   d. falls, falls

2. A sudden crash in the stock market shifts
   a. the aggregate-demand curve.
   b. the short-run aggregate-supply curve, but not the long-run aggregate-supply curve.
   c. the long-run aggregate-supply curve, but not the short-run aggregate-supply curve.
   d. both the short-run and the long-run aggregate-supply curves.

3. A change in the expected price level shifts
   a. the aggregate-demand curve.
   b. the short-run aggregate-supply curve, but not the long-run aggregate-supply curve.
   c. the long-run aggregate-supply curve, but not the short-run aggregate-supply curve.
   d. both the short-run and the long-run aggregate-supply curves.

4. An increase in the aggregate demand for goods and services has a larger impact on output _____ and a larger impact on the price level _____.
   a. in the short run, in the long run
   b. in the long run, in the short run
   c. in the short run, also in the short run
   d. in the long run, also in the long run

5. Stagflation is caused by
   a. a leftward shift in the aggregate-demand curve.
   b. a rightward shift in the aggregate-demand curve.
   c. a leftward shift in the aggregate-supply curve.
   d. a rightward shift in the aggregate-supply curve.

6. The idea that economic downturns result from an inadequate aggregate demand for goods and services is derived from the work of which economist?
   a. Adam Smith
   b. David Hume
   c. David Ricardo
   d. John Maynard Keynes

SUMMARY

- All societies experience short-run economic fluctuations around long-run trends. These fluctuations are irregular and largely unpredictable. When recessions occur, real GDP and other measures of income, spending, and production fall, while unemployment rises.

- Classical economic theory is based on the assumption that nominal variables such as the money supply and the price level do not influence real variables such as output and employment. Most economists believe that this assumption is accurate in the long run but not in the short run. Economists analyze short-run economic fluctuations using the model of aggregate demand and aggregate supply. According to this model, the output of goods and services and the overall level of prices adjust to balance aggregate demand and aggregate supply.

- The aggregate-demand curve slopes downward for three reasons. The first is the wealth effect: A lower price level raises the real value of households' money holdings, which stimulates consumer spending. The second is the interest-rate effect: A lower price level reduces the quantity of money households demand; as households try to convert money into interest-bearing assets, interest rates fall, which stimulates investment spending. The third is the exchange-rate effect: As a lower price level reduces interest rates, the dollar depreciates in the market for foreign-currency exchange, which stimulates net exports.

- Any event or policy that raises consumption, investment, government purchases, or net exports at a given price level increases aggregate demand. Any event or policy that reduces consumption, investment, government purchases, or net exports at a given price level decreases aggregate demand.

- The long-run aggregate-supply curve is vertical. In the long run, the quantity of goods and services supplied depends on the economy's labor, capital, natural resources, and technology but not on the overall level of prices.

- Three theories have been proposed to explain the upward slope of the short-run aggregate-supply curve. According to the sticky-wage theory, an unexpected fall in the price level temporarily raises real wages, which induces firms to reduce employment and production. According to the sticky-price theory, an unexpected fall in the price level leaves some firms with prices that are temporarily too high, which reduces their sales and causes them to cut back production. According to the misperceptions theory, an unexpected fall in the price level leads suppliers to mistakenly believe that their relative prices have fallen, which induces them to reduce production. All three theories imply that output deviates from its natural level when the actual price level deviates from the price level that people expected.

- Events that alter the economy's ability to produce output, such as changes in labor, capital, natural resources, or technology, shift the short-run aggregate-supply curve (and may shift the long-run aggregate-supply curve as well). In addition, the position of the short-run aggregate-supply curve depends on the expected price level.

- One possible cause of economic fluctuations is a shift in aggregate demand. When the aggregate-demand curve shifts to the left, for instance, output and prices fall in the short run. Over time, as a change in the expected price level causes wages, prices, and perceptions to adjust, the short-run aggregate-supply curve shifts to the right. This shift returns the economy to its natural level of output at a new, lower price level.

- A second possible cause of economic fluctuations is a shift in aggregate supply. When the short-run aggregate-supply curve shifts to the left, the effect is falling output and rising prices—a combination called stagflation. Over time, as wages, prices, and perceptions adjust, the short-run aggregate-supply curve shifts back to the right, returning the price level and output to their original levels.

KEY CONCEPTS

recession, p. 702
depression, p. 702

model of aggregate demand and
   aggregate supply, p. 706
aggregate-demand curve, p. 706

aggregate-supply curve, p. 707
natural level of output, p. 714
stagflation, p. 730

QUESTIONS FOR REVIEW

1. Name two macroeconomic variables that decline when the economy goes into a recession. Name one macroeconomic variable that rises during a recession.

2. Draw a diagram with aggregate demand, short-run aggregate supply, and long-run aggregate supply. Be careful to label the axes correctly.

3. List and explain the three reasons the aggregate-demand curve slopes downward.

4. Explain why the long-run aggregate-supply curve is vertical.

5. List and explain the three theories for why the short-run aggregate-supply curve slopes upward.

6. What might shift the aggregate-demand curve to the left? Use the model of aggregate demand and aggregate supply to trace through the short-run and long-run effects of such a shift on output and the price level.

7. What might shift the aggregate-supply curve to the left? Use the model of aggregate demand and aggregate supply to trace through the short-run and long-run effects of such a shift on output and the price level.

PROBLEMS AND APPLICATIONS

1. Suppose the economy is in a long-run equilibrium.
   a. Draw a diagram to illustrate the state of the economy. Be sure to show aggregate demand, short-run aggregate supply, and long-run aggregate supply.
   b. Now suppose that a stock market crash causes aggregate demand to fall. Use your diagram to show what happens to output and the price level in the short run. What happens to the unemployment rate?
   c. Use the sticky-wage theory of aggregate supply to explain what will happen to output and the price level in the long run (assuming no change in policy). What role does the expected price level play in this adjustment? Be sure to illustrate your analysis in a graph.

2. Explain whether each of the following events will increase, decrease, or have no effect on long-run aggregate supply.
   a. The United States experiences a wave of immigration.
   b. Congress raises the minimum wage to $15 per hour.
   c. Intel invents a new and more powerful computer chip.
   d. A severe hurricane damages factories along the East Coast.

3. Suppose an economy is in long-run equilibrium.
   a. Use the model of aggregate demand and aggregate supply to illustrate the initial equilibrium (call it point A). Be sure to include both short-run and long-run aggregate supply.
   b. The central bank raises the money supply by 5 percent. Use your diagram to show what happens to output and the price level as the economy moves from the initial to the new short-run equilibrium (call it point B).

   c. Now show the new long-run equilibrium (call it point C). What causes the economy to move from point B to point C?
   d. According to the sticky-wage theory of aggregate supply, how do nominal wages at point A compare to nominal wages at point B? How do nominal wages at point A compare to nominal wages at point C?
   e. According to the sticky-wage theory of aggregate supply, how do real wages at point A compare to real wages at point B? How do real wages at point A compare to real wages at point C?
   f. Judging by the impact of the money supply on nominal and real wages, is this analysis consistent with the proposition that money has real effects in the short run but is neutral in the long run?

4. In 1939, with the U.S. economy not yet fully recovered from the Great Depression, President Roosevelt proclaimed that Thanksgiving would fall a week earlier than usual so that the shopping period before Christmas would be longer. Explain what President Roosevelt might have been trying to achieve, using the model of aggregate demand and aggregate supply.

5. Explain why the following statements are false.
   a. "The aggregate-demand curve slopes downward because it is the horizontal sum of the demand curves for individual goods."
   b. "The long-run aggregate-supply curve is vertical because economic forces do not affect long-run aggregate supply."
   c. "If firms adjusted their prices every day, then the short-run aggregate-supply curve would be horizontal."
   d. "Whenever the economy enters a recession, its long-run aggregate-supply curve shifts to the left."

6. For each of the three theories for the upward slope of the short-run aggregate-supply curve, carefully explain the following:
   a. how the economy recovers from a recession and returns to its long-run equilibrium without any policy intervention
   b. what determines the speed of that recovery

7. The economy begins in long-run equilibrium. Then one day, the president appoints a new chair of the Federal Reserve. This new chairman is well known for her view that inflation is not a major problem for an economy.
   a. How would this news affect the price level that people would expect to prevail?
   b. How would this change in the expected price level affect the nominal wage that workers and firms agree to in their new labor contracts?
   c. How would this change in the nominal wage affect the profitability of producing goods and services at any given price level?
   d. How does this change in profitability affect the short-run aggregate-supply curve?
   e. If aggregate demand is held constant, how does this shift in the aggregate-supply curve affect the price level and the quantity of output produced?
   f. Do you think this Fed chairman was a good appointment?

8. Explain whether each of the following events shifts the short-run aggregate-supply curve, the aggregate-demand curve, both, or neither. For each event that does shift a curve, draw a diagram to illustrate the effect on the economy.
   a. Households decide to save a larger share of their income.
   b. Florida orange groves suffer a prolonged period of below-freezing temperatures.
   c. Increased job opportunities overseas cause many people to leave the country.

9. For each of the following events, explain the short-run and long-run effects on output and the price level, assuming policymakers take no action.
   a. The stock market declines sharply, reducing consumers' wealth.
   b. The federal government increases spending on national defense.
   c. A technological improvement raises productivity.
   d. A recession overseas causes foreigners to buy fewer U.S. goods.

10. Suppose firms become very optimistic about future business conditions and invest heavily in new capital equipment.
   a. Draw an aggregate-demand/aggregate-supply diagram to show the short-run effect of this optimism on the economy. Label the new levels of prices and real output. Explain in words why the aggregate quantity of output *supplied* changes.
   b. Now use the diagram from part (a) to show the new long-run equilibrium of the economy. (For now, assume there is no change in the long-run aggregate-supply curve.) Explain in words why the aggregate quantity of output *demanded* changes between the short run and the long run.
   c. How might the investment boom affect the long-run aggregate-supply curve? Explain.

To find additional study resources, visit cengagebrain.com, and search for "Mankiw."

The Influence of Monetary and Fiscal Policy on Aggregate Demand

Imagine that you are a member of the Federal Open Market Committee, the group at the Federal Reserve that sets monetary policy. You observe that the president and Congress have agreed to raise taxes. How should the Fed respond to this change in fiscal policy? Should it expand the money supply, contract the money supply, or leave it unchanged?

To answer this question, you need to consider the impact of monetary and fiscal policy on the economy. In the preceding chapter, we used the model of aggregate demand and aggregate supply to explain short-run economic

fluctuations. We saw that shifts in the aggregate-demand curve or the aggregate-supply curve cause fluctuations in the economy's overall output of goods and services and its overall level of prices. As we noted in the previous chapter, both monetary and fiscal policy influence aggregate demand. Thus, a change in one of these policies can lead to short-run fluctuations in output and prices. Policymakers will want to anticipate this effect and, perhaps, adjust the other policy in response.

In this chapter, we examine in more detail how the government's policy tools influence the position of the aggregate-demand curve. These tools include monetary policy (the supply of money set by the central bank) and fiscal policy (the levels of government spending and taxation set by the president and Congress). We have previously discussed the long-run effects of these policies. In Chapters 25 and 26, we saw how fiscal policy affects saving, investment, and long-run economic growth. In Chapters 29 and 30, we saw how monetary policy influences the price level in the long run. We now look at how these policy tools can shift the aggregate-demand curve and thereby affect macroeconomic variables in the short run.

As we have already learned, many factors influence aggregate demand besides monetary and fiscal policy. In particular, desired spending by households and firms determines the overall demand for goods and services. When desired spending changes, aggregate demand shifts. If policymakers do not respond, such shifts in aggregate demand cause short-run fluctuations in output and employment. As a result, monetary and fiscal policymakers sometimes use the policy levers at their disposal to try to offset these shifts in aggregate demand and stabilize the economy. Here we discuss the theory behind these policy actions and some of the difficulties that arise in using this theory in practice.

34-1 How Monetary Policy Influences Aggregate Demand

The aggregate-demand curve shows the total quantity of goods and services demanded in the economy for any price level. The preceding chapter discussed three reasons why the aggregate-demand curve slopes downward:

- *The wealth effect:* A lower price level raises the real value of households' money holdings, which are part of their wealth. Higher real wealth stimulates consumer spending and thus increases the quantity of goods and services demanded.
- *The interest-rate effect:* A lower price level reduces the amount of money people want to hold. As people try to lend out their excess money holdings, the interest rate falls. The lower interest rate stimulates investment spending and thus increases the quantity of goods and services demanded.
- *The exchange-rate effect:* When a lower price level reduces the interest rate, investors move some of their funds overseas in search of higher returns. This movement of funds causes the real value of the domestic currency to fall in the market for foreign-currency exchange. Domestic goods become less expensive relative to foreign goods. This change in the real exchange rate stimulates spending on net exports and thus increases the quantity of goods and services demanded.

These three effects occur simultaneously to increase the quantity of goods and services demanded when the price level falls and to decrease it when the price level rises.

Although all three effects work together to explain the downward slope of the aggregate-demand curve, they are not of equal importance. Because money holdings are a small part of household wealth, the wealth effect is the least important of the three. In addition, because exports and imports represent only a small fraction of U.S. GDP, the exchange-rate effect is not large for the U.S. economy. (This effect is more important for smaller countries, which typically export and import a higher fraction of their GDP.) *For the U.S. economy, the most important reason for the downward slope of the aggregate-demand curve is the interest-rate effect.*

To better understand aggregate demand, we now examine the short-run determination of interest rates in more detail. Here we develop the **theory of liquidity preference**. This theory of interest rates helps explain the downward slope of the aggregate-demand curve, as well as how monetary and fiscal policy can shift this curve. By shedding new light on aggregate demand, the theory of liquidity preference expands our understanding of what causes short-run economic fluctuations and what policymakers can potentially do about them.

theory of liquidity preference
Keynes's theory that the interest rate adjusts to bring money supply and money demand into balance

34-1a   The Theory of Liquidity Preference

In his classic book *The General Theory of Employment, Interest, and Money*, John Maynard Keynes proposed the theory of liquidity preference to explain the factors that determine an economy's interest rate. The theory is, in essence, an application of supply and demand. According to Keynes, the interest rate adjusts to balance the supply of and demand for money.

You may recall that economists distinguish between two interest rates: The *nominal interest rate* is the interest rate as usually reported, and the *real interest rate* is the interest rate corrected for the effects of inflation. When there is no inflation, the two rates are the same. But when borrowers and lenders expect prices to rise over the course of the loan, they agree to a nominal interest rate that exceeds the real interest rate by the expected rate of inflation. The higher nominal interest rate compensates for the fact that they expect the loan to be repaid in less valuable dollars.

Which interest rate are we now trying to explain with the theory of liquidity preference? The answer is both. In the analysis that follows, we hold constant the expected rate of inflation. This assumption is reasonable for studying the economy in the short run, because expected inflation is typically stable over short periods of time. In this case, nominal and real interest rates differ by a constant. When the nominal interest rate rises or falls, the real interest rate that people expect to earn rises or falls by a similar amount. For the rest of this chapter, when we discuss changes in the interest rate, these changes refer to both the real and nominal interest rates.

Let's now develop the theory of liquidity preference by considering the supply and demand for money and how each depends on the interest rate.

Money Supply   The first piece of the theory of liquidity preference is the supply of money. As we first discussed in Chapter 29, the money supply in the U.S. economy is controlled by the Federal Reserve. The Fed alters the money supply primarily by changing the quantity of reserves in the banking system through the purchase and sale of government bonds in open-market operations. When the Fed buys government bonds, the dollars it pays for the bonds are typically deposited in banks, and these dollars are added to bank reserves. When the Fed sells government bonds, the dollars it receives for the bonds are withdrawn from the banking system, and bank reserves fall. These changes in bank reserves, in turn, lead to changes in banks' ability to make loans and create money. Thus, by buying and selling bonds in open-market operations, the Fed alters the supply of money in the economy.

In addition to open-market operations, the Fed can influence the money supply using a variety of other tools. One option is for the Fed to change how much it lends to banks. For example, a decrease in the discount rate (the interest rate at which banks can borrow reserves from the Fed) encourages more bank borrowing, which increases bank reserves and thereby the money supply. Conversely, an increase in the discount rate discourages bank borrowing, which decreases bank reserves and the money supply. The Fed also alters the money supply by changing reserve requirements (the amount of reserves banks must hold against deposits) and by changing the interest rate it pays banks on the reserves they are holding.

These details of monetary control are important for the implementation of Fed policy, but they are not crucial for the analysis in this chapter. Our goal here is to examine how changes in the money supply affect the aggregate demand for goods and services. For this purpose, we can ignore the details of how Fed policy is implemented and assume that the Fed controls the money supply directly. In other words, the quantity of money supplied in the economy is fixed at whatever level the Fed decides to set it.

Because the quantity of money supplied is fixed by Fed policy, it does not depend on other economic variables. In particular, it does not depend on the interest rate. Once the Fed has made its policy decision, the quantity of money supplied is the same, regardless of the prevailing interest rate. We represent a fixed money supply with a vertical supply curve, as in Figure 1.

FIGURE 1

Equilibrium in the Money Market

According to the theory of liquidity preference, the interest rate adjusts to bring the quantity of money supplied and the quantity of money demanded into balance. If the interest rate is above the equilibrium level (such as at r_1), the quantity of money people want to hold (M_1^d) is less than the quantity the Fed has created, and this surplus of money puts downward pressure on the interest rate. Conversely, if the interest rate is below the equilibrium level (such as at r_2), the quantity of money people want to hold (M_2^d) is greater than the quantity the Fed has created, and this shortage of money puts upward pressure on the interest rate. Thus, the forces of supply and demand in the market for money push the interest rate toward the equilibrium interest rate, at which people are content holding the quantity of money the Fed has created.

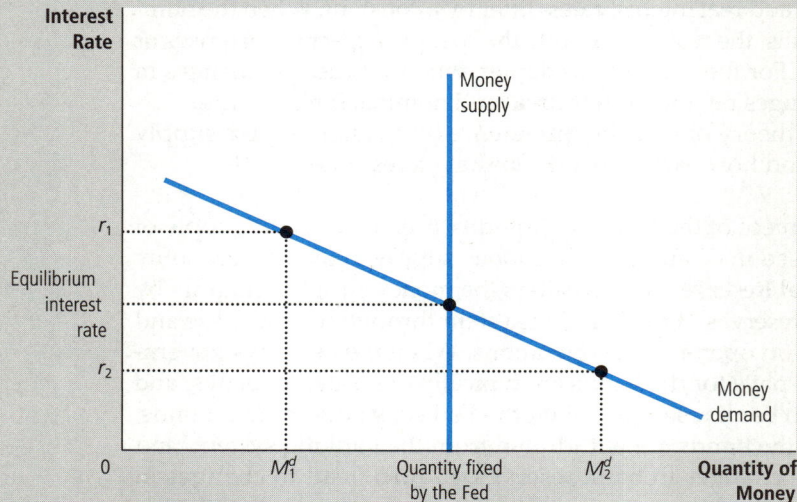

Money Demand   The second piece of the theory of liquidity preference is the demand for money. As a starting point for understanding money demand, recall that an asset's *liquidity* refers to the ease with which that asset can be converted into the economy's medium of exchange. Because money is the economy's medium of exchange, it is by definition the most liquid asset available. The liquidity of money explains the demand for it: People choose to hold money instead of other assets that offer higher rates of return because money can be used to buy goods and services.

Although many factors determine the quantity of money demanded, the one emphasized by the theory of liquidity preference is the interest rate. The reason is that the interest rate is the opportunity cost of holding money. That is, when you hold wealth as cash in your wallet, instead of as an interest-bearing bond, you lose the interest you could have earned. An increase in the interest rate raises the cost of holding money and, as a result, reduces the quantity of money demanded. A decrease in the interest rate reduces the cost of holding money and raises the quantity demanded. Thus, as shown in Figure 1, the money demand curve slopes downward.

Equilibrium in the Money Market   According to the theory of liquidity preference, the interest rate adjusts to balance the supply and demand for money. There is one interest rate, called the *equilibrium interest rate*, at which the quantity of money demanded exactly balances the quantity of money supplied. If the interest rate is at any other level, people will try to adjust their portfolios of assets and, as a result, drive the interest rate toward the equilibrium.

For example, suppose that the interest rate is above the equilibrium level, such as r_1 in Figure 1. In this case, the quantity of money that people want to hold, M_1^d, is less than the quantity of money that the Fed has supplied. Those people who are holding the surplus of money will try to get rid of it by buying interest-bearing bonds or by depositing it in interest-bearing bank accounts. Because bond issuers and banks prefer to pay lower interest rates, they respond to this surplus of money by lowering the interest rates they offer. As the interest rate falls, people become more willing to hold money until, at the equilibrium interest rate, people are happy to hold exactly the amount of money the Fed has supplied.

Conversely, at interest rates below the equilibrium level, such as r_2 in Figure 1, the quantity of money that people want to hold, M_2^d, is greater than the quantity of money that the Fed has supplied. As a result, people try to increase their holdings of money by reducing their holdings of bonds and other interest-bearing assets. As people cut back on their holdings of bonds, bond issuers find that they have to offer higher interest rates to attract buyers. Thus, the interest rate rises until it reaches the equilibrium level.

34-1b The Downward Slope of the Aggregate-Demand Curve

Having seen how the theory of liquidity preference explains the economy's equilibrium interest rate, we now consider the theory's implications for the aggregate demand for goods and services. As a warm-up exercise, let's begin by using the theory to reexamine a topic we already understand—the interest-rate effect and the downward slope of the aggregate-demand curve. In particular, suppose that the overall level of prices in the economy rises. What happens to the interest rate that balances the supply and demand for money, and how does that change affect the quantity of goods and services demanded?

As we discussed in Chapter 30, the price level is one determinant of the quantity of money demanded. At higher prices, more money is exchanged every time a good or service is sold. As a result, people will choose to hold a larger quantity of money. That is, a higher price level increases the quantity of money demanded for any given interest rate. Thus, an increase in the price level from P_1 to P_2 shifts the money demand curve to the right from MD_1 to MD_2, as shown in panel (a) of Figure 2.

Notice how this shift in money demand affects the equilibrium in the money market. For a fixed money supply, the interest rate must rise to balance money supply and money demand. Because the higher price level has increased the amount of money people want to hold, it has shifted the money demand curve to the right. Yet the quantity of money supplied is unchanged, so the interest rate must rise from r_1 to r_2 to discourage the additional demand.

This increase in the interest rate has ramifications not only for the money market but also for the quantity of goods and services demanded, as shown in panel (b). At

FYI

Interest Rates in the Long Run and the Short Run

In an earlier chapter, we said that the interest rate adjusts to balance the supply of loanable funds (national saving) and the demand for loanable funds (desired investment). Here we just said that the interest rate adjusts to balance the supply of and demand for money. Can we reconcile these two theories?

To answer this question, we need to focus on three macroeconomic variables: the economy's output of goods and services, the interest rate, and the price level. According to the classical macroeconomic theory we developed earlier in the book, these variables are determined as follows:

1. *Output* is determined by the supplies of capital and labor and the available production technology for turning capital and labor into output. (We call this the natural level of output.)
2. For any given level of output, the *interest rate* adjusts to balance the supply and demand for loanable funds.
3. Given output and the interest rate, the *price level* adjusts to balance the supply and demand for money. Changes in the supply of money lead to proportionate changes in the price level.

These are three of the essential propositions of classical economic theory. Most economists believe that these propositions do a good job of describing how the economy works *in the long run*.

Yet these propositions do not hold in the short run. As we discussed in the preceding chapter, many prices are slow to adjust to changes in the money supply; this fact is reflected in a short-run aggregate-supply curve that is upward-sloping rather than vertical. As a result, *in the short run*, the overall price level cannot, by itself, move to balance the supply of and demand for money. This stickiness of the price level requires the interest rate to move to bring the money market into equilibrium. These changes in the interest

rate, in turn, affect the aggregate demand for goods and services. As aggregate demand fluctuates, the economy's output of goods and services moves away from the level determined by factor supplies and technology.

To think about the operation of the economy in the short run (day to day, week to week, month to month, or quarter to quarter), it is best to keep in mind the following logic:

1. The *price level* is stuck at some level (based on previously formed expectations) and, in the short run, is relatively unresponsive to changing economic conditions.
2. For any given (stuck) price level, the *interest rate* adjusts to balance the supply of and demand for money.
3. The interest rate that balances the money market influences the quantity of goods and services demanded and thus the level of *output*.

Notice that this precisely reverses the order of analysis used to study the economy in the long run.

The two different theories of the interest rate are useful for different purposes. When thinking about the long-run determinants of the interest rate, it is best to keep in mind the loanable-funds theory, which highlights the importance of an economy's saving propensities and investment opportunities. By contrast, when thinking about the short-run determinants of the interest rate, it is best to keep in mind the liquidity-preference theory, which highlights the importance of monetary policy. ■

An increase in the price level from P_1 to P_2 shifts the money demand curve to the right, as in panel (a). This increase in money demand causes the interest rate to rise from r_1 to r_2. Because the interest rate is the cost of borrowing, the increase in the interest rate reduces the quantity of goods and services demanded from Y_1 to Y_2. This negative relationship between the price level and quantity demanded is represented with a downward-sloping aggregate-demand curve, as in panel (b).

FIGURE 2

The Money Market and the Slope of the Aggregate-Demand Curve

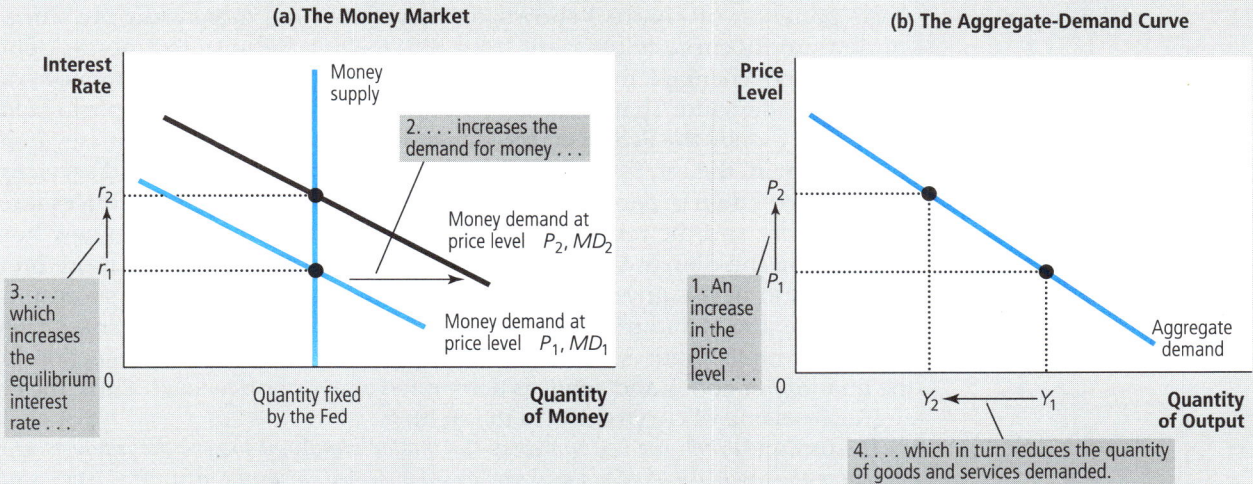

(a) The Money Market

(b) The Aggregate-Demand Curve

a higher interest rate, the cost of borrowing and the return to saving are greater. Fewer households choose to borrow to buy a new house, and those who do buy smaller houses, so the demand for residential investment falls. Fewer firms choose to borrow to build new factories and buy new equipment, so business investment falls. Thus, when the price level rises from P_1 to P_2, increasing money demand from MD_1 to MD_2 and raising the interest rate from r_1 to r_2, the quantity of goods and services demanded falls from Y_1 to Y_2.

This analysis of the interest-rate effect can be summarized in three steps: (1) A higher price level raises money demand. (2) Higher money demand leads to a higher interest rate. (3) A higher interest rate reduces the quantity of goods and services demanded. The same logic works for a decline in the price level: A lower price level reduces money demand, which leads to a lower interest rate, and this in turn increases the quantity of goods and services demanded. The result of this analysis is a negative relationship between the price level and the quantity of goods and services demanded, as illustrated by a downward-sloping aggregate-demand curve.

34-1c Changes in the Money Supply

So far, we have used the theory of liquidity preference to explain more fully how the total quantity of goods and services demanded in the economy changes as the price level changes. That is, we have examined movements along a downward-sloping aggregate-demand curve. The theory also sheds light, however, on some of the other events that alter the quantity of goods and services demanded. Whenever the quantity of goods and services demanded changes for any given price level, the aggregate-demand curve shifts.

One important variable that shifts the aggregate-demand curve is monetary policy. To see how monetary policy affects the economy in the short run, suppose that the Fed increases the money supply by buying government bonds in open-market operations. (Why the Fed might do this will become clear later, after we understand the effects of such a move.) Let's consider how this monetary injection influences the equilibrium interest rate for a given price level. This will tell us what the injection does to the position of the aggregate-demand curve.

As panel (a) of Figure 3 shows, an increase in the money supply shifts the money supply curve to the right from MS_1 to MS_2. Because the money demand curve has not changed, the interest rate falls from r_1 to r_2 to balance money supply and money demand. That is, the interest rate must fall to induce people to hold the additional money the Fed has created, restoring equilibrium in the money market.

Once again, the interest rate influences the quantity of goods and services demanded, as shown in panel (b) of Figure 3. The lower interest rate reduces the cost of borrowing and the return to saving. Households spend more on new homes, stimulating the demand for residential investment. Firms spend more on new factories and new equipment, stimulating business investment. As a result, the quantity of goods and services demanded at a given price level, $\overline{P}$, rises from Y_1 to Y_2. Of course, there is nothing special about $\overline{P}$: The monetary injection raises the quantity of goods and services demanded at every price level. Thus, the entire aggregate-demand curve shifts to the right.

To sum up: *When the Fed increases the money supply, it lowers the interest rate and increases the quantity of goods and services demanded for any given price level, shifting the aggregate-demand curve to the right. Conversely, when the Fed contracts the money supply, it raises the interest rate and reduces the quantity of goods and services demanded for any given price level, shifting the aggregate-demand curve to the left.*

FIGURE 3

A Monetary Injection

In panel (a), an increase in the money supply from MS_1 to MS_2 reduces the equilibrium interest rate from r_1 to r_2. Because the interest rate is the cost of borrowing, the fall in the interest rate raises the quantity of goods and services demanded at a given price level from Y_1 to Y_2. Thus, in panel (b), the aggregate-demand curve shifts to the right from AD_1 to AD_2.

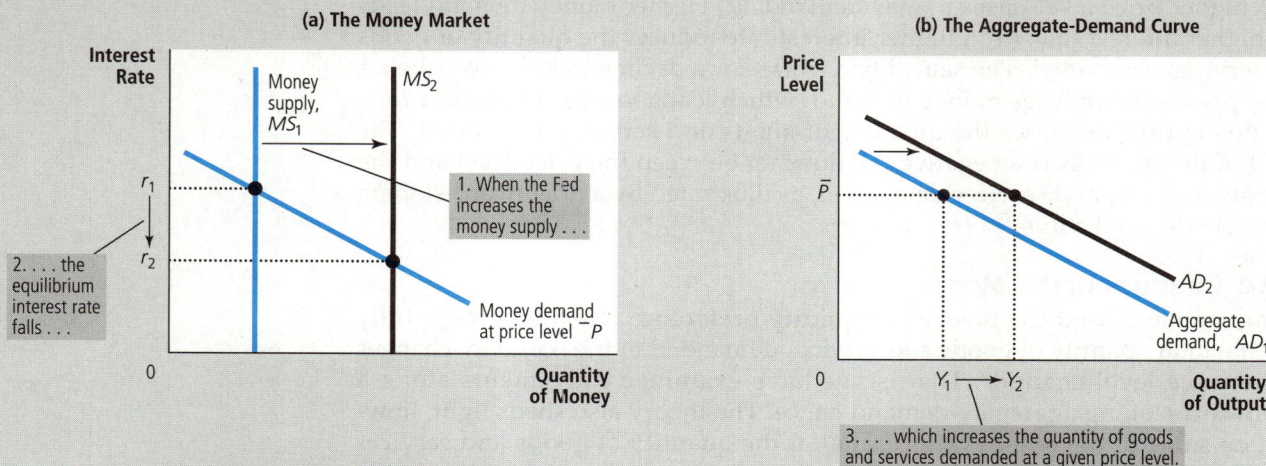

(a) The Money Market

(b) The Aggregate-Demand Curve

34-1d The Role of Interest-Rate Targets in Fed Policy

How does the Federal Reserve affect the economy? Our discussion here and earlier in the book has treated the money supply as the Fed's policy instrument. When the Fed buys government bonds in open-market operations, it increases the money supply and expands aggregate demand. When the Fed sells government bonds in open-market operations, it decreases the money supply and contracts aggregate demand.

Discussions of Fed policy often treat the interest rate, rather than the money supply, as the Fed's policy instrument. Indeed, in recent years, the Federal Reserve has conducted policy by setting a target for the *federal funds rate*—the interest rate that banks charge one another for short-term loans. This target is reevaluated every six weeks at meetings of the Federal Open Market Committee (FOMC). The FOMC has chosen to set a target for the federal funds rate, rather than for the money supply, as it did at times in the past.

There are several related reasons for the Fed's decision to use the federal funds rate as its target. One is that the money supply is hard to measure with sufficient precision. Another is that money demand fluctuates over time. For any given money supply, fluctuations in money demand would lead to fluctuations in interest rates, aggregate demand, and output. By contrast, when the Fed announces a target for the federal funds rate, it essentially accommodates the day-to-day shifts in money demand by adjusting the money supply accordingly.

The Fed's decision to target an interest rate does not fundamentally alter our analysis of monetary policy. The theory of liquidity preference illustrates an important principle: *Monetary policy can be described either in terms of the money supply or in terms of the interest rate.* When the FOMC sets a target for the federal funds rate of, say, 6 percent, the Fed's bond traders are told: "Conduct whatever open-market operations are necessary to ensure that the equilibrium interest rate is 6 percent." In other words, when the Fed sets a target for the interest rate, it commits itself to adjusting the money supply to make the equilibrium in the money market hit that target.

As a result, changes in monetary policy can be viewed either in terms of changing the interest rate target or in terms of changing the money supply. When you read in the newspaper that "the Fed has lowered the federal funds rate from 6 to 5 percent," you should understand that this occurs only because the Fed's bond traders are doing what it takes to make it happen. To lower the federal funds rate, the Fed's bond traders buy government bonds, and this purchase increases the money supply and lowers the equilibrium interest rate (just as in Figure 3). Similarly, when the FOMC raises the target for the federal funds rate, the bond traders sell government bonds, and this sale decreases the money supply and raises the equilibrium interest rate.

The lessons from this analysis are simple: *Changes in monetary policy aimed at expanding aggregate demand can be described either as increasing the money supply or as lowering the interest rate. Changes in monetary policy aimed at contracting aggregate demand can be described either as decreasing the money supply or as raising the interest rate.*

CASE STUDY

WHY THE FED WATCHES THE STOCK MARKET (AND VICE VERSA)
"The stock market has predicted nine out of the past five recessions." So quipped Paul Samuelson, the famed economist (and textbook author). Samuelson was right that the stock market is highly volatile and can give wrong signals about the economy. But fluctuations in stock prices are often a sign of broader economic developments. The economic boom of the 1990s, for example, appeared not only in rapid GDP growth and falling unemployment but also in rising stock prices, which increased about fourfold during this decade.

Similarly, the deep recession of 2008 and 2009 was reflected in falling stock prices: From November 2007 to March 2009, the stock market lost about half its value.

How should the Fed respond to stock market fluctuations? The Fed has no reason to care about stock prices in themselves, but it does have the job of monitoring and responding to developments in the overall economy, and the stock market is a piece of that puzzle. When the stock market booms, households become wealthier, and this increased wealth stimulates consumer spending. In addition, a rise in stock prices makes it more attractive for firms to sell new shares of stock, and this stimulates investment spending. For both reasons, a booming stock market expands the aggregate demand for goods and services.

As we discuss more fully later in the chapter, one of the Fed's goals is to stabilize aggregate demand, because greater stability in aggregate demand means greater stability in output and the price level. To promote stability, the Fed might respond to a stock market boom by keeping the money supply lower and interest rates higher than it otherwise would. The contractionary effects of higher interest rates would offset the expansionary effects of higher stock prices. In fact, this analysis does describe Fed behavior: Real interest rates were kept high by historical standards during the stock market boom of the late 1990s.

The opposite occurs when the stock market falls. Spending on consumption and investment tends to decline, depressing aggregate demand and pushing the economy toward recession. To stabilize aggregate demand, the Fed would increase the money supply and lower interest rates. And indeed, that is what it typically does. For example, on October 19, 1987, the stock market fell by 22.6 percent—one of the biggest one-day drops in history. The Fed responded to the market crash by increasing the money supply and lowering interest rates. The federal funds rate fell from 7.7 percent at the beginning of October to 6.6 percent at the end of the month. In part because of the Fed's quick action, the economy avoided a recession. Similarly, as we discussed in a case study in the preceding chapter, the Fed also reduced interest rates during the economic downturn and stock market decline of 2008 and 2009, but this time monetary policy was not sufficient to avert a deep recession.

While the Fed keeps an eye on the stock market, stock market participants also keep an eye on the Fed. Because the Fed can influence interest rates and economic activity, it can alter the value of stocks. For example, when the Fed raises interest rates by reducing the money supply, it makes owning stocks less attractive for two reasons. First, a higher interest rate means that bonds, the alternative to stocks, are earning a higher return. Second, the Fed's tightening of monetary policy reduces the demand for goods and services, which reduces profits. As a result, stock prices often fall when the Fed raises interest rates. ●

Quick Quiz   *Use the theory of liquidity preference to explain how a decrease in the money supply affects the equilibrium interest rate. How does this change in monetary policy affect the aggregate-demand curve?*

34-1e The Zero Lower Bound

As we have just seen, monetary policy works through interest rates. This conclusion raises a question: What if the Fed's target interest rate has fallen as far as it can? In the recession of 2008 and 2009, the federal funds rate fell to about zero. In this situation, what, if anything, can monetary policy do to stimulate the economy?

Some economists describe this situation as a *liquidity trap*. According to the *theory of liquidity preference*, expansionary monetary policy works by reducing interest rates and stimulating investment spending. But if interest rates have already fallen to around zero, monetary policy may no longer be effective. Nominal interest rates cannot fall much below zero: Rather than making a loan at a negative nominal interest rate, a person would just hold cash. In this environment, expansionary monetary policy raises the supply of money, making the public's asset portfolio more liquid, but because interest rates can't fall any further, the extra liquidity might not have any effect. Aggregate demand, production, and employment may be "trapped" at low levels.

Other economists are skeptical about the relevance of liquidity traps and believe that a central bank continues to have tools to expand the economy, even after its interest rate target hits its lower bound of zero. One possibility is that the central bank could commit itself to keeping interest rates low for an extended period of time. Such a policy is sometimes called *forward guidance.* Even if the central bank's current target for the interest rate cannot fall any further, the promise that interest rates will remain low may help stimulate investment spending.

A second possibility is that the central bank could conduct expansionary open-market operations with a larger variety of financial instruments. Normally, the Fed conducts expansionary open-market operations by buying short-term government bonds. But it could also buy mortgages, corporate debt, and longer-term government bonds and thereby lower the interest rates on these kinds of loans. The Federal Reserve actively pursued this last option in the aftermath of the financial crisis of 2008 and 2009. This type of unconventional monetary policy is sometimes called *quantitative easing* because it increases the quantity of bank reserves.

Some economists have suggested that the possibility of hitting the zero lower bound for interest rates justifies setting the target rate of inflation well above zero. Under zero inflation, the real interest rate, like the nominal interest, can never fall below zero. But if the normal rate of inflation is, say, 4 percent, then the central bank can easily push the real interest rate to negative 4 percent by lowering the nominal interest rate toward zero. Thus, moderate inflation gives monetary policymakers more room to stimulate the economy when needed, reducing the risk of hitting the zero lower bound and having the economy fall into a liquidity trap.

34-2   How Fiscal Policy Influences Aggregate Demand

The government can influence the behavior of the economy not only with monetary policy but also with fiscal policy. **Fiscal policy** refers to the government's choices regarding the overall level of government purchases and taxes. Earlier in the book, we examined how fiscal policy influences saving, investment, and growth in the long run. In the short run, however, the primary effect of fiscal policy is on the aggregate demand for goods and services.

fiscal policy
the setting of the level of government spending and taxation by government policymakers

34-2a   Changes in Government Purchases
When policymakers change the money supply or the level of taxes, they shift the aggregate-demand curve indirectly by influencing the spending decisions of firms or households. By contrast, when the government alters its own purchases of goods and services, it shifts the aggregate-demand curve directly.

Suppose, for instance, that the U.S. Department of Defense places a $20 billion order for new fighter planes with Boeing, the large aircraft manufacturer. This order raises the demand for the output produced by Boeing, which induces the company to hire more workers and increase production. Because Boeing is part of the economy, the increase in the demand for Boeing planes means an increase in the total quantity of goods and services demanded at each price level. As a result, the aggregate-demand curve shifts to the right.

By how much does this $20 billion order from the government shift the aggregate-demand curve? At first, one might guess that the aggregate-demand curve shifts to the right by exactly $20 billion. It turns out, however, that this is not the case. There are two macroeconomic effects that cause the size of the shift in aggregate demand to differ from the change in government purchases. The first—the multiplier effect—suggests the shift in aggregate demand could be *larger* than $20 billion. The second—the crowding-out effect—suggests the shift in aggregate demand could be *smaller* than $20 billion. We now discuss these two effects in turn.

34-2b The Multiplier Effect

When the government buys $20 billion of goods from Boeing, that purchase has repercussions. The immediate impact of the higher demand from the government is to raise employment and profits at Boeing. Then, as the workers see higher earnings and the firm owners see higher profits, they respond to this increase in income by raising their own spending on consumer goods. As a result, the government purchase from Boeing raises the demand for the products of many other firms in the economy. Because each dollar spent by the government can raise the aggregate demand for goods and services by more than a dollar, government purchases are said to have a **multiplier effect** on aggregate demand.

multiplier effect
the additional shifts in aggregate demand that result when expansionary fiscal policy increases income and thereby increases consumer spending

This multiplier effect continues even after this first round. When consumer spending rises, the firms that produce these consumer goods hire more people and experience higher profits. Higher earnings and profits stimulate consumer spending once again and so on. Thus, there is positive feedback as higher demand leads to higher income, which in turn leads to even higher demand. Once all these effects are added together, the total impact on the quantity of goods and services demanded can be much larger than the initial impulse from higher government spending.

Figure 4 illustrates the multiplier effect. The increase in government purchases of $20 billion initially shifts the aggregate-demand curve to the right from AD_1 to AD_2 by exactly $20 billion. But when consumers respond by increasing their spending, the aggregate-demand curve shifts still further to AD_3.

This multiplier effect arising from the response of consumer spending can be strengthened by the response of investment to higher levels of demand. For instance, Boeing might respond to the higher demand for planes by deciding to buy more equipment or build another plant. In this case, higher government demand spurs higher demand for investment goods. This positive feedback from demand to investment is sometimes called the *investment accelerator*.

34-2c A Formula for the Spending Multiplier

Some simple algebra permits us to derive a formula for the size of the multiplier effect that arises when an increase in government purchases induces increases in consumer spending. An important number in this formula is the *marginal propensity to consume (MPC)*—the fraction of extra income that a household consumes rather than saves. For example, suppose that the marginal propensity to consume is ¾. This means that for every extra dollar that a household earns, the household

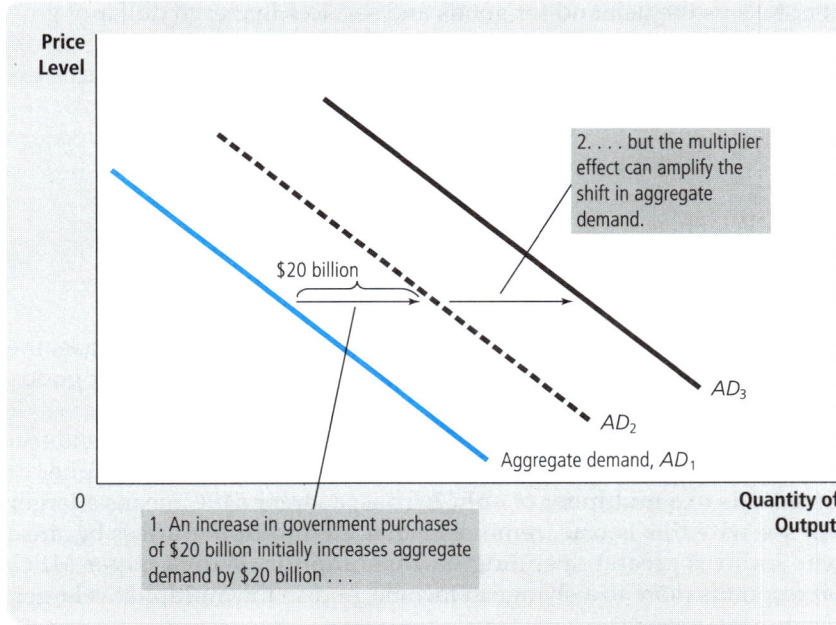

FIGURE 4

The Multiplier Effect
An increase in government purchases of $20 billion can shift the aggregate-demand curve to the right by more than $20 billion. This multiplier effect arises because increases in aggregate income stimulate additional spending by consumers.

spends $0.75 (¾ of the dollar) and saves $0.25. With an MPC of ¾, when the workers and owners of Boeing earn $20 billion from the government contract, they increase their consumer spending by ¾ × $20 billion, or $15 billion.

To gauge the impact on aggregate demand of a change in government purchases, we follow the effects step-by-step. The process begins when the government spends $20 billion, which implies that national income (earnings and profits) also rises by this amount. This increase in income in turn raises consumer spending by MPC × $20 billion, which raises the income for the workers and owners of the firms that produce the consumption goods. This second increase in income again raises consumer spending, this time by MPC × (MPC × $20 billion). These feedback effects go on and on.

To find the total impact on the demand for goods and services, we add up all these effects:

Change in government purchases =	$20 billion
First change in consumption	= MPC × $20 billion
Second change in consumption	= MPC^2 × $20 billion
Third change in consumption	= MPC^3 × $20 billion
•	•
•	•
•	•

Total change in demand
= $(1 + MPC + MPC^2 + MPC^3 + \ldots) \times \$20$ billion.

Here "..." represents an infinite number of similar terms. Thus, we can write the multiplier as follows:

$$\text{Multiplier} = 1 + MPC + MPC^2 + MPC^3 + \ldots.$$

This multiplier tells us the demand for goods and services that each dollar of government purchases generates.

To simplify this equation for the multiplier, recall from math class that this expression is an infinite geometric series. For x between -1 and $+1$,

$$1 + x + x^2 + x^3 + \ldots = 1 / (1 - x).$$

In our case, $x = MPC$. Thus,

$$\text{Multiplier} = 1/(1 - MPC).$$

For example, if MPC is ¾, the multiplier is $1/(1 - \text{¾})$, which is 4. In this case, the $20 billion of government spending generates $80 billion of demand for goods and services.

This formula for the multiplier shows that the size of the multiplier depends on the marginal propensity to consume. While an MPC of ¾ leads to a multiplier of 4, an MPC of ½ leads to a multiplier of only 2. Thus, a larger MPC means a larger multiplier. To see why this is true, remember that the multiplier arises because higher income induces greater spending on consumption. With a larger MPC, consumption responds more to a change in income, and so the multiplier is larger.

34-2d Other Applications of the Multiplier Effect

Because of the multiplier effect, a dollar of government purchases can generate more than a dollar of aggregate demand. The logic of the multiplier effect, however, is not restricted to changes in government purchases. Instead, it applies to any event that alters spending on any component of GDP—consumption, investment, government purchases, or net exports.

For example, suppose that a recession overseas reduces the demand for U.S. net exports by $10 billion. This reduced spending on U.S. goods and services depresses U.S. national income, which reduces spending by U.S. consumers. If the marginal propensity to consume is ¾ and the multiplier is 4, then the $10 billion fall in net exports leads to a $40 billion contraction in aggregate demand.

As another example, suppose that a stock market boom increases households' wealth and stimulates their spending on goods and services by $20 billion. This extra consumer spending increases national income, which in turn generates even more consumer spending. If the marginal propensity to consume is ¾ and the multiplier is 4, then the initial impulse of $20 billion in consumer spending translates into an $80 billion increase in aggregate demand.

The multiplier is an important concept in macroeconomics because it shows how the economy can amplify the impact of changes in spending. A small initial change in consumption, investment, government purchases, or net exports can end up having a large effect on aggregate demand and, therefore, the economy's production of goods and services.

34-2e The Crowding-Out Effect

The multiplier effect seems to suggest that when the government buys $20 billion of planes from Boeing, the resulting expansion in aggregate demand is necessarily larger than $20 billion. Yet another effect works in the opposite direction. While an increase in government purchases stimulates the aggregate demand for goods and services, it also causes the interest rate to rise, which reduces investment spending and puts downward pressure on aggregate demand. The reduction in aggregate demand that results when a fiscal expansion raises the interest rate is called the **crowding-out effect**.

To see why crowding out occurs, let's consider what happens in the money market when the government buys planes from Boeing. As we have discussed, this increase in demand raises the incomes of the workers and owners of this firm (and, because of the multiplier effect, of other firms as well). As incomes rise, households plan to buy more goods and services and, as a result, choose to hold more of their wealth in liquid form. That is, the increase in income caused by the fiscal expansion raises the demand for money.

The effect of the increase in money demand is shown in panel (a) of Figure 5. Because the Fed has not changed the money supply, the vertical supply curve remains the same. When the higher level of income shifts the money demand curve to the right from MD_1 to MD_2, the interest rate must rise from r_1 to r_2 to keep supply and demand in balance.

The increase in the interest rate, in turn, reduces the quantity of goods and services demanded. In particular, because borrowing is more expensive, the demand for residential and business investment goods declines. In other words, as the increase in government purchases increases the demand for goods and services, it may also crowd out investment. This crowding-out effect partially offsets the impact of government purchases on aggregate demand, as illustrated in panel (b) of Figure 5. The increase in government purchases initially shifts the aggregate-demand curve from AD_1 to AD_2, but once crowding out takes place, the aggregate-demand curve drops back to AD_3.

crowding-out effect
the offset in aggregate demand that results when expansionary fiscal policy raises the interest rate and thereby reduces investment spending

Panel (a) shows the money market. When the government increases its purchases of goods and services, the resulting increase in income raises the demand for money from MD_1 to MD_2, and this causes the equilibrium interest rate to rise from r_1 to r_2. Panel (b) shows the effects on aggregate demand. The initial impact of the increase in government purchases shifts the aggregate-demand curve from AD_1 to AD_2. Yet because the interest rate is the cost of borrowing, the increase in the interest rate tends to reduce the quantity of goods and services demanded, particularly for investment goods. This crowding out of investment partially offsets the impact of the fiscal expansion on aggregate demand. In the end, the aggregate-demand curve shifts only to AD_3.

FIGURE 5

The Crowding-Out Effect

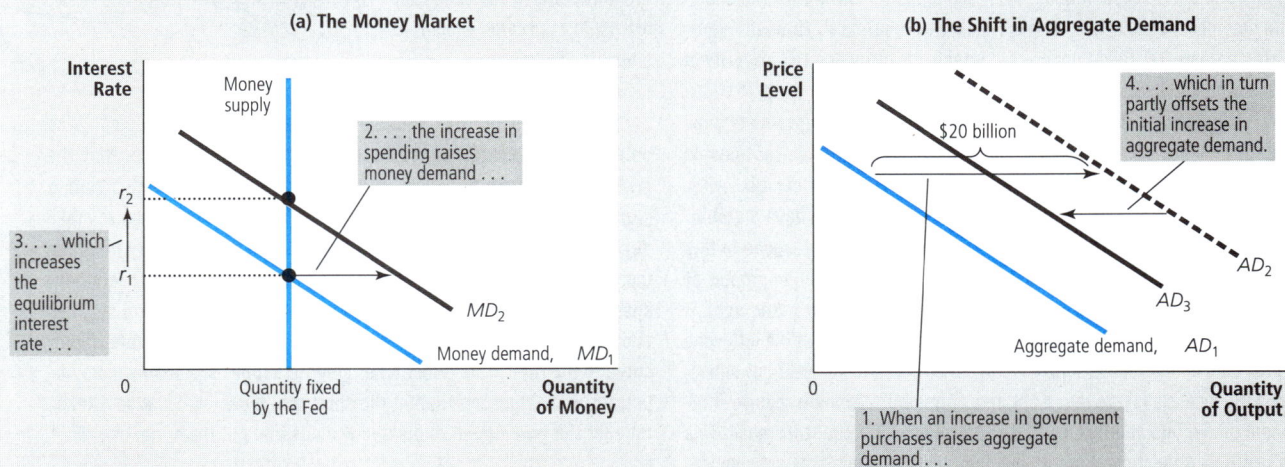

(a) The Money Market

(b) The Shift in Aggregate Demand

To sum up: *When the government increases its purchases by $20 billion, the aggregate demand for goods and services could rise by more or less than $20 billion depending on the sizes of the multiplier and crowding-out effects*. The multiplier effect makes the shift in aggregate demand greater than $20 billion. The crowding-out effect pushes the aggregate-demand curve in the opposite direction and, if large enough, could result in an aggregate-demand shift of less than $20 billion.

34-2f Changes in Taxes

The other important instrument of fiscal policy, besides the level of government purchases, is the level of taxation. When the government cuts personal income taxes, for instance, it increases households' take-home pay. Households will save some of this additional income, but they will also spend some of it on consumer goods. Because it increases consumer spending, the tax cut shifts the aggregate-demand curve to the right. Similarly, a tax increase depresses consumer spending and shifts the aggregate-demand curve to the left.

The size of the shift in aggregate demand resulting from a tax change is also affected by the multiplier and crowding-out effects. When the government cuts taxes and stimulates consumer spending, earnings and profits rise, which further stimulates consumer spending. This is the multiplier effect. At the same time, higher income leads to higher money demand, which tends to raise interest rates. Higher interest rates make borrowing more costly, which reduces investment spending. This is the crowding-out effect. Depending on the sizes of the multiplier and crowding-out effects, the shift in aggregate demand could be larger or smaller than the tax change that causes it.

FYI

How Fiscal Policy Might Affect Aggregate Supply

So far, our discussion of fiscal policy has stressed how changes in government purchases and changes in taxes influence the quantity of goods and services demanded. Most economists believe that the short-run macroeconomic effects of fiscal policy work primarily through aggregate demand. Yet fiscal policy can potentially influence the quantity of goods and services supplied as well.

For instance, consider the effects of tax changes on aggregate supply. One of the *Ten Principles of Economics* in Chapter 1 is that people respond to incentives. When government policymakers cut tax rates, workers get to keep more of each dollar they earn, so they have a greater incentive to work and produce goods and services. If they respond to this incentive, the quantity of goods and services supplied will be greater at each price level, and the aggregate-supply curve will shift to the right.

Some economists, called *supply siders*, have argued that the influence of tax cuts on aggregate supply is large. According to some supply siders, the influence is so large that a cut in tax rates will stimulate enough additional production and income that tax revenue will actually increase. This is certainly a theoretical possibility, but most economists do not consider

it the normal case. While the supply-side effects of taxes are important to consider, they are usually not large enough to cause tax revenue to rise when tax rates fall.

Like changes in taxes, changes in government purchases can also potentially affect aggregate supply. Suppose, for instance, that the government increases expenditure on a form of government-provided capital, such as roads. Roads are used by private businesses to make deliveries to their customers; an increase in the quantity of roads increases these businesses' productivity. Hence, when the government spends more on roads, it increases the quantity of goods and services supplied at any given price level and, thus, shifts the aggregate-supply curve to the right. This effect on aggregate supply is probably more important in the long run than in the short run, however, because it takes time for the government to build new roads and put them into use. ■

In addition to the multiplier and crowding-out effects, there is another important determinant of the size of the shift in aggregate demand that results from a tax change: households' perceptions about whether the tax change is permanent or temporary. For example, suppose that the government announces a tax cut of $1,000 per household. In deciding how much of this $1,000 to spend, households must ask themselves how long this extra income will last. If they expect the tax cut to be permanent, they will view it as adding substantially to their financial resources and, therefore, increase their spending by a large amount. In this case, the tax cut will have a large impact on aggregate demand. By contrast, if households expect the tax change to be temporary, they will view it as adding only slightly to their financial resources and, therefore, will increase their spending by only a small amount. In this case, the tax cut will have a small impact on aggregate demand.

An extreme example of a temporary tax cut was the one announced in 1992. In that year, President George H. W. Bush faced a lingering recession and an upcoming reelection campaign. He responded to these circumstances by announcing a reduction in the amount of income tax that the federal government was withholding from workers' paychecks. Because legislated income tax rates did not change, however, every dollar of reduced withholding in 1992 meant an extra dollar of taxes due on April 15, 1993, when income tax returns for 1992 were to be filed. Thus, this "tax cut" actually represented only a short-term loan from the government. Not surprisingly, the impact of the policy on consumer spending and aggregate demand was relatively small.

QuickQuiz *Suppose that the government reduces spending on highway construction by $10 billion. Which way does the aggregate-demand curve shift? Explain why the shift might be larger or smaller than $10 billion.*

34-3 Using Policy to Stabilize the Economy

We have seen how monetary and fiscal policy can affect the economy's aggregate demand for goods and services. These theoretical insights raise some important policy questions: Should policymakers use these instruments to control aggregate demand and stabilize the economy? If so, when? If not, why not?

34-3a The Case for Active Stabilization Policy

Let's return to the question that began this chapter: When the president and Congress raise taxes, how should the Federal Reserve respond? As we have seen, the level of taxation is one determinant of the position of the aggregate-demand curve. When the government raises taxes, aggregate demand will fall, depressing production and employment in the short run. If the Federal Reserve wants to prevent this adverse effect of the fiscal policy, it can expand aggregate demand by increasing the money supply. A monetary expansion would reduce interest rates, stimulate investment spending, and expand aggregate demand. If monetary policy is set appropriately, the combined changes in monetary and fiscal policy could leave the aggregate demand for goods and services unaffected.

This analysis is exactly the sort followed by members of the Federal Open Market Committee. They know that monetary policy is an important determinant of aggregate demand. They also know that there are other important determinants as well, including fiscal policy set by the president and Congress. As a result, the FOMC watches the debates over fiscal policy with a keen eye.

This response of monetary policy to the change in fiscal policy is an example of a more general phenomenon: the use of policy instruments to stabilize aggregate demand and, as a result, production and employment. Economic stabilization has been an explicit goal of U.S. policy since the Employment Act of 1946. This act states that "it is the continuing policy and responsibility of the federal government to . . . promote full employment and production." In essence, the government has chosen to hold itself accountable for short-run macroeconomic performance.

The Employment Act has two implications. The first, more modest, implication is that the government should avoid being a cause of economic fluctuations. Thus, most economists advise against large and sudden changes in monetary and fiscal policy, for such changes are likely to cause fluctuations in aggregate demand. Moreover, when large changes do occur, it is important that monetary and fiscal policymakers be aware of and respond to each others' actions.

The second, more ambitious, implication of the Employment Act is that the government should respond to changes in the private economy to stabilize aggregate demand. The act was passed not long after the publication of Keynes's *The General Theory of Employment, Interest, and Money*, which has been one of the most influential books ever written about economics. In it, Keynes emphasized the key role of aggregate demand in explaining short-run economic fluctuations. Keynes

---

IN THE NEWS

How Large Is the Fiscal Policy Multiplier?

In the global economic downturn of 2008 and 2009, governments around the world turned to fiscal policy to prop up aggregate demand. This episode ignited a debate about the size of the multipliers, which remains a topic of much research.

Much Ado about Multipliers

It is the biggest peacetime fiscal expansion in history. Across the globe countries have countered the recession by cutting taxes and by boosting government spending. The G20 group of economies, whose leaders meet this week in Pittsburgh, have introduced stimulus packages worth an average of 2% of GDP this year [2009] and 1.6% of GDP in 2010. Coordinated action on this scale might suggest a consensus about the effects of fiscal stimulus. But economists are in fact deeply divided about how well, or indeed whether, such stimulus works.

The debate hinges on the scale of the "fiscal multiplier." This measure, first formalised in 1931 by Richard Kahn, a student of John Maynard Keynes, captures how effectively tax cuts or increases in government spending stimulate output. A multiplier of one means that a $1 billion increase in government spending will increase a country's GDP by $1 billion.

The size of the multiplier is bound to vary according to economic conditions. For an economy operating at full capacity, the fiscal multiplier should be zero. Since there are no spare resources, any increase in government demand would just replace spending elsewhere. But in a recession, when workers and factories lie idle, a fiscal boost can increase overall demand. And if the initial stimulus triggers a cascade of expenditure among consumers and businesses, the multiplier can be well above one.

The multiplier is also likely to vary according to the type of fiscal action. Government spending on building a bridge may have a bigger multiplier than a tax cut if consumers save a portion of their tax windfall. A tax cut targeted at poorer people may have a bigger impact on spending than one for the affluent, since poorer folk tend to spend a higher share of their income.

Crucially, the overall size of the fiscal multiplier also depends on how people react to higher government borrowing. If the government's actions bolster confidence and revive animal spirits, the multiplier could rise as demand goes up and private investment is "crowded in." But if interest rates climb in response to government borrowing then some private investment that would otherwise have occurred could get "crowded out." And if consumers expect higher future taxes in order to finance new government borrowing, they could spend less today. All that would reduce the fiscal multiplier, potentially to below zero.

claimed that the government should actively stimulate aggregate demand when aggregate demand appeared insufficient to maintain production at its full-employment level.

Keynes (and his many followers) argued that aggregate demand fluctuates because of largely irrational waves of pessimism and optimism. He used the term "animal spirits" to refer to these arbitrary changes in attitude. When pessimism reigns, households reduce consumption spending and firms reduce investment spending. The result is reduced aggregate demand, lower production, and higher unemployment. Conversely, when optimism reigns, households and firms increase spending. The result is higher aggregate demand, higher production, and inflationary pressure. Notice that these changes in attitude are, to some extent, self-fulfilling.

In principle, the government can adjust its monetary and fiscal policy in response to these waves of optimism and pessimism and, thereby, stabilize the economy. For example, when people are excessively pessimistic, the Fed can expand the money supply to lower interest rates and expand aggregate demand. When they are excessively optimistic, it can contract the money supply to raise interest rates and dampen aggregate demand. Former Fed Chairman William McChesney Martin described this view of monetary policy very simply: "The Federal Reserve's job is to take away the punch bowl just as the party gets going."

Different assumptions about the impact of higher government borrowing on interest rates and private spending explain wild variations in the estimates of multipliers from today's stimulus spending. Economists in the Obama administration, who assume that the federal funds rate stays constant for a four-year period, expect a multiplier of 1.6 for government purchases and 1.0 for tax cuts from America's fiscal stimulus. An alternative assessment by John Cogan, Tobias Cwik, John Taylor and Volker Wieland uses models in which interest rates and taxes rise more quickly in response to higher public borrowing. Their multipliers are much smaller. They think America's stimulus will boost GDP by only one-sixth as much as the Obama team expects.

When forward-looking models disagree so dramatically, careful analysis of previous fiscal stimuli ought to help settle the debate. Unfortunately, it is extremely tricky to isolate the impact of changes in fiscal policy. One approach is to use microeconomic case studies to examine consumer behaviour in response to specific tax rebates and cuts. These studies, largely based on tax changes in America, find that permanent cuts have a bigger impact on consumer spending than temporary ones and that consumers who find it hard to borrow, such as those close to their credit-card limit, tend to spend more of their tax windfall. But case studies do not measure the overall impact of tax cuts or spending increases on output.

An alternative approach is to try to tease out the statistical impact of changes in government spending or tax cuts on GDP. The difficulty here is to isolate the effects of fiscal-stimulus measures from the rises in social-security spending and falls in tax revenues that naturally accompany recessions. This empirical approach has narrowed the range of estimates in some areas. It has also yielded interesting cross-country comparisons. Multipliers are bigger in closed economies than open ones (because less of the stimulus leaks abroad via imports). They have traditionally been bigger in rich countries than emerging ones (where investors tend to take fright more quickly, pushing interest rates up). But overall economists find as big a range of multipliers from empirical estimates as they do from theoretical models.

To add to the confusion, the post-war experiences from which statistical analyses are drawn differ in vital respects from the current situation. Most of the evidence on multipliers for government spending is based on military outlays, but today's stimulus packages are heavily focused on infrastructure. Interest rates in many rich countries are now close to zero, which may increase the potency of, as well as the need for, fiscal stimulus. Because of the financial crisis relatively more people face borrowing constraints, which would increase the effectiveness of a tax cut. At the same time, highly indebted consumers may now be keen to cut their borrowing, leading to a lower multiplier. And investors today have more reason to be worried about rich countries' fiscal positions than those of emerging markets.

Add all this together and the truth is that economists are flying blind. They can make relative judgments with some confidence. Temporary tax cuts pack less punch than permanent ones, for instance. Fiscal multipliers will probably be lower in heavily indebted economies than in prudent ones. But policymakers looking for precise estimates are deluding themselves. ■

Source: *The Economist*, September 24, 2009.

KEYNESIANS IN THE WHITE HOUSE

CASE STUDY

When a reporter in 1961 asked President John F. Kennedy why he advocated a tax cut, Kennedy replied, "To stimulate the economy. Don't you remember your Economics 101?" Kennedy's policy was, in fact, based on the analysis of fiscal policy we have developed in this chapter. His goal was to enact a tax cut, which would raise consumer spending, expand aggregate demand, and increase the economy's production and employment.

In choosing this policy, Kennedy was relying on his team of economic advisers. This team included such prominent economists as James Tobin and Robert Solow, both of whom would later win Nobel Prizes for their contributions to the field. As students in the 1940s, these economists had closely studied John Maynard Keynes's *General Theory*, which was then only a few years old. When the Kennedy advisers proposed cutting taxes, they were putting Keynes's ideas into action.

Although tax changes can have a potent influence on aggregate demand, they have other effects as well. In particular, by changing the incentives that people face, taxes can alter the aggregate supply of goods and services. Part of the Kennedy proposal was an investment tax credit, which gives a tax break to firms that invest in new capital. Higher investment would not only stimulate aggregate demand immediately but also increase the economy's productive capacity over time. Thus, the short-run goal of increasing production through higher aggregate demand was coupled with a long-run goal of increasing production through higher aggregate supply. And indeed, when the tax cut Kennedy proposed was finally enacted in 1964, it helped usher in a period of robust economic growth.

Since the 1964 tax cut, policymakers have from time to time used fiscal policy as a tool for controlling aggregate demand. For example, when President Barack Obama moved into the Oval Office in 2009, he faced an economy in the midst of a recession. One of his first policy initiatives was a stimulus bill, called the American Recovery and Reinvestment Act (ARRA), which included substantial increases in government spending. The In the News box on the preceding two pages discusses some of the debate over this policy initiative. ●

ASK THE EXPERTS

Economic Stimulus

"Because of the American Recovery and Reinvestment Act of 2009, the U.S. unemployment rate was lower at the end of 2010 than it would have been without the stimulus bill."

What do economists say?

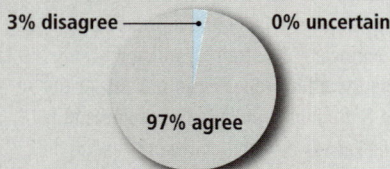

3% disagree   0% uncertain

97% agree

"Taking into account all of the ARRA's economic consequences—including the economic costs of raising taxes to pay for the spending, its effects on future spending, and any other likely future effects—the benefits of the stimulus will end up exceeding its costs."

What do economists say?

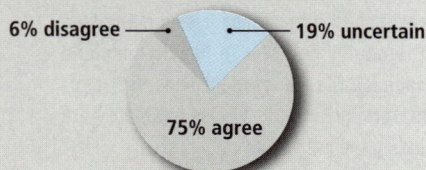

6% disagree   19% uncertain

75% agree

Source: IGM Economic Experts Panel, July 29, 2014.

34-3b The Case against Active Stabilization Policy

Some economists argue that the government should avoid active use of monetary and fiscal policy to try to stabilize the economy. They claim that these policy instruments should be set to achieve long-run goals, such as rapid economic growth and low inflation, and that the economy should be left to deal with short-run fluctuations on its own. These economists may admit that monetary and fiscal policy can stabilize the economy in theory, but they doubt whether it can do so in practice.

The primary argument against active monetary and fiscal policy is that these policies affect the economy with a long lag. As we have seen, monetary policy works by changing interest rates, which in turn influence investment spending. But many firms make investment plans far in advance. Thus, most economists believe that it takes at least 6 months for changes in monetary policy to have much effect on output and employment. Moreover, once these effects occur, they can last for several years. Critics of stabilization policy argue that because of this lag, the Fed should not try to fine-tune the economy. They claim that the Fed often reacts too late to changing economic conditions and, as a result, ends up being a cause of rather than a cure for economic fluctuations. These critics advocate a passive monetary policy, such as slow and steady growth in the money supply.

Fiscal policy also works with a lag, but unlike the lag in monetary policy, the lag in fiscal policy is largely attributable to the political process. In the United States, most changes in government spending and taxes must go through congressional committees in both the House and the Senate, be passed by both legislative bodies, and then be signed by the president. Completing this process can take months or, in some cases, years. By the time the change in fiscal policy is passed and ready to implement, the condition of the economy may have changed.

These lags in monetary and fiscal policy are a problem in part because economic forecasting is so imprecise. If forecasters could accurately predict the condition of the economy a year in advance, then monetary and fiscal policymakers could look ahead when making policy decisions. In this case, policymakers could stabilize the economy despite the lags they face. In practice, however, major recessions and depressions arrive without much advance warning. The best that policymakers can do is to respond to economic changes as they occur.

34-3c Automatic Stabilizers

automatic stabilizers
changes in fiscal policy that stimulate aggregate demand when the economy goes into a recession without policymakers having to take any deliberate action

All economists—both advocates and critics of stabilization policy—agree that the lags in implementation reduce the efficacy of policy as a tool for short-run stabilization. The economy would be more stable, therefore, if policymakers could find a way to avoid some of these lags. In fact, they have. **Automatic stabilizers** are changes in fiscal policy that stimulate aggregate demand when the economy goes into a recession without policymakers having to take any deliberate action.

The most important automatic stabilizer is the tax system. When the economy goes into a recession, the amount of taxes collected by the government falls automatically because almost all taxes are closely tied to economic activity. The personal income tax depends on households' incomes, the payroll tax depends on workers' earnings, and the corporate income tax depends on firms' profits. Because incomes, earnings, and profits all fall in a recession, the government's tax revenue falls as well. This automatic tax cut stimulates aggregate demand and, thereby, reduces the magnitude of economic fluctuations.

Some government spending also acts as an automatic stabilizer. In particular, when the economy goes into a recession and workers are laid off, more people apply for unemployment insurance benefits, welfare benefits, and other forms of income support. This automatic increase in government spending stimulates aggregate demand at exactly the time when aggregate demand is insufficient to maintain full employment. Indeed, when the unemployment insurance system was first enacted in the 1930s, economists who advocated this policy did so in part because of its power as an automatic stabilizer.

The automatic stabilizers in the U.S. economy are not sufficiently strong to prevent recessions completely. Nonetheless, without these automatic stabilizers, output and employment would probably be more volatile than they are. For this reason, many economists oppose a constitutional amendment that would require the federal government always to run a balanced budget, as some politicians have proposed. When the economy goes into a recession, taxes fall, government spending rises, and the government's budget moves toward deficit. If the government faced a strict balanced-budget rule, it would be forced to look for ways to raise taxes or cut spending in a recession. In other words, a strict balanced-budget rule would eliminate the automatic stabilizers inherent in our current system of taxes and government spending.

Quick Quiz   *Suppose a wave of negative "animal spirits" overruns the economy, and people become pessimistic about the future. What happens to aggregate demand? If the Fed wants to stabilize aggregate demand, how should it alter the money supply? If it does this, what happens to the interest rate? Why might the Fed choose not to respond in this way?*

34-4 Conclusion

Before policymakers make any change in policy, they need to consider all the effects of their decisions. Earlier in the book, we examined classical models of the economy, which describe the long-run effects of monetary and fiscal policy. There we saw how fiscal policy influences saving, investment, and long-run growth and how monetary policy influences the price level and the inflation rate.

In this chapter, we examined the short-run effects of monetary and fiscal policy. We saw how these policy instruments can change the aggregate demand for goods and services and alter the economy's production and employment in the short run. When Congress reduces government spending to balance the budget, it needs to consider both the long-run effects on saving and growth and the short-run effects on aggregate demand and employment. When the Fed reduces the growth rate of the money supply, it must take into account the long-run effect on inflation as well as the short-run effect on production. In all parts of government, policymakers must keep in mind both long-run and short-run goals.

CHAPTER QuickQuiz

1. If the central bank wants to expand aggregate demand, it can _____ the money supply, which would _____ the interest rate.
   a. increase, increase
   b. increase, decrease
   c. decrease, increase
   d. decrease, decrease

2. If the government wants to contract aggregate demand, it can _____ government purchases or _____ taxes.
   a. increase, increase
   b. increase, decrease
   c. decrease, increase
   d. decrease, decrease

3. The Federal Reserve's target rate for the federal funds rate
   a. is an extra policy tool for the central bank, in addition to and independent of the money supply.
   b. commits the Fed to set a particular money supply so that it hits the announced target.
   c. is a goal that is rarely achieved, because the Fed can determine only the money supply.
   d. matters to banks that borrow and lend federal funds but does not influence aggregate demand.

4. With the economy in a recession because of inadequate aggregate demand, the government increases its purchases by $1,200. Suppose the central bank adjusts the money supply to hold the interest rate constant, investment spending is fixed, and the marginal propensity to consume is $2/3$. How large is the increase in aggregate demand?
   a. $400
   b. $800
   c. $1,800
   d. $3,600

5. If the central bank in the preceding question instead holds the money supply constant and allows the interest rate to adjust, the change in aggregate demand resulting from the increase in government purchases will be
   a. larger.
   b. the same.
   c. smaller but still positive.
   d. negative.

6. Which of the following is an example of an automatic stabilizer? When the economy goes into a recession,
   a. more people become eligible for unemployment insurance benefits.
   b. stock prices decline, particularly for firms in cyclical industries.
   c. Congress begins hearings about a possible stimulus package.
   d. the Federal Reserve changes its target for the federal funds rate.

SUMMARY

- In developing a theory of short-run economic fluctuations, Keynes proposed the theory of liquidity preference to explain the determinants of the interest rate. According to this theory, the interest rate adjusts to balance the supply and demand for money.
- An increase in the price level raises money demand and increases the interest rate that brings the money market into equilibrium. Because the interest rate represents the cost of borrowing, a higher interest rate reduces investment and, thereby, the quantity of goods and services demanded. The downward-sloping aggregate-demand curve expresses this negative relationship between the price level and the quantity demanded.
- Policymakers can influence aggregate demand with monetary policy. An increase in the money supply reduces the equilibrium interest rate for any given price level. Because a lower interest rate stimulates investment spending, the aggregate-demand curve shifts to the right. Conversely, a decrease in the money supply raises the equilibrium interest rate for any given price level and shifts the aggregate-demand curve to the left.

- Policymakers can also influence aggregate demand with fiscal policy. An increase in government purchases or a cut in taxes shifts the aggregate-demand curve to the right. A decrease in government purchases or an increase in taxes shifts the aggregate-demand curve to the left.

- When the government alters spending or taxes, the resulting shift in aggregate demand can be larger or smaller than the fiscal change. The multiplier effect tends to amplify the effects of fiscal policy on aggregate demand. The crowding-out effect tends to dampen the effects of fiscal policy on aggregate demand.

- Because monetary and fiscal policy can influence aggregate demand, the government sometimes uses these policy instruments in an attempt to stabilize the economy. Economists disagree about how active the government should be in this effort. According to advocates of active stabilization policy, changes in attitudes by households and firms shift aggregate demand; if the government does not respond, the result is undesirable and unnecessary fluctuations in output and employment. According to critics of active stabilization policy, monetary and fiscal policy work with such long lags that attempts at stabilizing the economy often end up being destabilizing.

KEY CONCEPTS

theory of liquidity preference, p. 739
fiscal policy, p. 747

multiplier effect, p. 748
crowding-out effect, p. 751

automatic stabilizers, p. 758

QUESTIONS FOR REVIEW

1. What is the theory of liquidity preference? How does it help explain the downward slope of the aggregate-demand curve?

2. Use the theory of liquidity preference to explain how a decrease in the money supply affects the aggregate-demand curve.

3. The government spends $3 billion to buy police cars. Explain why aggregate demand might increase by more or less than $3 billion.

4. Suppose that survey measures of consumer confidence indicate a wave of pessimism is sweeping the country. If policymakers do nothing, what will happen to aggregate demand? What should the Fed do if it wants to stabilize aggregate demand? If the Fed does nothing, what might Congress do to stabilize aggregate demand?

5. Give an example of a government policy that acts as an automatic stabilizer. Explain why the policy has this effect.

PROBLEMS AND APPLICATIONS

1. Explain how each of the following developments would affect the supply of money, the demand for money, and the interest rate. Illustrate your answers with diagrams.
   a. The Fed's bond traders buy bonds in open-market operations.
   b. An increase in credit-card availability reduces the amount of cash people want to hold.
   c. The Federal Reserve reduces banks' reserve requirements.
   d. Households decide to hold more money to use for holiday shopping.
   e. A wave of optimism boosts business investment and expands aggregate demand.

2. The Federal Reserve expands the money supply by 5 percent.
   a. Use the theory of liquidity preference to illustrate in a graph the impact of this policy on the interest rate.
   b. Use the model of aggregate demand and aggregate supply to illustrate the impact of this change in the interest rate on output and the price level in the short run.
   c. When the economy makes the transition from its short-run equilibrium to its new long-run equilibrium, what will happen to the price level?

d. How will this change in the price level affect the demand for money and the equilibrium interest rate?

e. Is this analysis consistent with the proposition that money has real effects in the short run but is neutral in the long run?

3. Suppose a computer virus disables the nation's automatic teller machines, making withdrawals from bank accounts less convenient. As a result, people want to keep more cash on hand, increasing the demand for money.

a. Assume the Fed does not change the money supply. According to the theory of liquidity preference, what happens to the interest rate? What happens to aggregate demand?

b. If instead the Fed wants to stabilize aggregate demand, how should it change the money supply?

c. If it wants to accomplish this change in the money supply using open-market operations, what should it do?

4. Consider two policies—a tax cut that will last for only one year and a tax cut that is expected to be permanent. Which policy will stimulate greater spending by consumers? Which policy will have the greater impact on aggregate demand? Explain.

5. The economy is in a recession with high unemployment and low output.

a. Draw a graph of aggregate demand and aggregate supply to illustrate the current situation. Be sure to include the aggregate-demand curve, the short-run aggregate-supply curve, and the long-run aggregate-supply curve.

b. Identify an open-market operation that would restore the economy to its natural rate.

c. Draw a graph of the money market to illustrate the effect of this open-market operation. Show the resulting change in the interest rate.

d. Draw a graph similar to the one in part *a* to show the effect of the open-market operation on output and the price level. Explain in words why the policy has the effect that you have shown in the graph.

6. In the early 1980s, new legislation allowed banks to pay interest on checking deposits, which they could not do previously.

a. If we define money to include checking deposits, what effect did this legislation have on money demand? Explain.

b. If the Federal Reserve had maintained a constant money supply in the face of this change, what would have happened to the interest rate? What

would have happened to aggregate demand and aggregate output?

c. If the Federal Reserve had maintained a constant market interest rate (the interest rate on nonmonetary assets) in the face of this change, what change in the money supply would have been necessary? What would have happened to aggregate demand and aggregate output?

7. Suppose economists observe that an increase in government spending of $10 billion raises the total demand for goods and services by $30 billion.

a. If these economists ignore the possibility of crowding out, what would they estimate the marginal propensity to consume (*MPC*) to be?

b. Now suppose the economists allow for crowding out. Would their new estimate of the *MPC* be larger or smaller than their initial one?

8. An economy is operating with output that is $400 billion below its natural level, and fiscal policymakers want to close this recessionary gap. The central bank agrees to adjust the money supply to hold the interest rate constant, so there is no crowding out. The marginal propensity to consume is $4/5$, and the price level is completely fixed in the short run. In what direction and by how much would government spending need to change to close the recessionary gap? Explain your thinking.

9. Suppose government spending increases. Would the effect on aggregate demand be larger if the Federal Reserve held the money supply constant in response or if the Fed were committed to maintaining a fixed interest rate? Explain.

10. In which of the following circumstances is expansionary fiscal policy more likely to lead to a short-run increase in investment? Explain.

a. When the investment accelerator is large or when it is small?

b. When the interest sensitivity of investment is large or when it is small?

11. Consider an economy described by the following equations:

$$Y = C + I + G$$
$$C = 100 + 0.75(Y - T)$$
$$I = 500 - 50\,r$$
$$G = 125$$
$$T = 100$$

where Y is GDP, C is consumption, I is investment, G is government purchases, T is taxes, and r is the interest rate. If the economy were at full employment (that is, at its natural rate), GDP would be 2,000.

a. Explain the meaning of each of these equations.

b. What is the marginal propensity to consume in this economy?

c. Suppose the central bank's policy is to adjust the money supply to maintain the interest rate at 4 percent, so $r = 4$. Solve for GDP. How does it compare to the full-employment level?

d. Assuming no change in monetary policy, what change in government purchases would restore full employment?

e. Assuming no change in fiscal policy, what change in the interest rate would restore full employment?

To find additional study resources, visit cengagebrain.com, and search for "Mankiw."

术语表
GLOSSARY

ability-to-pay principle 支付能力原则

absolute advantage 绝对优势

accounting profit 会计利润

adverse selection 逆向选择

agent 代理人

aggregate-demand curve 总需求曲线

aggregate-supply curve 总供给曲线

appreciation 升值

Arrow's impossibility theorem 阿罗不可能性定理

automatic stabilizers 自动稳定器

average fixed cost 平均固定成本

average revenue 平均收益

average tax rate 平均税率

average total cost 平均总成本

average variable cost 平均可变成本

behavioral economics 行为经济学

balanced trade 贸易平衡

benefits principle 受益原则

bond 债券

budget constraint 预算约束线

budget deficit 预算赤字

budget surplus 预算盈余

business cycle 经济周期

capital 资本

capital flight 资本外逃

cartel 卡特尔

catch-up effect 追赶效应

central bank 中央银行

circular-flow diagram 循环流量图

classical dichotomy 古典二分法

closed economy 封闭经济

Coase theorem 科斯定理

collective bargaining 集体谈判

collusion 共谋，勾结

commodity money 商品货币

common resources 公共资源

comparative advantage 比较优势

compensating differential 补偿性工资差别

competitive market 竞争市场

complements 互补品

compounding 复利

Condorcet paradox 康多塞悖论

constant returns to scale 规模收益不变

consumer price index (CPI) 消费物价指数

consumer surplus 消费者剩余

consumption 消费

cost 成本

cost-benefit analysis 成本 - 收益分析

cross-price elasticity of demand 需求的交叉价格弹性

crowding out 挤出

crowding-out effect 挤出效应

currency 现金

cyclical unemployment 周期性失业

deadweight loss 无谓损失

demand curve 需求曲线

demand deposits 活期存款

demand schedule 需求表

depreciation 贬值

depression 萧条

diminishing marginal product 边际产量递减

diminishing returns 收益递减

discount rate 贴现率

discouraged workers 丧失信心的工人

discrimination 歧视

diseconomies of scale 规模不经济

diversification 多元化

dominant strategy 优势战略

economic profit 经济利润

economics 经济学

economies of scale 规模经济

efficiency 效率

efficiency wages 效率工资

efficient markets hypothesis 有效市场假说

efficient scale 有效规模

elasticity 弹性

equality 平等

equilibrium 均衡

equilibrium price 均衡价格

equilibrium quantity 均衡数量

excludability 排他性

explicit costs 显性成本

exports 出口

externality 外部性

factors of production 生产要素

federal funds rate 联邦基金利率

Federal Reserve (Fed) 联邦储备

fiat money 法定货币

finance 金融学

financial intermediaries 金融中介机构

financial markets 金融市场

financial system 金融体系

firm-specific risk 企业特有风险

fiscal policy 财政政策

Fisher effect 费雪效应

fixed costs 固定成本

fractional-reserve banking 部分准备金银行

free rider 搭便车者

frictional unemployment 摩擦性失业

fundamental amalysis 基本分析

future value 未来值

game theory 博弈论

GDP deflator GDP 平减指数

Giffen good 吉芬物品

government purchases 政府购买

gross domestic product(GDP) 国内生产总值

horizontal equity 横向公平

human capital 人力资本

implicit costs 隐性成本

imports 进口

incentive 激励

income effect 收入效应

income elasticity of demand 需求收入弹性

indexation 指数化

indifference curve 无差异曲线

inferior good 低档物品

inflation 通货膨胀

inflation rate 通货膨胀率

inflation tax 通货膨胀税

informational efficiency 信息有效

in-kind transfers 实物转移支付

internalizing an externality 外部性的内在化

investment 投资

job search 寻找工作

labor force 劳动力

labor-force participation rate 劳动力参工率

law of demand 需求定理

law of supply 供给定理

law of supply and demand 供求定理

leverage 杠杆

leverage ratio 杠杆率

liberalism 自由主义

libertarianism 自由至上主义

life cycle 生命周期

liquidity 流动性

lump-sum tax 定额税

macroeconomics 宏观经济学

marginal changes 边际变动

marginal cost 边际成本

marginal product 边际产量

marginal product of labor 劳动的边际产量

marginal rate of substitution 边际替代率

marginal revenue 边际收益

marginal tax rate 边际税率

market 市场

market economy 市场经济

market failure 市场失灵

market for loanable funds 可贷资金市场

market power 市场势力

market risk 市场风险

maximin criterion 最大最小准则

median voter theorem 中值选民定理

medium of exchange 交换媒介

menu costs 菜单成本

microeconomics 微观经济学

model of aggregate demand and aggregate supply 总需求与总供给模型

monetary neutrality 货币中性

monetary policy 货币政策

money 货币

money multiplier 货币乘数

money supply 货币供给

monopolistic competition 垄断竞争

monopoly 垄断

moral hazard 道德危险

multiplier effect 乘数效应

mutual fund 共同基金

Nash equilibrium 纳什均衡

national saving 国民储蓄

natural monopoly 自然垄断

natural-rate hypothesis 自然率假说

natural rate of unemployment 自然失业率

natural resources 自然资源

negative income tax 负所得税

net capital outflow 资本净流出

net exports 净出口

nominal exchange rate 名义汇率

nominal GDP 名义 GDP

nominal interest rate 名义利率

nominal variables 名义变量

normal good 正常物品

normative statements 规范表述

oligopoly 寡头

open economy 开放经济

open-market operations 公开市场活动

opportunity cost 机会成本

perfect complements 完全互补品

perfect substitutes 完全替代品

permanent income 持久收入

Phillips curve 菲利普斯曲线

physical capital 物质资本

political economy 政治经济学

positive statements 实证表述

poverty line 贫困线

poverty rate 贫困率

present value 现值

price ceiling 价格上限

price discrimination 价格歧视

price elasticity of demand 需求价格弹性

price elasticity of supply 供给价格弹性

price floor 价格下限

principal 委托人

prisoners-dilemma 囚徒困境

private goods 私人物品

private saving 私人储蓄

producer price index 生产物价指数

producer surplus 生产者剩余

production function 生产函数

production possibilities frontier 生产可能性边界

productivity 生产率

profit 利润

progressive tax 累进税

proportional tax 比例税

public goods 公共物品

public saving 公共储蓄

purchasing-power parity 购买力平价

quantity demanded 需求量

quantity equation 数量方程式

quantity supplied 供给量

quantity theory of money 货币数量论

random walk 随机行走

rational expectations 理性预期

real exchange rate 实际汇率

real GDP 实际 GDP

real interest rate 实际利率

real variables 实际变量

recession 衰退

regressive tax 累退税

reserve ratio 准备率

reserve requirements 法定准备率

reserves 准备金

risk averse 风险厌恶

rivalry 竞争性

sacrifice ratio 牺牲率

scarcity 稀缺性

screening 筛选

shoeleather costs 皮鞋成本

shortage 短缺

signaling 发信号

social insurance 社会保险

stagflation 滞胀

stock 股票

store of value 价值储藏

strike 罢工

structural unemployment 结构性失业

substitutes 替代品

substitution effect 替代效应

sunk cost 沉没成本

supply curve 供给曲线

supply schedule 供给表

supply shock 供给冲击

surplus 过剩

tariff 关税

tax incidence 税收归宿

technological knowledge 技术知识

theory of liquidity preference 流动偏好理论

total cost 总成本

total revenue(for a firm) （企业）总收益

total revenue(in a market) （市场）总收益

trade balance 贸易余额

trade deficit 贸易赤字

trade policy 贸易政策

trade surplus 贸易盈余

Tragedy of the Commons 公有地悲剧

transaction costs 交易成本

unemployment insurance 失业保障

unemployment rate 失业率

union 工会

unit of account 计价单位

utilitarianism 功利主义

utility 效用

value of the marginal product 边际产量值

variable costs 可变成本

velocity of money 货币流通速度

vertical equity 纵向公平

welfare 福利

welfare economics 福利经济学

willingness to pay 支付意愿

world price 世界价格

电子书阅读平台使用说明
MindTap Guide

曼昆《经济学原理》（第8版）配套的MindTap在线学习平台是由Cengage开发的个性化学习平台，包括交互电子书（Interactive Book）、视频导读（Video Application）、视频讲解（Video Problem Walk-Through）、学习指南（Study Guide）、在线测试（Adaptive Test）、拓展阅读（Additional Topics）等丰富的学习资源。

新用户注册

打开网址https://student.cengage.com，点击SIGN IN→点击下方Create Account→Are you a student? **选择YES**（务必选择YES，选择NO会导致账户无法注册）→输入**邮箱地址（这是你的用户名，请记住）**，点击NEXT→依次填写相关信息，完成Cengage账户注册。【注册信息表中的Institution**请输入并选择TSINGHUA UNIVERSITY PRESS (Beijing)**，选择其他Institution会导致无法使用MindTap电子图书。可扫描右方二维码获取详细流程指导。】

已注册账户登录

打开网址https://student.cengage.com，点击SIGN IN→输入邮箱地址，登录系统。

电子图书激活

登录系统后，点击主页中间的 **+** Enter a Course Key，输入Course Key：**MTPNPPM5S4QB**，点击Register加入课程；加入课程后点击网页中的OPEN MINDTAP或右上方的Enter Access Code or Course Key，输入本书Access Code（**刮开本书封底的刮刮卡，获取你的专属Access Code**），点击Register激活，即可进入电子书阅读平台。

技术支持

EMAIL：cn.hedtechsupport@cengage.com

Cengage

教辅资源申请表（Supplements Request Form）

鉴于部分教辅资源仅适用于老师，烦请索取的老师填写如下情况说明表。

Lecturer Details（教师信息）			
Name: （姓名）		Title: （职务）	
School/University: （学校）		Department: （学院/系）	
Official E-mail: （学校邮箱）		Lecturer's Address / Post Code: （通讯地址/邮编）	
Tel:（座机）			
Mobile:（手机）			

Textbook Details（教材信息）			
Adoption Types（教材类型）	原版□　　翻译版□　　影印版□		
Title:（英文书名） ISBN:（13位书号） Edition:（版次） Author:（作者）			
Local Publisher: （国内出版社名称）			

Other Details（其他信息）			
是否已购买教材？（Have you bought This Textbook?）	是□　　否□		
Enrolment: （学生人数）		Semester: （学期起止日期时间）	

获取教辅资源方式（Methods for Obtaining Supplements）

方式1： 请将此表格扫描或拍照，同时发送至以下邮箱：

tupfuwu@163.com; asia.infochina@cengage.com

方式2： 扫描右方二维码，关注公众号，线上申请教辅资源。

清华大学出版社

Tsinghua University Press

北京市海淀区清华园学研大厦 B 座 509 室

邮编：100084

Tel：(8610)83470142

Email：tupfuwu@163.com

Cengage

CENGAGE GROUP

ATTN : Higher Education Division

Tel: (86) 10-83435112

Email: asia.infochina@cengage.com

北京市海淀区魏公村路6号院丽金智地中心西塔807室

Post Code: 100081